# SpringerBriefs in Rights-Based Approaches to Social Work

AF711923

**Series Editor**
Shirley Gatenio Gabel, Fordham University, New York, USA

For further volumes:
http://www.springer.com/series/11694

S. Megan Berthold

# Human Rights-Based Approaches to Clinical Social Work

Springer

S. Megan Berthold
School of Social Work
University of Connecticut
West Hartford
Connecticut
USA

ISSN 2195-9749 ISSN 2195-9757 (electronic)
ISBN 978-3-319-08559-3 ISBN 978-3-319-08560-9 (eBook)
DOI 10.1007/978-3-319-08560-9
Springer Cham Heidelberg New York Dordrecht London

Library of Congress Control Number: 2014952037



Printed on acid-free paper

Springer is part of Springer Science+Business Media (www.springer.com)

*To the trafficked, the tortured, and sufferers of intimate partner violence—my teachers, my inspiration: with hope for a world where human rights exist for all.*

# Foreword by Shirley Gatenio Gabel

For over a century social workers have worked to improve the lives and situations of individuals, families, and communities. Social workers, often acting on behalf of the state's interests, typically intervened according to what they themselves perceived to be deficits in the lives and behaviors of persons in need. This approach to working with people patronizes, stigmatizes, and too often revictimizes those we seek to assist. It is long past time to revitalize and reframe our approach to working with those we seek to serve. The books in this series reframe deficit models used by social work practitioners and instead propose a human rights perspective. Rights-based social work shifts the focus from human needs to human rights and calls on social workers and the populations they work with to actively participate in decision making processes of the state so that the state can better serve the interests of the population. The authors in the series share their strategies for empowering the populations and individuals we, as social workers, engage with as clinicians, community workers, researchers, and policy analysts.

The roots of social work in the United States can be traced to the pioneering efforts of upper-class men and women who established church-based and secular charitable organizations that sought to address the consequences of poverty, urbanization, and immigration. These were issues that were ignored by the public sphere at the time. Little in the way of training or methods was offered to those who volunteered their resources, efforts, and time in these charitable organizations until later in the nineteenth century when concepts derived from business and industry were applied to distribution of relief efforts in what became known as "scientific charity." This scientific approach led to the use of investigation, registration, and supervision of applicants for charity, and in 1877 the first American Charity Organization Society (COS) was founded in Buffalo, NY. The popularity of the approach grew quickly across the country. COS leaders wanted to reform charity by including an agent's investigation of the case's "worthiness" before distributing aid because they believed that unregulated and unsupervised relief led to more calls for relief.

Around the same time, an alternative response to the impact of industrialization and immigration was introduced and tested by the settlement house movement. The first US settlement, the Neighborhood Guild in New York City, was established in 1886 and less than 3 years later, Jane Addams and Ellen Gates Starr founded Hull

House in Chicago, which came to symbolize the settlement house movement in the United States. Unlike the individually oriented COS, the settlement house movement focused on the environmental causes of poverty, seeking economic and social reforms for the poor, and providing largely immigrant and migrant populations with the skills needed to stake their claims in American society.

The settlement house movement spread rapidly in the United States and by 1910, there were more than 400 settlements (Trolander, 1987; Friedman & Friedman, 2006). Advocacy for rights and social justice became an important component of the settlement activities and led to the creation of national organizations like the National Consumers' League, Urban League, Women's Trade Union League, and the National Association for the Advancement of Colored People (NAACP). The leaders of the movement led major social movements of the period, including women's suffrage, peace, labor, civil rights, and temperance and were instrumental in establishing a federal level Children's Bureau in 1912, headed by Julia Lathrop from Hull House.

During this same period, the Charity Organization Societies set to standardize the casework skills for their work with individuals. Their methods became a distinct area of practice and were formalized as a social work training program in 1898 known as the New York School of Philanthropy and eventually, the Columbia University School of Social Work. In 1908, the Chicago Commons offered a full curriculum through the Chicago School of Civics and Philanthropy (now the University of Chicago's School of Social Service Administration) based on the practices and principles of the settlement movement. By 1919, there were 17 schools of social work.

Efforts already underway to secure and strengthen pragmatically derived casework knowledge into a standardized format were accelerated, following Abraham Flexner's provocative lecture in 1915, questioning whether social work was a profession because he believed it lacked specificity, technical skills, or specialized knowledge (Morris, 2008). By the 1920s casework emerged as the dominant form of professional social work in the United States and remained primarily focused on aiding impoverished children and families but was rapidly expanding to work with veterans and middle class individuals in child guidance clinics.

As social work branched out to other populations, it increasingly focused on refining clinical treatment modalities and over time clinical work too often stood apart from community work, advocacy, and social policy. Although social work education standards today require all students to be exposed to clinical and casework, community practice, advocacy, research and policy, most schools do not prioritize the integrated practice of these areas in the advanced year of social work education (Austin & Ezell, 2004; Knee & Folsom, 2012).

Despite the development of sophisticated methods for helping others, social work practice overly relies on charity and needs based approaches. These approaches are built on the deficit model of practice in which professionals or individuals with greater means diagnose what is "needed" in a situation and the "treatment" or services required to yield the desired outcome set by the profession or other persons of advantage. Judgments of need are based on professional research, practice wisdom, and theory steeped in values (Ife, 2012). These values, research, theories, and practices typically reflect the beliefs of the persons pronouncing judgment, not necessarily the values and theories of the person who is being judged. This has the effect of disempowering and diminishing control of one's own life while privileging professionals (Ife, 2012). In turn this risks reinforcing passiveness and perpetuating the violation of rights among the marginalized populations we seek to empower and at best maintains the status quo in society.

Needs-based approaches typically arise from charitable intentions. In social welfare, charity-based efforts have led to the labeling of persons worthy and unworthy of assistance, attributing personal behaviors as the cause of marginalization, poverty, disease, and disenfranchisement, and restricted the types of aid available accordingly. Judgments are cast by elites regarding who is deserving and who is not based on criteria that serve to perpetuate existing social, economic, and political relationships in charity based approaches. Needs-based approaches attempt to introduce greater objectivity into the process of selecting who is helped and how by using evidence to demonstrate need and introducing effective and efficient interventions to improve the lot of the needy and society as a whole. Yet the solutions of needs-based efforts like charity-based ones are laden with the values of professionals and the politically elite and do not necessarily reflect the values and choices of the persons who are the object of assistance. Needs-based approaches prioritize the achievement of professionally established goals over the process of developing the goals, and, too often, the failure of outcomes is attributed to personal attributes or behaviors of individuals or groups who receive assistance. For example, the type of services a person diagnosed with a mental disorder receives in a needs-based approach will be often decided by authorities or experts according to their determination of what is best for the person and is likely to assume that a person with a mental disorder is incapable of making choices or at least not "good" choices. Programmatic success would then be evaluated according to adherence to the treatment plan prescribed by the persons with authority in the situation that may omit consumers' objections or own assessments of well-being.

Unlike needs-based and charity-based approaches, a rights-based approach places equal value on process and outcome. In rights-based work, goals are temporary markers that are adjusted as people perpetually reevaluate and understand rights in new ways calling for new approaches to social issues. For example having nearly achieved universal access to primary education, a reevaluation of the right to education might lead to a new goal to raise the quality of education or promote universal enrollment in secondary education among girls. Rights-based approaches are anchored in a normative framework that are based in a set of internationally agreed upon legal covenants and conventions, which in and of themselves can provide a different and potentially more powerful approach. A key aspect of this approach posits the right of all persons to participate in societal decision making, especially those persons or groups who are affected by the decisions. For example, Article 12 of the United Nations Convention on the Rights of the Child (CRC) asserts that states "shall assure to the child who is capable of forming his or her own views the right to express those views freely in all matters affecting the child, the views of the child being given due weight in accordance with the age and maturity of the child." (UNCRC, 1989) Likewise, the preamble to the United Nations Convention on the Rights of Persons with Disabilities holds states responsible for "redressing the profound social disadvantage of persons with disabilities and (to) promote their participation in the civil, political, economic, social and cultural spheres with equal opportunities." (UNCRPD, 2006)

A rights-based approach requires consideration of the universally recognized principles of human rights: the equality of each individual as a human being, the inherent dignity of each person, and the rights to self-determination, peace, and security. Respect for all human rights and dignity set the foundation for all civil, political, social, and economic goals that seek to establish certain standards of well-being for all persons. Rights-based efforts remove the charity dimension by recognizing people not only as beneficiaries, but as active rights holders.

One of the areas of value added by the human rights approach is the emphasis it places on the *accountability* of policymakers and other actors whose actions have an impact on the rights of people. Unlike needs, rights imply duties, and duties demand accountability (UN OHCHR, 2002). Whereas needs may be met or satisfied, rights are realized and as such must be respected, protected, facilitated, and fulfilled. Human rights are indivisible and interdependent, and unlike needs that can be ranked, all human rights are of equal importance. A central dynamic of a rights-based approach is thus about identifying root causes of social issues and empowering rights-holders to understand and if possible claim their rights while duty-bearers are enabled to meet their obligations. Under international law, the state is the principal duty-bearer with respect to the human rights of the people living within its jurisdiction. However, the international community at large also has a responsibility to help realize universal human rights. Thus, monitoring and accountability procedures extend beyond states to global actors—such as the donor community, intergovernmental organizations, international nongovernmental organizations (NGOs), and transnational corporations—whose actions bear upon the enjoyment of human rights in any country (UN OHCHR, 2002, paragraph 230).

Table 1 summarizes the differences between charity-, needs-, and rights-based approaches.

It can be argued that rights-based practice is not strikingly different from the way many social workers practice. For example, the strengths perspective that has become a popular approach in social work practice since the 1990s focuses on strengths, abilities, and potential rather than problems, deficits, and pathologies (Chapin, 1995; Early & GlenMaye, 2000; Saleebey, 1992b) and "interventions are directed to the uniqueness, skills, interests, hopes, and desires of each consumer, rather than a categorical litany of deficits" (Kisthardt, 1992, pp. 60–61). In the strengths-based approach clients are usually seen as the experts on their own situation and professionals are understood as not necessarily having the "best vantage point from which to appreciate client strengths" (Saleebey, 1992a, p. 7). The focus is on "collaboration and partnership between social workers and clients" (Early & GlenMaye, 2000, p. 120).

The strengths perspective has provided a way for many social workers to engage themselves and the populations they work with in advocacy and empowerment that builds upon capabilities and more active processes of social change. Indeed, strengths-based and rights-based approaches build upon the strengths of individuals

**Table 1** Comparison of charity, needs, and rights-based approaches to social issues

| | Charity-based | Needs-based | Rights-based |
|---|---|---|---|
| Goals | Assistance to deserving and disadvantaged individuals or populations to relieve immediate suffering | Fulfilling an identified deficit in individuals or community through additional resources for marginalized and disadvantaged groups | Realization of human rights that will lead to the equitable allocation of resources and power |
| Motivation | Religious or moral imperative of rich or endowed to help the less fortunate who are deserving of assistance | To help those deemed in need of help so as to promote well-being of societal members | Legal obligation to entitlements |
| Accountability | May be accountable to private organization | Generally accountable to those who identified the need and developed the intervention | Governments and global bodies such as the donor community, intergovernmental organizations, international NGOs, and transnational corporations |
| Process | Philanthropic with emphasis on donor | Expert identification of need, its dimensions, and strategy for meeting need within political negotiation. Affected population is the object of interventions | Political with a focus on participatory process in which individuals and groups are empowered to claim their rights |
| Power relationships | Preserves status quo | Largely maintain existing structure, change might be incremental | Must change |
| Target population of efforts | Individuals and populations worthy of assistance | Disadvantaged individuals or populations | All members of society with an emphasis on marginalized populations |
| Emphasis | On donor's benevolent actions | On meeting needs | On the realization of human rights |
| Interventions respond to | Immediate manifestation of problems | Symptomatic deficits and may address structural causes | Fundamental structural causes while providing alleviation from symptomatic manifestations |

and communities and both involve a shift from a deficit approach to one that reinforces the potential of individuals and communities. Both approaches acknowledge the unique sets of strengths and challenges of individuals and communities, and engage them as partners in developing and implementing interventions to improve well-being, giving consideration to the complexities of environments. However, the strengths-based perspective falls short of empowering individuals to claim their rights within a universal, normative framework that goes beyond social work to cut across every professional discipline and applies to all human beings. Rights-based approaches tie social work practice into a global strategy that asserts universal entitlements and the accountability of governments and other actors who bear responsibility for furthering the realization of human rights.

The link between social work and human rights normative standards is an important one as history has repeatedly demonstrated. In many ways social work has been moving toward these standards (Healy, 2008) but has yet to fully embrace it. Social work has been a contradictory and perplexing profession functioning both to help and also to control the disadvantaged. At times social workers have engaged in roles that have furthered oppression (Ife, 2012) and served as a "handmaiden" to those who seek to preserve the status quo (Abramovitz, 1998, p. 512). Social benefits can be used to integrate marginalized populations but also be used to privilege and exclude, particularly, when a charity-based approach is utilized. When conditional, benefits can also be used as a way to modify behaviors and as a means of collecting information on private individual and family matters.

This contradictory and perplexing role of social work is shown albeit, in an extreme case, by social work involvement in the social eugenics movement specifically promulgated by National Socialists leaders in the 1930s and 1940s (Johnson & Moorehead, 2011). Leading up to and during World War II, social workers were used as instruments to implement Nazi policies in Europe. Though the history of social work and social work education is different in each European country, in at least Germany, Austria, Switzerland, Czechoslovakia, and Hungary, authorities used social workers to exclude what the state considered at the time to be undesirable populations from assistance, to reward those who demonstrated loyalty and pledged to carry forth the ideology of the state, and to collect information on personal and family affairs for the state (Hauss & Schulte, 2009). University-based and other forms of social work training were closed down in Germany in 1933 when the National Socialists assumed control because welfare was regarded as superfluous and a "waste for persons useless to the national community" (*Volksgemeinschaft* as quoted in Hauss, 2009, p. 9). "Inferiors" were denied support and social workers were reeducated in Nazi ideology to train mothers on how to raise children who were loyal and useful to the ambitions of the National Socialists (Kruse, 2009). Similarly in Hungary, where social workers were referred to as "social sisters," social workers were reeducated to train mothers about the value of their contributions to the state (mainly their reproductive capacity and rearing of strong children for the state) and were instrumental in the implementation of Hungary's major welfare program that rewarded "worthy" clients with the redistribution of assets from Jewish estates (Szikra, 2009). As Szikra notes, "In the 1930s social policy and social work constituted a central part of social and economic policy-making that was fueled by nationalist and anti-Semitic ideology, influenced by similar practices in Germany, Italy and Czechoslavakia" (p. 116). Following Nazi ideological inoculation based on eugenics and race hate, social workers in Austria were charged with the responsibility of collecting incriminating information regarding mental illness, venereal disease, prostitution, alcoholism, hereditary diseases, and disabilities that would then be used to deny social benefits, prohibit marriages and even select children for Austria's euthanasia program (Melinz, 2009).

Using social workers to realize state ideology was also used usher in and to advance the Soviet agenda beginning in 1918 (Iarskaia-Smirnova & Romanov, 2009). The provision of social services was distributed across multiple disciplines among the helping professions, and the term social work was not used because of its association to western social welfare (Iarskaia-Smirnova & Romanov, 2009). These professionals, often referred to as social agents (workers in nurseries and youth centers, activists in women's organizations and trade unions, nurses, educators, and domestic affairs officials), were charged with the double-task of social care and control. Early on social agents contributed to the establishment of standards designating worthy and unworthy behavior and activities and practices such as censure and social exclusion designed to alienate those who did not comply with state goals (Iarskaia-Smirnova & Romanov, 2009).

The use of social workers to carry out goals seemingly in contradiction of social work's ethics can be found in many examples in the United States as well (Abramovitz, 1998). In his book, *The Child Savers: The Invention of Delinquency* (1965), Anthony Platt demonstrates that despite well-intentioned efforts to protect youth, the establishment of the juvenile justice system in the United States removed youth from the adult justice systems and in doing so created a class of delinquents who were judged without due process. Platt argues that "child savers should in no sense be considered libertarians or humanists" (Platt, 1965, p. 176). The juvenile justice system that these reformers—many of whom were social work pioneers—created in the United States purposefully blurred the distinction between delinquent and dependent young people. Labeling dependent children as delinquents, most of whom had committed no crime, robbed them of their opportunity to due process. The state and various religious organizations were given open reign to define delinquency as they saw fit and children who were perceived to be out of order or young women who were viewed as immoral, were committed to institutions or other forms of state supervision with no means of redress.

More recently, Bumiller's analysis of domestic violence in the United States rouses our consciousness of the ways in which social workers engaged with persons involved in domestic violence and/or rape may inadvertently squash rather than empower individuals and families (Bumiller, 2008). Bumiller uses sexual violence to demonstrate how lawyers, medical professionals, and social workers may be contributing to passivity of social service beneficiaries and in doing so, enlarge the state's ability to control the behaviors of its members (Bumiller, 2008). As Bumiller explains, our public branding perpetrators of sexual violence as deserving of severe punishment and isolation allows us then to deem them incapable of rehabilitation and so we offer few opportunities for perpetrators to rejoin society as functioning members. In contrast, we expend resources toward "treating" victims to turn them into successful survivors and in the process of doing so instill their dependency on the state. We do this by requiring victims who seek support and protection from the state to comply with authorities, which in many cases are social workers, and acquiesce to the invasion of state control into their lives. In return for protection and assistance, needy women and children often relinquish control of their own lives and are forced to become individuals who need constant oversight and regulation. "As women have become the subjects of a more expansive welfare state, social service agencies have viewed women and their needs in ways that have often discouraged them from resisting regulations and from being active participants in their own decisions" (Bumiller, 2008). Some social workers use professional authority to support a deficit approach that allows social workers to scrutinize the parenting skills, education, housing, relationships, and psychological coping skills of those who have experienced sexual violence, and then prescribe behaviors necessary to access to benefits. Those who voice complaints and resist scrutiny may be denied benefits such as disqualifying women from temporary assistance for needy families (TANF) benefits who fail to comply with work requirements or cutting off assistance to women who return to violent relationships. As key actors in this process, social workers have the opportunity to legitimize women's voice both within social welfare institutions and within the confines of relationships rather than reinforcing dependency and in some circumstances, revictimizing the individuals by making compliance a prerequisite for assistance.

The commonality of these examples lies in the omission of a normative frame that transcends national borders. The foundation of a rights-based approach is nested in universal legal guarantees to protect individuals and groups against the actions and omissions that interfere with fundamental freedoms, entitlements, and human dignity as first presented in the Universal Declaration of Human Rights. International human rights law is based on a series of international conventions, covenants, and treaties ratified by states and other nonbinding instruments such as declarations, guidelines, and principles. Taken together these inalienable, interdependent, interrelated and indivisible human rights are owned by people everywhere and responsibility to respect, protect, and fulfill these rights is primarily the obligation of the state.

Bonding social work practice to these international legal instruments obligates social workers to look beyond their own government's responses to social issues, to empower the populations they work with to have their voice heard, and to recast the neglected sovereignty of marginalized individuals and communities. It moves social workers away from being agents of the state to being change agents in keeping with the founding vision of social work. It reunites the different methods of social work practice by obligating all social workers to reflect on how public policies affect the rights of individuals and communities and how individual actions affect the rights of others (see Table 2). A rights-based approach compels social workers to look beyond existing methods of helping that too often exist to justify state intervention without addressing the root causes of the situation. It calls upon social workers who often act as agents of the state to acknowledge and act on their responsibility as moral

**Table 2** Rights-based approaches to social work practice at different levels of intervention

| |
|---|
| *Individuals* seeking assistance are not judged to be worthy or unworthy of assistance but rather are viewed as rights holders. Social workers assist others in claiming their rights and helping others understand how individual rights have been violated. Interventions offered are not patronizing or stigmatizing, rather methods provide assistance based on the dignity of and respect for all individuals.<br>Example of individual-centered change: *Sexually trafficked persons are viewed as rights holders whose rights were violated rather than as criminals, and are offered healing services and other benefits to restore their wholeness.* |
| *Community/group/organization* efforts are redirected away from proving that they deserve or need a resource toward learning about how they can claim their entitlements to resources. Social workers facilitate human rights education among group members including knowledge of human rights instruments, principles, and methods for accessing rights.<br>Example of group-centered change: Groups are offered opportunities to learn about their housing rights, the change process in their community, and learn skills so that they can claim their right to participation in community decision making. |
| *Society* redirects its social policies and goals to facilitate the realization of human rights including addressing human needs. Macro practicing social workers affect the policy process and goals by expanding means for all members of a society to have their voices heard in the decision making process.<br>Example of society-centered change: Persons with disabilities are able to participate in the policymaking process through the use of technology that allows them to participate in meetings from their homes. |

duty bearers who have the obligation to respect, protect, and fulfill the rights of rights-holders.

Rights-based approaches in social work have gained international acceptance in the past two decades more so outside of the United States than within. Social workers in the United States are relatively new to human rights practice, in part because of longstanding resistance known as “American exceptionalism” which allows the United States to initiate and even demand compliance of human rights abroad while repeatedly rejecting the application of international standards for human rights in the United States (Hertel & Libal, 2011). Most Americans are knowledgeable about civil and political rights, yet far fewer are as familiar with economic, social, and cultural rights. Relatively limited engagement in this area by social workers also stems from the perception that human rights activism is best led and achieved by lawyers or elite policy advocates. The books in this series are written to facilitate rights-based approaches to social work practice both in the United States and around the world and recognize that exposure to human rights multilateral treaties and applications may vary depending on where the reader was educated or trained.

A rights-based approach brings a holistic perspective with regards to civil, political, social, economic, and cultural roles we hold as human beings and a more holistic understanding of well-being that goes beyond the meeting of material needs. Our understanding of human rights is always evolving and our methods, practices, research, interventions, and processes should evolve as our understanding deepens. The purpose of this series is to assist social work practitioners, educators, and students toward operationalizing a new approach to social work practice that is grounded in human rights. It is hoped that the books will stimulate discussion and the introduction of new methods of practice around maximizing the potential of individuals, communities, and societies. The books, like social work, reflect the wide-range of practice methods, social issues, and populations while specifically addressing an essential area of social work practice. By using current issues as examples of rights-based approaches, the books facilitate the ability of social workers familiar with human rights to apply rights-based approaches in their practice. Each book in the series calls on social work practitioners in clinical, community, research, or policymaking settings to be knowledgeable about the laws in their jurisdiction but to also look beyond and hold state's accountability to the international human rights laws and framework.

Shirley Gatenio Gabel
Fordham University New York, NY

## References

Abramovitz, M. (1998). Social work and social reform: An arena of struggle. *Social Work, 43*(6), 512–526.

Austin, M. J., & Ezell, M. (2004). Educating future social work administrators. *Administration in Social Work, 28*(1), 1–3.

Bumiller, K. (2008). *In an abusive state: How neoliberalism appropriated the feminist movement against sexual violence*. Durham, NC: Duke University Press.

Chapin, R. (1995). Social policy development: The strengths perspective. *Social Work, 40*(4), 506–514.

Early, T., & GlenMaye, L. (2000). Valuing families: Social work practice with families from a strengths perspective. *Social Work, 45*(2), 118–130.

Friedman, M., & Friedman, B. (2006). *Settlement houses: Improving the welfare of America's immigrants*. New York, NY: Rosen.

Hauss, G. & Schulte, D. (2009). *Amid social contradictions: Toward a history of social work in Europe*. Opladen, Farmington Hills: Barbara Budrich Publishers.

Healy, L. M. (2008). Exploring the history of social work as a human rights profession. *International Social Work, 51*(6), 735–746.

Hertel, S. Libal, K. (2011). *Human Rights in the United States: Beyond Exceptionalism.* Cambridge.

Iarskaia-Smirnova, E. & Romanov, P. (2009) Rhetoric and practice of modernisation: Soviet social policy (1917-1930). In G. Hauss & D. Schulte (Eds.), *Amid social contradictions: Towards a history of social work in Europe.* MI: Barbara Budrich Publishers.

Ife, J. (2012). *Human rights and social work: Towards rights-based practice*. Cambridge, UK: Cambridge University Press.

Johnson, S., & Moorhead, B. (2011). Social eugenics practices with children in Hitler's Nazi Germany and the role of social work: Lessons for current practice. *Journal of Social Work Values and Ethics, 8*(1), 1–10.

Kisthardt, W. (1992). A strengths model of case management: The principles and functions of a helping partnership with persons with persistent mental illness. In D. Saleebey (Ed.), *The strengths perspective in social work practice*. New York, NY: Longman.

Knee, R. T., & Folsom, J. (2012). Bridging the crevasse between direct practice social work and management by increasing the transferability of core skills. *Administration in Social Work, 36,* 390–408.

Kruse, E. (2009). Toward a history of social work training Germany—Discourses and struggle for power at the turning points. In G. Hauss & D. Schulte (Eds.), *Amid social contradictions: Towards a history of social work in Europe*. Opladen, Germany: Barbara Budrich.

Melinz, G. (2009). In the interest of children: Modes of intervention in family privacy in Austria (1914–1945). In G. Hauss & D. Schulte (Eds.), *Amid social contradictions: Towards a history of social work in Europe*. Opladen, Germany: Barbara Budrich.

Morris, P. M. (2008). Reinterpreting Abraham Flexner's speech, "Is social work a profession?" Its meaning and influence on the Field's early professional development. *Social Service Review, 82*(1), 29–60.

Platt, A. M. (1965). *The child savers: The invention of delinquency.* Chicago, IL: University of Chicago Press.

Saleebey, D. (1992b). Introduction: Beginnings of a strengths approach to practice. In D. Saleebey (Ed.), *The strengths perspective in social work practice*. New York, NY: Longman.

Saleebey, D. (Ed.). (1992d). *The strengths perspective in social work practice*. New York, NY: Longman.

Szikra, D. (2009). Social policy and anti-semitic exclusion before and during WW II in Hungary: The case of productive social policy. In G. Hauss & D. Schulte (Eds.), *Amid social contradictions: Towards a history of social work in Europe*. Opladen, Germany: Barbara Budrich Publishers.

Trolander, J. A. (1987). *Professionalism and social change: From the settlement house movement to neighborhood centers, 1886 to the present.* New York, NY: Columbia University Press.

United Nations Office of the High Commissioner for Human Rights (OHCHR) (2002). Draft Guidelines for a Human Rights Approach to Poverty Reduction Strategies 2002: paragraph 23.

United Nations. (1989, November 20). Convention on the rights of the child. New York: United Nations. Retrieved from http://www2.ohchr.org/english/law/pdf/crc.pdf.

United Nations. (2006, December 13). Convention on the rights of persons with disabilities. New York: United Nations. Retrieved from http://www2.ohchr.org/english/law/pdf/disabilitiesconvention.pdf.

# Acknowledgements

To my editor, Shirley Gatenio Gabel, who encouraged me to write this book and has been a huge support throughout. Her insightful guidance and critical feedback have been invaluable.

I am indebted to Kathryn Libal for her expert consultation and substantive feedback on an early draft of this manuscript.

I also would like to thank Jennifer Hadley and her staff at Springer US for their expertise and assistance in ushering the manuscript to press.

Above all I want to thank my family who believed in me and supported me through long hours over many months: most especially to my husband Craig, my granddaughter Tallulah, my son Satyam, and my parents Fred and Laura. I could not have written this manuscript without you.

# Contents

1 Introduction: Rights-Based versus Conventional Needs-Based Approaches to Clinical Practice .................................. 1

2 Rights-Based Approach to Working with Torture Survivors ......... 31

3 Rights-Based Clinical Practice with Survivors of Human Trafficking .......................................... 63

4 Intimate Partner Violence and a Rights-Based Approach to Healing .......................................... 85

5 The Use and Care of Self when Engaging in Rights-Based Clinical Practice ............................................. 115

# Chapter 1
# Introduction: Rights-Based versus Conventional Needs-Based Approaches to Clinical Practice

> Henry[1], a white male 45-year-old former schoolteacher, has come for the first time to a homeless shelter where Susan works as a social worker. As Susan sits down to get to know Henry, she notices that he occasionally appears to be laughing and talking as though he were having a conversation with someone in the corner of the room, although nobody is there. Henry informs her that he ran out of his medicine for diabetes a week ago. Upon questioning by Susan, Henry says that he was dumped on the street after a short stay at a local psychiatric hospital with only a 3-day supply of medicine and no follow-up appointment. He had nowhere to go and no resources. A man he met on the street introduced him to Susan's shelter.

How might you approach your work with Henry if you were Susan? What, if anything, might a clinical social worker contribute that would be valuable to Henry? A referral to a physician? Assistance in applying for stable housing? Both? Or might there be a different approach to interacting with and working with Henry? A social worker operating from a human rights frame would likely conceptualize and engage with Henry in a very different manner than one focused on identifying and addressing Henry's immediate needs. Mentally ill individuals facing homelessness like Henry have had their rights violated, their dignity trampled on, and their most basic needs ignored.

## Overview of the Book

Clinical social workers that seek to apply a rights-based frame to guide their practice or inform their ethical decision making can find little explicit direction in the existing literature. Fundamentally, a rights-based approach goes deeper than addressing individuals' immediate needs (Jewell, Collins, Gargotto, & Dishon, 2009), both working to realize their rights through service provision and advocating for the advancement of human rights more broadly (Libal, Berthold, Thomas, & Healy, 2014).

[1] The names and other identifying information in all case materials have been changed to protect confidentiality, and aspects of each case are a composite from more than one person.

 
S. M. Berthold, *Human Rights-Based Approaches to Clinical Social Work*,
SpringerBriefs in Rights-Based Approaches to Social Work, DOI 10.1007/978-3-319-08560-9_1

Children, the mentally ill, the disabled, homeless individuals and families, and those who are incarcerated are among those who are often marginalized, left without a voice, and are at particular risk for having their rights violated. It can be argued that social and clinical service providers, our schools, and society at large do not appear to be engaged in sufficient prevention or the early identification or treatment of mental health and other serious problems that have been linked to perpetration of violence or other human rights abuses. Those who perpetrate mass murder and other human rights violations often show signs of distress earlier in life, such as Adam Lanza who shot and killed 26 members of the Sandy Hook Elementary School and his mother in Connecticut in 2012. In hindsight, these tragedies often uncover a failure to respond (or adequately respond) to the needs and rights of these individuals for treatment. Why are these individuals marginalized and left out of the system of care? Why are their rights not promoted and what difference would human rights-based approaches make in their lives and the lives of others? One of the lessons learned from Sandy Hook and other tragedies is arguably that a rights-based approach may help to prevent the perpetration of some rights violations. Clinical social workers are needed as part of a team that includes rights-based community, policy, legislative, and administrative partners to prevent distressed children and other marginalized individuals and groups from being left out. Their rights matter too.

Human rights, by their nature, are political. It is the responsibility of States (governments), the United Nations, and other official bodies to protect and ensure that the rights of all are respected and fulfilled. Unfortunately, even when governments sign and ratify human rights treaties, adherence to their treaty obligations are often overlooked, purposively ignored, or only partially implemented. Social workers, acting as individual clinical practitioners and collectively, can make a difference by practicing from a rights-base. Largely absent from the clinical practice curriculum and literature until recently, rights-based approaches to clinical practice are emerging (Berthold, 2014; New Haven Trauma Competencies, 2013).

This introductory chapter presents a framework for a human rights-based approach to clinical social work practice. It defines human rights and provides a conceptual overview of a rights-based approach to clinical social work practice and how this differs from conventional needs-based approaches. Core principles of a rights-based approach to clinical social work practice are examined and illustrated. These core principles include: reframing needs as entitlements or rights, operating from a stance of cultural humility and intersectionality, fostering a therapeutic relationship and reconstructing safety, providing trauma-informed care, and drawing from the recovery-model and a strengths and resilience orientation. These principles are reinforced throughout the book and applied to diverse case material. The similarities and differences between needs- and rights-based approaches to clinical practice at the various stages of work with individuals (e.g., preparation for the work, engagement phase, assessment, working phase, and termination) are discussed.

Chapters 2 to 4 provide a more in-depth look at rights-based clinical social work practice with survivors of several major human rights issues, including torture, human trafficking, and intimate partner violence (IPV) within a US context. A rights-based approach to working with perpetrators is also explored, in the context of IPV. Although examples of torture and human trafficking have often been used to point to human rights violations that have occurred outside of the United States, this text will present an argument against US exceptionalism (Hertel & Libal, 2011). Examination of the use of solitary confinement of minors and the US' involvement in the torture of enemy combatants in Chapter 2 will illustrate that human rights concerns are not solely external to a domestic US context.

Chapters 2 to 4 will include an opening case example followed by three main sections: (1) definitional and contextual issues; (2) relevant human rights mechanisms/tools; and (3) clinical interventions and illustration of selected core principles of a rights-based approach to clinical practice with the population discussed in each chapter. At the end of each chapter is a section that includes activities and resources for further study. The concluding chapter, Chapter 5, examines the social work practitioner's use and care of self in engaging in rights-based practice. It explores the impact of rights-based practice on the social work practitioner, including the risk of vicarious trauma. The chapter highlights the practitioner's ethical duty to remain deeply self-reflective and aware of the impact of his or her reactions to the work on the people he or she serves and emphasizes the importance of self-care.

The case material woven throughout this manuscript stems from the author's long-term experience in working with survivors of torture, trafficking, and IPV. While some of the case examples may not be representative of the types of cases encountered most frequently by social workers practicing in the United States, the rights-based principles illustrated can apply to work with a much broader range of populations. This text will not comprehensively address clinical approaches to work with these populations as that material has been covered elsewhere. The focus in this book is on rights-based aspects of the work and the intended audience includes social work practitioners, field instructors, students, and educators.

## Definitions and Context

### *Definition of Human Rights*

In order to apply a rights-based approach, it is necessary to understand what human rights are. Although the Universal Declaration of Human Rights (UDHR) never precisely defined what human rights are, the drafters agreed that the concepts of intrinsic fundamental rights for all by virtue of being human and shared human dignity were core features (Reichert, 2007). According to the United Nations, "Human rights are rights inherent to all human beings, whatever our nationality, place of residence, sex, national or ethnic origin, color, religion, language, or any other status. We are all equally entitled to our human rights without discrimination. These rights are all interrelated, interdependent, and indivisible" (Office of the High Commissioner for Human Rights, n.d., para. 1). Human rights are fundamentally universal and inalienable. Individuals have rights, for example, to bodily security, to family, to be free from arbitrary detention, to never be tortured, to adequate healthcare, to housing, and to food. Not only do human rights involve the rights of all persons but they also entail obligations on behalf of States to respect, protect, and fulfill peoples' rights.

## *Context for a Human Rights-Based Approach*

Advancing human rights was recognized as a core competency for social workers in the Global Standards put forth by the International Federation of Social Workers and International Association of the Schools of Social Work (IFSW/IASSW, 2004) as well as in the Educational Policy and Accreditation Standards of the Council on Social Work Education in the United States (CSWE, 2008). The CSWE Standards cite the IFSW/IASSW standards as providing a foundation for making ethical decisions in keeping with the ethical principles and codes of the social work profession[2]. This may be considered, perhaps, a linking of the obligation of social workers to uphold core human rights treaties with their obligations to adhere to the social work code of ethics (NASW, 1999). Social work has long been concerned with advancing social justice, including in clinical practice (Aldarondo, 2007; Council on Social Work Education, 2012; Finn & Jacobson, 2003; Sachs & Newdom, 2011). A human rights-based approach also promotes social justice.

## Core Principles of a Rights-Based Approach to Clinical Practice

The focus and scope of this book do not allow for a detailed and complete presentation of the theory and techniques of different treatment approaches, but rather highlight some core aspects of treatment that are particularly relevant to a rights-based clinical social work approach. Rights-based clinical social workers should draw on evidence-based research matched to the population they are working with, along with practice wisdom regarding best and promising practices. It is an ethical and professional responsibility for clinical social workers to keep abreast of the research literature regarding evidence-based and best practices in their field. Clinical social workers are encouraged to obtain advanced training in several evidence-based treatment approaches, including those developed for trauma survivors. Information is provided at the end of the chapter regarding where one can obtain further information about some of these treatment approaches.

Clinical social workers operating from a rights-base know that one of the core principles of a rights-based approach is reframing needs as entitlements or rights. Essential also is the practitioner's fundamental orientation toward cultural humility (explained below) (Ortega & Faller, 2011) and intersectionality, and advanced knowledge and expertise in providing trauma-informed care. In addition, they are oriented toward a recovery model that recognizes and builds on strengths and resilience and are informed by an indigenous rights perspective in the sense of not seeking to control or impose values or decisions on those they work with (Brydon, 2011). Rights-based

[2] Educational Policy 2.1.2 of the 2008 CSWE Standards adds that the IASSW/IFSW standards should be applied "as applicable," however, leaving in doubt which parts of the standards are deemed to be applicable and which are not.

practitioners eschew and organize against the common practice of acting as agents of social control through the implementation of policies that do not support the dignity or rights of others, such as with internal immigration controls (Humphries, 2004). Underlying all of their work is the importance of the therapeutic relationship itself, a key component that shapes the nature of the work and its outcomes. These core principles are relevant to work with diverse populations, including those covered in this book, and will be discussed below.

## *Reframing Needs as Entitlements or Rights*

Social workers have a long history of engaging in casework, group work, and family therapy (Gitterman & Germain, 2008; Toseland & Rivas, 2012). The dominant social work paradigm, however, that has been taught and practiced is aligned with a deficit-based medical model. It is focused on assessing and meeting needs rather than rights. Typically the emphasis is on the provision of clinical services to address disorders and overcoming obstacles to accessing services rather than a more fundamental critique of existing services, structures, and prevailing diagnostic and other systems. In addition, in some countries such as the United States, clinical services that promote the realization of peoples' rights are often not provided or even identified as an appropriate target.

One of the key principles of a rights-based approach to clinical practice is that clinicians empower those they work with by reframing needs as entitlements or rights (Cemlyn, 2008a, b; Lundy & van Wormer, 2007). Rather than a need for medical care or safety, for example, the social worker focuses on the individual's right to healthcare and safety. The voices of those served are honored and respected, and drive the clinical work. Rights-based clinicians work in a participatory and democratic style and their work may be repoliticized and in keeping with a critical theory of practice (Adams, Dominelli, & Payne, 2007; Lundy, 2011). Rather than pathologizing individuals, families and community members, problems are viewed within their sociopolitical and structural contexts, and these contexts become targets for intervention (Engstrom & Okamura, 2004; Lundy, 2011). In Henry's case, rights-based practitioners would target the policies and practices of the hospital that allowed him to be dumped on the streets in violation of his right to health and well-being. When rights are violated, individuals are supported in claiming their right to reparation or redress. Rights-based clinical social workers no longer confine themselves solely to micro practice concerns, but open themselves up to practicing across the micro/macro divide (Androff & McPherson, 2014).

While the rights of those engaged in clinical services are routinely addressed formally through the use of such documents as Privacy Practice forms to ensure compliance with the Health Insurance Portability and Accountability Act (HIPAA) and Consent for Services forms, in practice they often are not fully realized in conventional clinical work. In contrast, a rights-based approach to clinical practice goes well beyond the legalistic attention to the rights of those served to infuse attention and realization of rights throughout every phase of person-centered practice (Tondora, Miller, Slade, & Davidson, 2014). Rights-based clinical practice, for example, holds that the person's voice and active participation and partnership in the selection and delivery of clinical services is essential. Such an approach also holds governmental and societal institutions accountable for ensuring the individual's rights are upheld and informs every interaction between the individual and his or her practitioner.

## Cultural Humility

Increasingly, social workers engage with diverse individuals and communities and must be adequately prepared to do so in a way that respects the rights, dignity, unique perspective, ways of knowing, and experiences of each, as well as the self-defined meaning and impact of their cultures (Brydon, 2011; Ortega & Faller, 2011; Tervalon & Murray-Garcia, 1998). Brydon (2011) cautions of the dangers of what she calls the hegemony of Western social work and its values and characteristics that she describes as being inconsistent and incompatible with the cultural orientations of other non-Western societies. Healy (2007) argues for the benefit of a stance of moderate universalism to resolve the ethical dilemma of universalism and relativism in social work practice.

A rights-based approach to working with those who are culturally different from the practitioner is consonant with an approach grounded in cultural humility (rather than cultural competence). The concept of cultural competence, long advocated for in social work education, has been criticized by some for placing too strong an emphasis on characteristics shared by a group to the detriment of recognizing and working with individual differences, and for intensifying the power imbalance between the worker and the person they serve through the privileging of the social worker's knowledge and *expertise* about the person's culture (Ortega & Faller, 2011). Some critics of cultural competence have called for practitioners to develop their *critical awareness* capacities instead, and emphasize respect for each individual's own definition of their cultural experiences and associated meanings (Furlong & Wight, 2011). Cultural humility is offered as an alternative approach to cultural competence, one that supports the social worker in engaging those they serve more actively in the therapeutic process. This approach can be valuable for working with anyone, not just with those from cultural backgrounds dissimilar to the practitioner's own background. If someone appears to come from the same culture as the social worker, it is important that the social worker does not assume that the meaning and expression of that culture will be the same for everyone.

At its core, the cultural humility framework is a respectful and non-paternalistic approach that is fundamental to a human rights-based approach to clinical social work practice. As Ortega and Faller (2011) stress, individuals are, "in the best position to define for themselves the meaning of their culture and cultural experiences" (p. 43). Social workers who practice from a standpoint of cultural humility develop their abilities to work across difference; emphasizing strong communication and interaction skills that are attuned to the unique individual they are working with. Such an approach does not emphasize or require the social worker to learn all about the culture of the populations they work with. It reduces their need to seek mastery about the extensive range of cultural practices and beliefs that those they work with may possess (Ortega & Faller, 2011). Becoming "culturally competent" and an "expert" about multiple cultures is arguably an impossible task, and is furthermore fundamentally inconsistent with cultural humility. Putting oneself forth as an "expert" on a culture runs the risk of stereotyping and incomplete or inaccurate understanding of how culture influences the life experiences of a particular person. Rather, practicing with cultural humility opens the social worker to learn from those that he or she works with, recognizing that each individual is the expert on his or her own life. Cultural humility is not viewed as an outcome or a goal to be attained. Rather, the practitioner enters into a professional relationship with an individual, family, group, or community with an unknowing stance, ready to engage in an ongoing process of learning.

Ortega and Faller (2011) advocate that social workers working within the child welfare arena should embrace and follow the following six practice principles, principles that are relevant to practice grounded in cultural humility with other populations as well:

1. "Embrace the complexity of diversity" (p. 43)
2. "'Know thyself' and critically challenge one's 'openness' to learn from others" (p. 43)
3. "Accept cultural difference and relate to [others] in ways that are most understandable to them" (p. 43)
4. "Continuously engage in collaborative helping" (p. 44)
5. "Demonstrate familiarity with the living environment of [those] being served" (p. 44)
6. "Build organizational support that demonstrates cultural humility as an important and ongoing aspect of the work itself" (p. 44)

It is important to emphasize that a rights-based approach to clinical social work does not relegate the practitioner to narrowly focus on clinical issues with the particular individual, family, couple, or group they are working with. Instead, a rights-based approach requires that the clinical practitioner look beyond the micro into the structural or larger forces at play in the lives of those they work with, thereby breaking down and working across the micro/macro divide in social work (Androff & McPherson, 2014). The fifth Practice Principle put forth by Ortega and Faller (2011), as outlined above, relates to bridging this divide. This principle extends, for example, to examining whether the organization is structured in a fashion to promote and support cultural humility. Further, the practitioner must address structural contributions to rights violations through advocacy and other forms of collective action, ideally in collaboration with the person(s) they serve. Whenever possible, rights-based practitioners should support the individuals they work with to do for themselves rather than doing for them (Brydon, 2011). In understanding the environment(s) of the persons they work with, the worker "is challenged to identify, understand, and build on assets and adaptive strengths of [these individuals] and perhaps engage in efforts to disrupt or dismantle the kind of social forces that act to disenfranchise and disempower them as members of society" (Ortega & Faller, 2011, p. 44). For example, social workers must remain alert for and address the microaggressions (van Sluytman, 2013) that the individuals they serve may have experienced (particularly those who are of color or otherwise marginalized in society), including in the context of trying to access or receive services. Microaggressions are conscious and unconscious insults and expressions of bias that serve to minimize and silence others who have less power, and include microinsults, microinvalidation, and microassaults (Hopkins, 2010; Solórzano, Ceja, & Yosso, 2000; Sue, Bucceri, Lin, Nadal, & Torino, 2007). They can be verbal, nonverbal, or visual in nature. The subtlety and pervasiveness of microaggressions generally make them challenging to confront and contribute to their being frequently ignored or justified (Sue et al., 2007). The presence of microaggressions in settings where social workers practice may contribute to barriers to the fulfillment of rights and must be confronted and addressed.

Practicing from a stance of cultural humility has a lot in common with traditional social work practice (Hepworth, Rooney, Rooney, Strom-Gottfried, & Larsen, 2010; Ortega & Faller, 2011). Ortega and Faller (2011) emphasize that it is the social worker's responsibility to bridge the differing perspectives, cultural experiences, histories, and worldviews that they and the individuals they serve bring to their interactions. In order to bridge perspectives and demonstrate cultural humility, Ortega and Faller (2011) state that reserving judgment, active listening and reflecting, and entering the other person's world are all essential skills for practitioners. Strong foundational social work skills and putting the profession's values into practice are central to the practice of cultural humility (Ortega & Faller, 2011). This includes, in part, the practitioner's ongoing efforts at self-awareness, learning from those they work with and starting from where they are at, and affirming the dignity and positive worth of and demonstrating respect and empathy for those they serve.

## *Intersectionality*

Another critical concept for rights-based clinical social workers to be versed in is intersectionality, a concept closely linked to the human rights principles of the dignity and worth of the person, equality, and nondiscrimination. This perspective holds that individuals occupy various positionalities or positions at the same time in the structural and socio-cultural-political framework in their society (Crenshaw, 1995; Hill Collins, 2000; Hernandez & McDowell, 2010). A person's gender, age, race and ethnicity, socioeconomic class, gender identity, sexual orientation, religious or spiritual beliefs, and other factors all intersect and contribute to a person's positionality and individuality. These facets are all central to notions of dignity and humanity. According to Ortega and Faller (2011), "Intersecting group memberships affect people's expectations, quality of life, capacities as individuals and parents, life chances, and so on. They draw attention to the whole person, power differences in relationships, different past and present experiences based on positionalities and social contexts, and potential resources (or gaps)" (p. 43). The multiple positions or identities of the individual have an effect on the way he or she expresses his or her culture and on his or her worldview (Ortega & Faller, 2011). These must be attended to by the social worker practicing with cultural humility.

Social workers who approach their practice with cultural humility are grounded in an understanding and application of critical race theory and intersectionality (Abrams & Moio, 2009; Murphy, Hunt, Zajicek, Norris, & Hamilton, 2009; Ortiz & Jani, 2010). Such an approach is holistic and respects the diversity of each person. It attends to the power dynamics and differences between social workers and those they serve and the variety of microaggressions and other experiences that individuals who seek services may have had. In addition, it assesses the limitations and resources available and the impact of power, authority, and control on the social worker's decision making and the choices available to those they serve (Ortega & Faller, 2011). It works to counteract the forces of power, bias, discrimination, racism, sexism, and other forms of oppression that have resulted in the denial of or limited access to services and resources and ultimately, the denial of rights (Finn & Jacobson, 2003; Hernandez & McDowell, 2010; Sengupta, 2006).

## *Fostering a Therapeutic Relationship and Reconstructing Safety*

Rights-based clinical social work practitioners understand that the nature and quality of the relationship between the practitioner and those they serve matters. Mental health professionals who work with survivors of mass and other forms of complex trauma[3] have long understood this (Briere, 2002; Kinzie, 2001; Mollica, 2006). Of course, what is therapeutic to one person may not be to another. Expert panelists reviewed a series of meta-analyses on evidence-based therapy relationships as part of the American Psychological Associations' second Task Force on Evidence-Based Therapy Relationships. The task force found support for the effectiveness of various methods of treatment adaptation and elements of the therapeutic relationship (Norcross & Wampold, 2011). Some of the task force's conclusions are highlighted here. The task force found that the therapeutic relationship makes independent, consistent, and substantial contributions to the outcome of psychotherapy separate from the particular type of treatment. They determined that, in order to be complete and not misleading, evidence-based and best practice guidelines must include attention to the therapy relationship. Outcomes are improved when interventions tailor the therapy

[3] Experiences that involve exposure to repeated and prolonged trauma such as domestic violence, childhood sexual abuse, human trafficking, and torture, or exposure to multiple types of personal trauma are commonly referred to as complex trauma (Cloitre et al., 2012).

relationship to the characteristics of the particular individual in therapy. Treatment effectiveness is determined by the combined impact of the characteristics of the person seeking therapy, qualities of the practitioner, treatment approach, and nature of the therapy relationship.

The experts identified that the following elements of the therapy relationship were demonstrated to be effective: alliance in individual, youth, and family psychotherapy; collecting feedback from the person served; and cohesion in group therapy (Norcross & Wampold, 2011). Other aspects of the therapy relationship had less evidence of effectiveness. The task force concluded that collaboration, positive regard, and goal consensus were probably effective elements of the relationship, while managing countertransference, congruence/genuineness, and the repairing of ruptures to the alliance showed promise.

Research has also identified things that therapists should *not* do if they want to be effective, some of which are highly relevant for rights-based practitioners (Norcross & Wampold, 2011). For example, adopting a strongly confrontational approach was not effective (Miller, Wilbourne, & Hettema, 2003), nor was attacking the person rather than the unhealthy thoughts or behavior (Norcross & Wampold, 2011). Motivational interviewing techniques, in contrast (e.g., demonstrating empathy, supporting self-efficacy, rolling with resistance), showed large positive effects in relatively few sessions (Lundahl & Burke, 2009). The therapy alliance is enhanced and there is less premature termination when therapists respectfully and explicitly ask the persons they work with in therapy for their perceptions of and satisfaction with the therapy relationship and treatment rather than making assumptions (Lambert & Shimokawa, 2011). Treatment outcomes are better predicted by observations of the person receiving treatment about the relationship rather than those of the therapist (Orlinsky, Ronnestad, & Willutzki, 2004). Tailoring the therapy to the person being served (Norcross & Wampold, 2011) and avoidance of inflexible or strongly structured approaches (Ackerman & Hilsenroth, 2001) contributes to more efficacious and appropriate treatment and lessens the risk of empathic failures.

Fabri (2001) elaborates on techniques for and the importance of developing a therapeutic relationship and reconstructing safety with torture survivors that are in keeping with a rights-based approach to practice. She calls for empowering the survivor through, in part, adjusting the therapeutic frame to attend to issues of safety and power that are of paramount concern to survivors. Fabri's (2001) approach is consonant with cultural humility. The survivor serves as the guide and expert regarding modifications to the treatment approach in order to prevent his or her revictimization. Modifications may be made to seating arrangements, roles, boundary definitions, and meeting space.

Clinical social workers are advised to proactively look for opportunities for the survivors they work with to be in control of as many aspects of their work together. This includes whether or not the survivor chooses to disclose their traumatic experiences, and if they do, how much, when, at what pace, and to whom they chose to disclose. Social workers must ensure that informed consent is truly informed and that the consent is freely given rather than coerced. It is important to ensure that the survivor understands what the consent for services and other forms say, a goal that can be made harder if there is no professionally translated version in the survivor's language, if it is necessary to have the forms interpreted on the spot (particularly if the interpreter is not a trained professional interpreter), or if the survivor is not literate in any language (Miletic et al. 2006). Rather than rushing through the explanation of the consent and other forms or worse, merely telling the survivor that they need to sign the form(s) in order to be helped, a rights-based clinical social worker should patiently go over the meaning and detail of the form(s), using it as an opportunity to start building a therapeutic relationship.

Building trust in survivors of human rights violations for whom trust has been shattered is essential. Establishing trust and safety is a process that takes time and is furthered when the social worker follows through on the commitments they make to the survivor and when they are clear not to promise things that they may not be able to deliver or are unlikely to happen. Clinicians have been asked on many occasions by trauma survivors such things as whether their traumatic memories will ever stop completely and forever, and whether they will ever see their disappeared child again. While tempting to say yes, particularly when the survivor asks over and over, it is never a good idea clinically (or ethically) to give false hope. Rather, the clinician should work with the survivor to come to terms with the reality as it is, no matter how painful.

## *Trauma-Informed*

Rights-based clinical social workers must be competent trauma-informed practitioners. Many persons served by social workers have had one or more traumatic experiences and often have had significant rights violated prior to seeking treatment or in the course of seeking treatment (e.g., right not to be abused, right to informed choice). These rights violations are traumatic in and of themselves. The majority of those who utilize public mental health services have trauma histories (Jennings, 2004a, b). Potentially traumatic events (PTEs) are experienced by approximately one-quarter of all children and adolescents in the community in the United States (Costello, Erkanli, Fairbank, & Angold, 2002). Child abuse, community violence, and other traumas experienced by youth can result in profound developmental disruptions and short- and long-term negative consequences for these youth, their families, and society (Briere & Lanktree, 2011; Greeson et al., 2011; Putnam, 2006; Pynoos, Steinberg, Schreiber, & Brymer, 2006). Children who have experienced child abuse and multiple other adverse childhood experiences are significantly more likely to develop health and mental health problems and have negative social outcomes as adults (Anda, 2008; Edwards, Holden, Felitti, & Anda, 2003; Felitti et al., 1998; Wegman & Stetler, 2009).

The adverse effects associated with traumatic stress have led many to seek care in schools and healthcare systems, and to become involved with juvenile justice and child welfare systems where clinical social workers practice (Chapman, Ford, Hawke, & Albert, 2006; Garland et al., 2001). Until recently, many of these systems have not addressed the impact of trauma with a systematic or evidence-based approach (Ko et al., 2008). The National Child Traumatic Stress Network (NCTSN) advocates for a system-wide trauma-informed approach that ensures that all youth receive trauma exposure screening; practitioners use evidence-informed approaches; survivors, family members, and providers have ready access to resources about trauma; and service systems provide continuity of care across systems (Ko et al., 2008).

The Council on Social Work Education (2012), SAMHSA (n.d.), and the NCTSN (2006) have developed trauma-informed guidelines.[4] The NCTSN (2006) also developed 12 core concepts that are useful for understanding traumatic stress responses. SAMHSA (2014) recognizes trauma-informed care as an evidence-based practice that is "based on an understanding of the vulnerabilities or triggers of trauma survivors that traditional service delivery approaches may exacerbate, so that these services and programs can be more supportive and avoid re-traumatization" (para. 2).

Trauma-informed services are those that reflect a deep understanding and sensitivity to the full range of trauma-related psychological, biological, neurological, spiritual, and social effects that may be experienced by survivors of violence and other traumas (Briere & Lanktree, 2011; Cook et al., 2005; Harris & Fallot, 2001; Ko et al., 2008). A trauma-informed service systems approach reflects the complexity and multifaceted nature of the problem by targeting all relevant parts of the system that contribute to or are affected by the problem (Fallot & Harris, 2008; Ko et al., 2008). The Sanctuary Model (Bloom, 2013; Esaki et al., 2013) is an organizational change model that is evidence-supported and trauma-informed. It seeks to create a restorative culture and positive therapeutic relationships in organizations that serve trauma survivors in order to promote healing and the conditions necessary for resilience. Among the defining features of a certified Sanctuary Organization are: the community feels connected and safe; there is direct, open, and honest communication; all who are affected by a decision are included in the decision making process and responsibility for conflict resolution and problem-solving is shared in order to minimize any possible abuse of power; the organizational environment is just; injuries, critical incidents, staff turnover and the use of coercive measures are minimized; and increased satisfaction of staff and those they serve (Esaki et al., 2013; Sanctuary Model, n.d.).

The following hypothetical example of youth bullying illustrates the relevance of a trauma-informed approach for rights-based practice:

[4] A trauma-informed approach is central to the work of many trauma, mental, and behavioral health organizations such as the NCTSN, International Society for Traumatic Stress Studies (ISTSS), Center for Mental Health Services (CMHS), Substance Abuse and Mental Health Services Administration (SAMHSA), and the U.S. Department of Health and Human Services (DHHS) for addressing the impact of trauma on children and adults in school, community, mental health, and other settings.

> Karen is an eleven-year-old overweight girl who has been bullied by her schoolmates for the past 5 months. The problem started with two popular girls taunting her in the lunch line, loudly calling her "fatso" and pushing her out of the line. Soon, cartoon drawings of her shoving her face full of pizza or bursting out of her clothes appeared on the chalkboard during homeroom most mornings. Once a banner depicting her as a pig was unfurled from the bleachers in gym class. The homeroom and gym teachers, school staff, and administration did nothing to seek to find the perpetrator(s) or address the issue. The bullying escalated. For the past three months female classmates have assaulted Karen multiple times on her way to school, once leaving Karen with a broken arm. Karen was too afraid to report the incidents, as the girls threatened to beat up her younger brother if she told on them. She told her parents that she fell off her bike and broke her arm in the fall. Last week Karen discovered a Facebook page with images of her as a punching bag and animated masked figures punching her over and over. She has become increasingly anxious and depressed and has been using a razor to make cuts on her lower abdomen. Karen frequently stays home sick from school and has begged her parents to let her be home schooled.

A trauma-informed social worker would address the impact of trauma on all parts of the system, including on Karen (the youth directly targeted by bullying), as well as her caregivers, other family members, peers, school personnel, the larger community, and service providers. Emphasis is not only on treating the impact of trauma but on creating and sustaining safe environments to prevent bullying and other violence and promote a healthier community. Agencies and programs in a trauma-informed system instill and seek to sustain awareness, knowledge, and skills related to addressing trauma into the fabric of their organizational policies, practices, and cultures. Emphasis is placed on a collaborative multidisciplinary approach, engaging all individuals and systems involved with the affected child or youth. The best available scientific evidence-based practice approaches drive all interventions aimed at promoting the recovery and resilience of all parts of the system (NCTSN, n.d.; SAMHSA, n.d.).

Key elements of a trauma-informed systems approach to the problem of bullying and other youth violence include: (1) routine screening of youth for exposure to trauma and associated symptoms of distress; (2) assessment and treatment of traumatic stress and related mental health symptoms that are culturally appropriate and evidence-based; (3) making resources and information related to trauma exposure, its effects and treatment available to children, youth, families, schools, communities, and providers; (4) efforts to strengthen resilience and protective factors of children, youth, families, schools, and broader communities affected by or at risk of exposure to trauma; (5) focus on the impact of youth violence on caregivers, the family, and the broader system; (6) emphasis throughout on collaboration among all members of the system and continuity of care; and (7) development of an environment of care for all providers that attends to their secondary traumatic stress and increases their resilience (NCTSN, n.d.).

A rights-based practitioner would incorporate a trauma-informed approach but go one step further and systematically address Karen's rights such as her right to education free from abuse and threats, and her rights to safety and health. In addition, the practitioner would utilize specialized trauma-informed specific services to treat Karen's traumatic symptoms of distress. The social worker might employ Briere's self-trauma model (STM) (Briere, 2002; Briere & Scott, 2012), a non-pathologizing model for treating survivors of acute and chronic trauma that combines relational, affect regulation, cognitive-behavioral, mindfulness, and psychopharmacologic approaches. Using the STM, the clinician would work with Karen's trauma story, in gradual doses of exposure, making sure not to overwhelm Karen with more trauma work then she is able to handle given her coping skills (more details regarding the STM will be provided in Chapter 2). Her self-injury would be understood as behavior aimed at reducing tension and distress rather than pathologized. Teaching grounding and other skills may assist Karen in regulating her affect and dissociative symptoms and adopting less harmful coping strategies. The practitioner may also draw from Trauma-Focused Cognitive-Behavioral Therapy (TF-CBT) or other trauma-specific approaches appropriate for youth of Karen's age (Cohen, Mannarino, & Deblinger, 2006; Ford & Courtois, 2013). Ultimately, providing trauma-specific clinical services to Karen would be ineffective and unethical in the absence of addressing the larger rights and contributing systemic factors. Karen should not feel forced to switch schools or be home schooled due to her fear of continued bullying and fear for her own and her brother's safety.

Throughout the work with Karen or any individual, the social worker would seek to minimize his or her power and control and pay attention to the culture of the person they are working with. To ensure that the treatment approach is meaningful and perceived as helpful to an individual, it needs to be in keeping with his or her worldview. Informed by cultural humility, the rights-based practitioner would be alert to the need to make cultural adaptations to their trauma-informed and other clinical interventions as appropriate, ensuring that the interventions are well matched to what is healing to the person seeking care. One example of this is *Honoring Children, Mending the Circle,* an adaptation to TF-CBT with indigenous survivors of sexual abuse that incorporates traditional indigenous rituals and healing practices (BigFoot & Schmidt, 2010).

## Centrality of the Trauma Story

Listening to and working therapeutically with the trauma story is considered by many to be a central part of healing from trauma (Briere, 2002; Kinzie, 2001; Mollica, 2010). The trauma story can facilitate personal disclosure and self-healing as the survivor becomes the clinician's teacher (Mollica, 2010). The trauma narrative includes multiple elements: the accounting of the events, focus on the cultural meanings of trauma, facilitating insights and reframing the survivor's trauma experiences, and the central importance of the relationship between the storyteller and the listener (Mollica, 2006, 2010). The survivor's transformative growth, wisdom, and resilience emerge from their story of trauma. It is important to note that some survivors of human rights violations may not have sufficient affect regulation skills to be able to tolerate recounting their story initially in therapy as is discussed further in Chapter 2 (Briere, 2002).

## *Recovery Model*

The recovery model is consonant with a rights-based approach combating the stigmatization and oppression of those living with a mental illness and supporting them in reclaiming their lives as contributing and valuable community members (Davidson, 2008; McNamara, 2009; Tondora et al., 2014). While initially developed for use with those recovering from serious and persistent mental illness, the Recovery Model can valuably inform social work practice with other populations. It is consistent with the NASW Code of Ethics (NASW, 1999) and places emphasis on recognizing strengths and abilities and respecting the value and worth of each person as an important and equal member of society. The goals of the recovery model are the self-actualization and empowerment of individuals from historically disenfranchised populations (NASW, 2006).

In most traditional models of care, those seeking treatment are told what to do or staff do things for them with little or no consultation with the person to elicit their opinion or wishes (NASW, 2006; Walsh, 2013). In contrast, those recovering from mental illness are referred to as "consumers" in the recovery model and it is the consumers themselves who are in primary control over all decisions related to their care (Walsh, 2013). Recovery is defined as, "an individual's journey of healing and transformation to live a meaningful life in a community of his or her choice while striving to achieve maximum human potential" (U.S. Department of Health and Human Services, 2005, p. 4).

The NASW (2006) provides helpful practice recommendations for social workers that are working with individuals whose decisions are in conflict with available scientific evidence and/or the practitioner's clinical judgment. Social workers must uphold their ethical responsibility (and in most states, their legal obligations) to intervene in situations where there is a serious, imminent, and foreseeable danger of harm to an individual or another person. However, in other situations the social worker should support and respect the wishes and right of the person they are working with to make their own decisions (even those that may not seem rational or healthy to the social worker). This includes, for adults, whether or not to take medication or engage in treatment (unless directed to do so by a legal guardian or court order). The practitioner can explore with the person the possible consequences of their decisions and realistic alternatives. Above all, Pat Deegan, Director of Training and Education at The National Empowerment Center, reminds professionals that persons in recovery "must have the opportunity to try and to fail and to try again. In order to support the recovery process mental health professionals must not rob us of the opportunity to fail. Professionals must embrace the concept of the dignity of risk and the right to failure if they are to be supportive of us" (Deegan, 1996, p. 97).

## *Strengths and Resilience Orientation*

Clinical social work practice that is steeped in and driven by a rights framework fosters healing and growth, is aligned with the strengths base of the social work profession, and promotes resilience and the furthering of human rights. Many who rely on social work services have experienced violations of their rights, sometimes at the hands of those who were supposed to protect them or those who claim to be there to help such as in the case of Henry (described at the outset of this chapter). Henry was discharged from the hospital without an adequate supply of medications for his diabetes or schizophrenia, an aftercare plan, and any housing.

A fundamental part of clinical training for social workers is teaching them to identify and build on the strengths and resilience of those they serve (Gitterman, 2014; Saleebey, 2005). It is important for practitioners to be aware that individuals, families, and communities can experience posttraumatic growth following trauma and other stressors (Tedeschi & Calhoun, 1996; Weiss & Berger, 2010). Despite the risk for negative consequences from the considerable and ongoing stressors and adversity that many people face in their lives, many are resilient, able to persevere and thrive (Masten & Coatsworth, 1998). Individual resilience has been defined as the processes of, capacity for, or patterns of successful adaptation that take place during or after threatening or otherwise traumatic events (Masten & Obradovic, 2008). Recent research suggests that resilience is the most common outcome of potentially traumatic events (PTEs) (Bonanno, Westphal & Mancini, 2011). Resilience, however, is not the same as recovery. According to Bonanno (2004) resilience is, "the ability of adults in otherwise normal circumstances who are exposed to an isolated and potentially highly disruptive event such as the death of a close relation or a violent or life-threatening situation, to maintain relatively stable healthy levels of psychological and physical functioning" (p. 20).

A number of independent predictors of resilient outcomes from traumatic events have been identified, including: individual personality traits and attributional styles; having the ability to act with agency despite being afraid; feeling good about how one acted in the face of danger; learning from the stressful/traumatic event; practical, emotional, and financial support from family; effective and greater use of social support and other resources; adaptive processes and effective strategies of coping that are relational and developmental in nature; higher socioeconomic status; greater family stability; higher level of education; various biological factors; relative mental health and no history of diagnosable substance abuse or psychiatric problems; coping self-efficacy (i.e., one's perception that one has the ability to cope and control outcomes); and the capacity to cope flexibly with and tolerate emotions and other symptoms associated with bereavement and other traumas (Bonanno et al., 2011; Charney, 2004; Ehlers & Clark, 2000; Kaniasty & Norris, 1999; Southwick & Charney, 2012; U.S. DHHS, 2004; Walsh, 2003; Watson, Brymer & Bonanno, 2011).

Some coping strategies that may have been protective and served a person well during a traumatic or stressful experience and enabled them to survive, such as dissociation or self-injurious behavior, may no longer be healthy or adaptive in another context or once the environment is no longer dangerous. A social worker acting from a strengths-based approach and an orientation of cultural humility would work in partnership with the people they serve to identify and build on their strengths and assets in order to support their health and recovery in the current context. Further, Ortega and Faller (2011) identify that another important role for social workers acting with cultural humility is to "engage in efforts to change the kind of social forces that act to disempower [individuals] as members of society" (p. 35). This is well aligned also with a rights-based and person-in-environment approach.

## Clinical Interventions: Stages of Work

A clinician's work at each stage of the therapeutic process varies considerably depending on whether they utilize a needs- or rights-based approach. In addition, each stage is associated with tasks or aspects of the work that are particularly illustrative of a rights approach. Examples of how the core principles of a rights-based approach may be applied to key stages of clinical social work are provided below.

### *Preparation for the Work*

As a social worker prepares to work with a new person, group, or family, he or she often has some basic information about the presenting situation from the referral or preliminary intake. The social worker should routinely examine their own biases and assumptions about the individual(s) he or she will soon work with at this phase. While it is important for the social worker to continually be self-aware in this regard (as will be discussed in more depth in Chapter 5 of this book), it is helpful to initiate this process before the work begins. It is also valuable to remind oneself of the cultural and other stereotypes associated with the background of the individual(s), and ensure that one is consciously grounded in cultural humility as one prepares to meet them. Among the common pitfalls to avoid at this stage are overly relying on prior case notes from one's agency or other practitioners and not keeping an open mind in regards to the person(s) seeking services.

### *Engagement Phase*

Every person has the right to determine whether (in cases of those who voluntarily seek services) and/or to what extent (for those who engage in services either involuntarily or voluntarily) they engage in treatment or not (Rooney, 2009). They also have the right to determine what type of treatment they want and the practitioner who they will work with. In practice, individuals are not always afforded these rights. They often are not given a choice of practitioner (with the exception of those with ample financial resources or particular types of insurance). Individuals that seek treatment are also often provided with only limited information about the theoretical orientation and training of the practitioner they work with or about what to expect in their treatment. Rights-based practitioners provide people who contact them inquiring about services with details about their orientation and treatment approach, encourage them to ask questions and explore their full range of options before deciding if and with whom to engage in treatment with, and do not take offense if the person decides against engaging in treatment with them. These practitioners understand that such an approach is vital to ensuring that the rights and well-being of individuals are safeguarded and that not all persons are well served by the same approach to treatment.

Advances in the protection of the rights of those receiving clinical services have occurred over the decades. Clinical social workers and their colleagues in the United States routinely use such documents as Privacy Practice forms to ensure compliance with the Health Insurance Portability and Accountability Act (HIPAA) of 1996 (U.S. DHHS, 1996). HIPAA provides individuals with various rights and protections for their identifiable protected health information (PHI) through its Privacy Rule[5] while allowing for the disclosure of PHI in order to receive healthcare and protect public health.

On the first day that a person seeks clinical social work services, they routinely are asked to sign various legal documents including a Notice of Privacy Practice, a Consent for Services form, and sometimes a financial disclosure/proof of insurance form and/or a Release of Information form (as appropriate). This can be overwhelming under the best of circumstances. Some of these forms are rather lengthy and written in legalistic language not easily understood by most laypersons. Generally, the staff member administering these forms is a stranger to the person seeking services. It can be anxiety provoking to be required to sign legal documents before being able to access services, to the extent that it may create a barrier to care. A person's distress may be particularly intense if he or she experienced trauma associated with signing a document (such as if the person lost his or her right to child custody when signing custody papers). Being asked to sign privacy policy or consent for service documents at the start of treatment may trigger distressing memories of the earlier trauma.

A rights-based approach starts with ensuring that persons seeking services have true *informed consent* and not assuming that they know what these documents are. The practitioner invites and encourages dialogue, not rushing the person to make a decision and fully explaining the documents and services in accessible language. The social worker should provide opportunities to discuss the content and meaning in language that the person can understand, encouraging them to ask questions, and raising issues for discussion that may be confusing or of concern. If the service is being offered in a language that the person is not functionally literate (or sufficiently fluent) in, a rights-based practitioner ensures that translation of written material and professional interpreters bound by confidentiality are provided. All of these factors help to build a strong foundation for the development of a trusting and therapeutic relationship.

---

[5] See http://www.hhs.gov/ocr/privacy/hipaa for detailed and up to date information about the HIPAA Privacy Rule.

Rights-based clinical practitioners support individuals they serve in making choices and remaining in control at every opportunity, even about basic things such as where they sit in the therapy room and if the door to the therapy room is open or closed. This can be particularly important, for example, if the person has experienced being locked up, assaulted, or has claustrophobia. Those who embrace a human rights-based approach do not medicalize or problematize the person's situation and do not imply, even indirectly, that a person subjected to violence or another rights violation is to blame for their situation. Instead, a key focus in the engagement phase is on building rapport and a positive working relationship. The practitioner enlists the person's expertise on their own life to understand the person's strengths and what is going well in their life. This information is valuable, as the rights-based practitioner will be seeking to draw and build on the person's existing strengths and support system throughout. Of course, the practitioner will need to attend to any safety issues and critical needs in the early phase as well.

Attention to setting and maintaining appropriate boundaries throughout (e.g., avoiding dual relationships) is essential and will be discussed in more depth in Chapter 5 of this book. Not only is setting and upholding professional boundaries a cornerstone of ethical social work practice, but also by doing so, the practitioner ensures that he or she is not creating a new rights violation by the absence of appropriate boundaries.

## *Assessment*

Rights-based social work clinicians engage in a full, holistic assessment of the person's strengths and vulnerabilities, along with an analysis of any rights violations the person may have experienced and their impact. When a social work practitioner relies on a prior clinician's assessment in the absence of their own independent assessment and analysis, misdiagnosis and labeling can be perpetuated and lead to more rights violations. Assessment is not a one-time static phenomenon, but an ongoing process that the person in treatment is encouraged to be actively engaged in. The situations faced by people evolve and people grow. As a person's relationship with their practitioner develops over time, the person may open up and share more. This is particularly common when a person has experienced human-perpetrated violence and may find it difficult to trust initially. This challenge is exacerbated when the assessment leads to situating the presenting problem within the person seeking services rather than considering and identifying the structural contributions to the problem and other causes and influences external to the person (e.g., labeling a mentally ill person who does not take the medication prescribed to them as "non-compliant" versus identifying the negative side-effects they experience from the medication and lack of an alternative medication that they can afford as the problem).

### *Working Phase*

The initial assessment typically culminates in the development of a working agreement or service plan that guides the working phase. This agreement or plan should be modified to reflect evolving assessment information and the priorities of the person in treatment as appropriate. A fundamental question in this phase is who drives the work, the social worker or the person receiving services? The voice and rights of the person being served must be central in the mind of the rights-based practitioner at all times. Rights-based practitioners do not seek to impose on the person what the social worker thinks the person needs, nor do they frame their efforts as addressing the needs of the person. Rather, the driving framework and orientation of the work are the person's rights. In the process of promoting and ensuring that the person obtains their rights (e.g., in Henry's case, his right to life saving medication, right to housing, and right to food), his or her needs are met as well.

Rights-based practitioners do not impose an evidence-based practice (EBP) treatment modality on a person if the treatment has not been normed on or a good match for the population from which the person being served comes from. They may modify the intervention to attend to individual and/or cultural differences in the person they are treating. Manualized treatment models for PTSD, for example, generally use short-term, highly structured protocols that are not appropriate for individuals who have experienced complex trauma and are socially marginalized (Briere & Lanktree, 2013; Lanktree et al., 2012). Rights-based social work practitioners practice holistically and are actively engaged as interdisciplinary team members as appropriate. They address multiple contributing factors (including structural ones and rights violations) and ensure that people's rights are realized, honoring their voice and right to live in dignity and with respect.

### *Termination*

Rights-based practitioners must be vigilant to ensure that they do not try to coerce, subtly or not so subtly, the people they serve to remain in treatment longer than they want to. It should always be a person's own choice to decide when they want to terminate their treatment or no longer receive services from a given practitioner. This is true even when the practitioner does not believe that the person is ready to terminate. The only exceptions in the United States are when a person is deemed to be a danger to him or herself or others, or is gravely disabled (specifics vary based on the law in the state).

## Conclusion

This chapter has laid the framework for a rights-based approach to clinical social work practice, highlighting key themes, principles, and components. In particular, core principles of a rights-based approach were introduced and illustrated. Rights-based clinical social workers are adept at reframing needs as entitlements or rights. They approach their work with cultural humility and are grounded in seeking an understanding of the intersectionality of people's experiences. Interventions do not solely focus on the individual without considering and addressing the larger systemic and structural factors that contribute to the person's situation and violation of the person's rights. Rights-based practitioners incorporate a strengths and resilience orientation and a trauma-informed approach, as well as drawing from the recovery-model of care. The core principles also include reconstructing safety and fostering a therapeutic relationship.

Attention to rights must be infused throughout each stage of the clinical relationship and work. This extends to the organizational context and culture in which clinical practitioners work. The European Region of the IFSW (IFSW European Region e.V., 2010) established rights-based standards for social work that address the use and misuse of information, the need for appropriate caseloads, and other important dimensions of social work practice. The caseloads of child welfare and social service workers as well as those who work for public mental health agencies have long been notoriously high, limiting access to meaningful services. Clinical social workers in these specialty services are among those with high levels of stress and high rates of burnout. Clinicians need more structural supports in order to be able to truly engage in rights-based practice.

Rights-based clinical social work practice not only fosters healing and growth and is aligned with the strengths base of the social work profession, but it also promotes the furthering of human rights. This goal is particularly relevant for many who rely on social work services and have experienced violations of their rights, sometimes by the very persons who are charged with ensuring their protection and well-being. The next three chapters will apply a rights-based approach to specific areas of clinical social work practice.

## Suggested Activity/Resources

*Case Discussion* Have students read the following case vignette and engage in discussion in small groups, reflecting on the discussion questions provided.

> Roger is about to turn 18 and "age out" of the foster care system that he has been in since he was 7 and removed from his parents' home after a long history of child abuse. You are the social worker assigned to work with Roger and develop a plan for his emancipation. In meeting with Roger, you learn that he has bounced around from one foster home to another over the past decade, rarely staying longer than six months. Notes in his file label Roger as a "trouble maker" and recount that many of the foster parents reported that they could not keep

Roger in their home due to his aggressive and angry behavior toward their other children. In the past three years, he has resided at several group homes. While he was identified as suffering from clinical depression and dyslexia, he has apparently not received sustained or in-depth treatment for his depression or specialized services for his dyslexia. He is in danger of not graduating from high school and has received little in the way of preparation to function independently as an adult.

Discussion Questions: The Case of Roger

1. What additional information would you want about Roger and his situation to guide you in your work with him?
2. How do the core principles of a rights-based approach to clinical social work presented in this chapter help us to understand Roger's case from a rights-based perspective? What human rights violations appear to be present in the case of Roger?
3. What human rights instrument(s) may be particularly relevant to your work with Roger? Discuss which principles apply and how.
4. How would you work with Roger from a rights-based perspective? In what way(s) might this differ from a more traditional needs-based social work approach?

Note: The following resource may be useful for students as they think through Roger's case: Human Rights Watch (2010). *My so-called emancipation: From foster care to homelessness for California youth.* New York: Human Rights Watch.

## *Teaching Resources*

1. Hokenstad, M. C. "Terry", Healy, L. M., & Segal, U. A. (Eds.). (2013). *Teaching human rights: Curriculum resources for social work educators.* Alexandria, VA: Council on Social Work Education.
2. Libal, K. R., Berthold, S. M., Thomas, R. L., & Healy, L. M. (Eds.). (2014). *Advancing human rights in social work education.* Alexandria, VA: Council on Social Work Education.

## *For Further Information*

Evidence-Based Social Work Practice

- Social Work Policy Institute: Evidence-Based Practice (EBP) (http://www.socialworkpolicy.org/research/evidence-based-practice-2.html). This website seeks to advance the integration of evidence-based mental health treatments into research and social work education. It includes resources to facilitate the identification of EBPs and relevant publications. It also provides examples of practitioner/researcher partnerships that promote the development of EBP.

Trauma-Informed Resources

- The Substance Abuse and Mental Health Service Administration's (SAMHSA's) Center for Mental Health Service's National Center for Trauma-Informed Care (NCTIC) (http://mentalhealth.samhsa.gov/nctic/): offers a number of resources and technical assistance related to trauma-informed care.
- The National Child Traumatic Stress Network (NCTSN) website (http://www.nctsnet.org/): includes a wealth of resources and online educational materials related to child traumatic stress and creating trauma-informed services and systems. Materials are tailored to different groups, including: professionals, parents and caregivers, military families and children, the media, and educators.
- Link to National Child Traumatic Stress Network's (NCTSN) 12 Core Concepts for Understanding Traumatic Stress Responses in Children and Families: http://www.nctsn.org/resources/audiences/parents-caregivers/what-is-cts/12-core-concepts
- Trauma-Informed Care Information and Resources from a social work perspective (developed by the University at Buffalo School of Social Work): http://www.socialwork.buffalo.edu/facstaff/tic_resources.asp
- The Indian Country Child Trauma Center (ICCTC) (http://www.icctc.org/): trauma-related outreach materials, treatment protocols, and guidelines for service delivery specifically designed for American Indian and Alaska Native (AI/AN) children and their families.

Trauma Specific Treatment Models (selected)

- TF-CBT Web—A Web-based learning course for Trauma-Focused Cognitive-Behavioral Therapy (http://tfcbt.musc.edu/): This course teaches how to conduct TF-CBT with children and adolescents, complete with video demonstrations and work with parents/caregivers. This is a project of the National Crime Victims Research and Treatment Center at the Medical University of South Carolina. The course is open to those who have a master's degree or higher in a mental health discipline, or are currently enrolled in a graduate training program in a mental health discipline.
- Self-Trauma Model (developed by John Briere, Ph.D.): www.johnbriere.com; includes a link to Drs. Briere and Lanktree's *Integrative Treatment of Complex Trauma for Adolescents (ITCT-A)* (a comprehensive trauma-informed assessment and treatment approach for survivors of complex trauma): http://www.johnbriere.com/itct_a.htm
- Narrative Exposure Therapy (NET): Information on NET training is available at www.vivo.net

Cultural Humility Resource

- Web-based course on cultural humility in child welfare practice (a multiple case-based, self-reflective and interactive training curriculum developed by Drs. Faller and Ortega from the University of Michigan School of Social Work): http://ssw.umich.edu/public/currentprojects/rrcwp/culturalHumility/

Recovery Model

- SAMHSA's Recovery to Practice website with resources for behavioral health professionals: http://www.samhsa.gov/recoverytopractice/
- The Program for Recovery and Community Health (PRCH) sponsored by the Connecticut Mental Health Center, Yale School of Medicine's Department of Psychiatry, and Yale's Institution for Social and Policy Studies: http://www.yale.edu/PRCH/
- Tools for Person-Centered Recovery Planning: *http://www.ct.gov/dmhas/cwp/view.asp?a=2913&q=456036*

## References

Abrams, L. S., & Moio, J. A. (2009). Critical race theory and the cultural competence dilemma in social work education. *Journal of Social Work Education, 45*(2), 245–261.

Ackerman, S. J., & Hilsenroth, M. J. (2001). A review of therapist characteristics and techniques negatively impacting the therapeutic alliance. *Psychotherapy, 38,* 171–185.

Adams, R., Dominelli, L., & Payne, M. (Eds.). (2007). *Critical practice in social work* (2nd ed.). New York, NY: Palgrave Macmillan.

Aldarondo, E. (2007). *Advancing social justice through clinical practice*. Hillsdale, NJ: Lawrence Erlbaum Associates.

Anda, R. G. (2008). The health and social impact of growing up with adverse childhood experiences: The human and economic costs of the status quo. Retrieved from http://www.aapweb.com/files/ReviewofACEStudywithreferencessummarytable.pdf.

Androff, D., & McPherson, J. (2014). Can human rights-based social work practice bridge the micro/macro divide? In K. R. Libal, S. M. Berthold, R. L. Thomas, & L. M. Healy (Eds.), *Advancing human rights in social work education*. Alexandria, VA: Council on Social Work Education.

Berthold, S. M. (2014). Teaching human rights in core micro foundation and clinical practice classes: Integration of clinical examples of human trafficking and torture. In K. R. Libal, S. M. Berthold, R. L. Thomas, & L. M. Healy (Eds.), *Advancing human rights in social work education*. Alexandria, VA: Council on Social Work Education.

BigFoot, D. S., & Schmidt, S. R. (2010). Honoring children, mending the circle: Cultural adaptation of Trauma-Focused Cognitive-Behavioral Therapy for American Indian and Alaska Native children. *Journal of Clinical Psychology: In Session, 66*(8), 847–856.

Bloom, S. L. (2013). *Creating sanctuary: Toward the evolution of sane societies* (revised ed.). New York, NY: Taylor & Francis.

Bonanno, G. A. (2004). Loss, trauma, and human resilience: Have we underestimated the human capacity to thrive after extremely aversive events? *American Psychologist, 59*(1), 20–28.

Bonanno, G. A., Westphal, M. & Mancini, A. D. (2011). Resilience to loss and potential trauma. *Annual Review of Clinical Psychology, 7,* 511–535.

Briere, J. (2002). Treating adult survivors of severe childhood abuse and neglect: Further development of an integrative model. In J. E. B. Myers, L. Berliner, J. Briere, C. T. Hendrix, T. Reid, & C. Jenny (Eds.), *The APSAC handbook on child maltreatment* (2nd ed., pp. 175–202). Newbury Park, CA: Sage.

Briere, J., & Lanktree, C. B. (2011). *Treating complex trauma in adolescents and young adults.* Thousand Oaks, CA: Sage.

Briere, J., & Lanktree, C. B. (2013). *Integrative treatment of complex trauma for adolescents (ITCT-A): A guide for the treatment of multiply-traumatized youth* (2nd ed.). Los Angeles, CA: USC Adolescent Trauma Treatment Training Center, National Child Traumatic Stress Network, U.S. Department of Substance Abuse and Mental Health Services Administration.

Briere, J. N., & Scott, C. (2012). *Principles of trauma therapy: A guide to symptoms, evaluation, and treatment* (2nd ed.). Thousand Oaks, CA: Sage.

Brydon, K. (2011). Promoting diversity or confirming hegemony? In search of new insights for social work. *International Social Work, 55*(2), 155–167.

Cemlyn, S. (2008a). Human rights practice: Possibilities and pitfalls for developing emancipatory social work. *Ethics and Social Welfare, 2*(3), 222–242.

Cemlyn, S. (2008b). Human rights and Gypsies and travellers: An exploration of the application of a human rights perspective to social work with a minority community in Britain. *British Journal of Social Work, 38,* 153–173.

Chapman, J., Ford, J. D., Hawke, J., & Albert, D. (2006). Traumatic stress: Exposure, identification, and intervention in correctional systems. Part I. *Correctional Health Care Report, 7*(5), 65–70. Retrieved from http://www.civicresearchinstitute.com/online/article_abstract.php?pid=10 & iid=322 & aid=2153.

Charney, D. S. (2004). Psychobiological mechanisms of resilience and vulnerability: Implications for successful adaptation to extreme stress. *American Journal of Psychiatry, 161*(2), 195–216.

Cloitre, M., Courtois, C. A., Ford, J. D., Green, B. L., Alexander, P., Briere, J., ... Van der Hart, O. (2012). The ISTSS Expert Consensus Treatment Guidelines for Complex PTSD in Adults. Retrieved from http://www.istss.org/ISTSS_Complex_PTSD_Treatment_Guidelines/5205.htm.

Cohen, J. A., Mannarino, A. P., & Deblinger, E. (2006). *Treating trauma and traumatic grief in children and adolescents.* New York, NY: Guilford Press.

Cook, A., Spinazzola, J., Ford, J., Lanktree, C., Blaustein, M., Cloitre, M., ... van der Kolk, B. (2005). Complex trauma in children and adolescents. *Psychiatric Annals, 35,* 390–398.

Costello, E. J., Erkanli, A., Fairbank, J. A., & Angold, A. (2002). The prevalence of potentially traumatic events in childhood and adolescence. *Journal of Traumatic Stress, 15,* 99–112.

Council on Social Work Education [CSWE]. (2008). *Educational policy and accreditation standards.* Alexandria, VA: Author.

Council on Social Work Education [CSWE]. (2012). *Advanced social work practice in trauma.* Alexandria, VA: Author.

Crenshaw, K. W. (1995). The intersection of race and gender. In K. Crenshaw, N. Gotanda, G. Peller, & K. Thomas (Eds.), *Critical race theory* (pp. 357–383). New York, NY: The New Press.

Davidson, L. (2008). Recovery as a response to oppressive social structures. *Chronic Illness, 4,* 305–306.

Deegan, P. E. (1996). Recovery as a journey of the heart. *Psychiatric Rehabilitation Journal, 19*(3), 91–97.

Edwards, V., Holden, G., Felitti, V., & Anda, R. (2003). Relationship between multiple forms of childhood maltreatment and adult mental health in community respondents: Results from the adverse childhood experiences study. *American Journal of Psychiatry, 160,* 1453–1460.

Ehlers, A., & Clark, D. M. (2000). A cognitive model of posttraumatic stress disorder. *Behaviour Research and Therapy, 38*(4), 319–345.

Engstrom, D. W., & Okamura, A. (2004). A plague of our era: Torture, human rights, and social work. *Families in Society, 85*(3), 291–300.

Esaki, N., Benamati, J., Yanosy, S., Middleton, J. S., Hopson, L. M., Hummer, V. L., & Bloom, S. L. (2013). The Sanctuary Model: Theoretical framework. *Families in Society: The Journal of Contemporary Social Services, 94*(2), 87–95.

Fabri, M. R. (2001). Reconstructing safety: Adjustments to the therapeutic frame in the treatment of survivors of political torture. *Professional Psychology: Research and Practice, 32*(5), 452–457.

Fallot, M. D., & Harris, M. (Eds.). (2008, Winter). Trauma-informed approaches to systems of care. *Trauma Psychology Newsletter,* 6–7.

Felitti, V., Anda, R., Nordenberg, D., Williamson, D., Spitz, A., Edwards, V., ... Marks, J. (1998). Childhood trauma tied to adult illness. *American Journal of Preventive Medicine, 14,* 245–258.

Finn, J. L., & Jacobson, M. (2003). *Just practice: Social justice approach to social work.* Peosta, IA: Eddie Bowers Publishing Co.

Ford, J. D., & Courtois, C. A. (Eds.). (2013). *Treating complex traumatic stress disorders in children and adolescents: Scientific foundations and therapeutic models.* New York, NY: Guilford Press.

Furlong, M., & Wight, J. (2011). Promoting "critical awareness" and critiquing "cultural competence": Towards disrupting received professional knowledge. *Australian Social Work, 64*(1), 38–54.

Garland, A. F., Hough, R. L., McCabe, K., Yeh, M., Wood, P. A., & Aarons, G. A. (2001). Prevalence of psychiatric disorders in youths across five sectors of care. *Journal of the American Academy of Child & Adolescent Psychiatry, 40,* 409–418.

Gitterman, A. (Ed.). (2014). *Handbook of social work practice with vulnerable and resilient populations* (3rd ed.). NewYork, NY: Columbia University Press.

Gitterman, A., & Germain, C. B. (2008). Social work practice and its historical traditions. *The life model of social work practice* (3rd ed., pp. 5–50). New York, NY: Columbia University Press.

Greeson, J. K. P., Pynoos, R. S., Fairbank, J. A., Briggs, E. C., Kisiel, C. L., Layne, C. M., ... Howard, M. L. (2011). Complex trauma and mental health in children and adolescents placed in foster care: Findings from the National Child Traumatic Stress Network. *Child Welfare, 90*(6), 91–108.

Harris, M., & Fallot, M., D. (Eds.). (2001). *Using trauma theory to design service systems* (New Directions for Mental Health Services Series). San Francisco, CA: Jossey-Bass.

Healy, L. M. (2007). Universalism and cultural relativism in social work ethics. *International Social Work, 50*(1), 11–26.

Hepworth, D., Rooney, R., Rooney, G., Strom-Gottfried, K., & Larsen, J. (2010). *Direct social work practice, theory and skills* (8th ed.). Belmont, CA: Thomson Brooks/Cole.

Hernandez, P., & McDowell, T. (2010). Intersectionality, power, and relational safety in context: Key concepts in clinical supervision. *Training and Education in Professional Psychology, 4*(1), 29–35.

Hertel, S., & Libal, K. (2011). *Human rights in the United States: Beyond exceptionalism.* New York, NY: Cambridge University Press.

Hill Collins, P. (2000). *Black feminist thought: Knowledge, consciousness, and the politics of empowerment* (2nd ed.). New York, NY: Routledge.

Hopkins, P. (2010). Practitioner know thyself! Reflections on the importance of self-work for diversity and social justice practitioners. *TAMARA: Journal of Critical Postmodern Organization Science, 8*(3/4), 157–171.

Humphries, B. (2004). An unacceptable role for social work: Implementing immigration policy. *British Journal of Social Work, 34*(1), 93–107.

IFSW European Region e.V. (2010). *Standards in social work practice meeting human rights.* Berlin: Author. Retrieved from http://cdn.ifsw.org/assets/ifsw_45904-8.pdf.

International Federation of Social Workers and International Association of Schools of Social Work [IFSW/IASSW]. (2004). *Ethics in social work, statement of principles.* Retrieved from http://www.ifsw.org.

Jennings, A. (2004a). *Damaging consequences of violence and trauma: Facts, discussion points, and recommendations for the behavioral health system.* Alexandria, VA: National Association of State Mental Health Program Directors.

Jennings, A. (2004b). *Models for developing trauma-informed behavioral health systems and trauma-specific services.* Alexandria, VA: National Center for Trauma-Informed Care.

Jewell, J. R., Collins, K. V., Gargotto, L., & Dishon, A. J. (2009). Building the unsettlingforce: Social workers and the struggle for human rights. *Journal of Community Practice, 17*(3), 309–322.

Kaniasty, K., & Norris, F. H. (1999). The experience of disaster: Individuals and communities sharing trauma. In R. Gist & B. Lubin (Eds.), *Response to disaster: Psychosocial, community, and ecological approaches* (pp. 25–61). Philadelphia, PA: Brunner/Maze.

Kinzie, J. D. (2001). Psychotherapy for massively traumatized refugees: The therapist variable. *American Journal of Psychotherapy, 55*(4), 475–490.

Ko, S. J., Ford, J. D., Kassam-Adams, N., Berkowitz, S. J., Wilson, C., Wong, M., . . . Layne, C. M. (2008). Creating trauma-informed systems: Child welfare, education, first responders, health care, juvenile justice. *Professional Psychology: Research and Practice, 39*(4), 396–404.

Lambert, M. T., & Shimokawa, K. (2011). Collecting client feedback. *Psychotherapy, 48,* 72–79.

Lanktree, C.B., Briere, J., Godbout, N., Hodges, M., Chen, K., Trimm, L., . . . Freed, W. (2012). Treating multi-traumatized, socially-marginalized children: Results of a naturalistic treatment outcome study. *Journal of Aggression, Maltreatment & Trauma, 21,* 813–828.

Libal, K. R., Berthold, S. M., Thomas, R. L., & Healy, L. M. (Eds.). (2014). *Advancing human rights in social work education*. Alexandria, VA: Council on Social Work Education.

Lundahl, B., & Burke, B. L. (2009). The effectiveness and applicability of motivational interviewing: A practice-friendly review of four metaanalyses. *Journal of Clinical Psychology: In Session, 11,* 1232–1245.

Lundy, C. (2011). *Social work, social justice, and human rights: A structural approach to practice* (2nd ed.). Toronto, CA: University of Toronto Press.

Lundy, C., & van Wormer, K. (2007). Social and economic justice, human rights and peace: The challenge for social work in Canada and the United States. *International Social Work, 50*(6), 727–739.

Masten, A. S., & Coatsworth, J. D. (1998). The development of competence in favorable and unfavorable environments: Lessons from successful children. *American Psychologist, 53*(2), 205–220.

Masten, A. S., & Obradović, J. (2008). Disaster preparation and recovery: Lessons from research on resilience in human development. *Ecology and Society, 13*(1), 9. Retrieved from http://www.ecologyandsociety.org/vol13/iss1/art9/

McNamara, S. (Ed). (2009). *Voices of recovery*. Boston, MA: Boston University, Center for Psychiatric Rehabilitation.

Miletic, T., Piu, M., Minas, H., Stankovska, M., Stolk, Y., & Klimidis, S. (2006). *Guidelines for working effectively with interpreters in mental health settings*. Victoria: Victorian Transcultural Psychiatry Unit. Retrieved from http://www.vtmh.org.au/docs/interpreter/VTPU_GuidelinesBooklet.pdf.

Miller, W. R., Wilbourne, P. L., & Hettema, J. E. (2003). What works? A summary of alcohol treatment outcome research. In R. K. Hester & W. R. Miller (Eds.), *Handbook of alcoholism treatment approaches: Effective alternatives* (3rd ed., pp. 13–63). Boston, MA: Allyn & Bacon.

Mollica, R. F. (2006). *Healing invisible wounds: Paths to hope and recovery in a violent world.* Boston, MA: Houghton Mifflin Harcourt.

Mollica, R. F. (2010, September 8). The trauma story and an empathic and therapeutic conversation with the survivor. [Webinar]. Retrieved from http://gulfcoastjewishfamily andcommunityservices.org/refugee/2013/06/01/dr-richard-mollica%E2%80%99s-webinar/.

Murphy, Y., Hunt, V., Zajicek, A. M., Norris, A. N., & Hamilton, L. (2009). *Incorporating intersectionality in social work practice, research, policy, and education*. Washington, DC: NASW Press.

National Association of Social Workers [NASW]. (Approved 1996, revised 1999). *Code of ethics for social workers*. Washington, DC: NASW.

National Association of Social Workers [NASW]. (2006). *NASW practice snapshot: The mental health recovery model*. Washington, DC: Author. Retrieved from www.naswdc.org/practice/behavioral_health/0206snapshot.asp.

National Child Traumatic Stress Network [NCTSN]. (2012). *The 12 core concepts: Concepts for understanding traumatic stress responses in children and families. Core Curriculum on Childhood Trauma*. Los Angeles, CA: Author.

National Child Traumatic Stress Network [NCTSN]. (n.d.). Creating trauma-informed systems. Retrieved from http://www.nctsnet.org/resources/topics/creating-trauma-informed- systems.

New Haven Trauma Competencies. (2013, April 25-28). *Advancing the science of education, training and practice in trauma: Developing the New Haven model*. Working conference held in New Haven, CT.

Norcross, J. C., & Wampold, B. E. (2011). Evidence-based therapy relationships: Research conclusions and clinical practices. *Psychotherapy, 48*(1), 98–102.

Office of the High Commissioner for Human Rights. (n.d.). What are human rights? Retrieved from http://www.ohchr.org/en/issues/pages/whatarehumanrights.aspx.

Orlinsky, D. E., Ronnestad, M. H., & Willutzki, U. (2004). Fifty years of psychotherapy process-outcome research: Continuity and change. In M. J. Lambert (Ed.), *Handbook of psychotherapy and behavior change* (5th ed., pp. 307–390). New York, NY: Wiley.

Ortega, R. M., & Faller, K. C. (2011). Training child welfare workers from an intersectional cultural humility perspective: A paradigm shift. *Child Welfare, 90*(5), 27–49.

Ortiz, L., & Jani, J. (2010). Critical race theory: A transformational model for teaching diversity. *Journal of Social Work Education, 46*(2), 175–193.

Putnam, F. (2006). The impact of trauma on child development. *Juvenile and Family Court Journal, 57*(1), 1–11.

Pynoos, R., Steinberg, A., Schreiber, M., & Brymer, M. (2006). Children and families: A new framework for preparedness and response to danger, terrorism, and trauma. In H. Spitz, Y. Danieli, L. Schein, G. Burlingame, & P. Muskin (Eds.), *Psychological effects of catastrophic disasters: Group approaches to treatment* (pp. 83–112). New York, NY: Haworth Press.

Reichert, E. (2007). Human rights in the twenty-first century: Creating a new paradigm for social work. In E. Reichert (Ed.), *Challenges in human rights: A social work perspective* (pp. 1–15). New York, NY: Columbia University Press.

Rooney, R. (2009). *Strategies for work with involuntary clients* (2nd ed.). New York, NY: Columbia University Press.

Sachs, J. & Newdom, F. (2011). *Clinical work and social action: An integrative approach*. New York: Routledge.

Saleebey, D. (2005). *The strengths perspective in social work practice* (4th ed.). Boston, MA: Allyn & Bacon.

Sanctuary Model (n.d.). The Sanctuary Model: An integrated theory. Retrieved from http://www.sanctuaryweb.com/sanctuary-model.php.

Sengupta, S. (2006). I/me/mine-Intersectional identities as negotiated minefields. *Signs: Journal of Women, Culture and Society, 31*(3), 629–639.

Solórzano, D., Ceja, M., & Yosso, T. (2000, Winter). Critical race theory, racial microaggressions, and campus racial climate: The experiences of African American college students. *Journal of Negro Education, 69*, 60–73.

Southwick, S. M., & Charney, D. S. (2012). *Resilience: The science of mastering life's greatest challenges*. New York, NY: Cambridge University Press.

Substance Abuse and Mental Health Services Association [SAMHSA]. (n.d.). Trauma-informed care and trauma services. Retrieved from http://www.samhsa.gov/nctic/trauma.asp.

Substance Abuse and Mental Health Services Association [SAMHSA]. (2014). SAMHSA's National Registry of Evidence-based Programs and Practices. Retrieved from http://www.nrepp.samhsa.gov.

Sue, D. W., Bucceri, J. M., Lin, A. I., Nadal, K. L., & Torino, G. C. (2007). Racial microaggressions and the Asian American experience. *Cultural Diversity & Ethnic Minority Psychology, 13,* 72–81.

Tedeschi, R. G., & Calhoun, L. G. (1996). The posttraumatic growth inventory: Measuring the positive legacy of trauma. *Journal of Traumatic Stress, 9*(3), 455–472.

Tervalon, M., & Murray-Garcia, J. (1998). Cultural humility versus cultural competence: A critical distinction in defining physician training outcomes in multicultural education. *Journal of Health Care for The Poor and Underserved, 9*(2), 117–125.

Tondora, J., Miller, R., Slade, M., & Davidson, L. (2014). *Partnering for recovery in mental health: A practical guide to person-centered planning*. Hoboken, NJ: Wiley-Blackwell.

Toseland, R. W., & Rivas, R. F. (2012). *An introduction to group work practice* (7th ed.). Boston, MA: Allyn Bacon.

U.S. Department of Health and Human Services [U.S. DHHS]. (1996). Health Insurance Portability and Accountability Act of 1996. Public Law 104–191, 104th Congress.

U.S. Department of Health and Human Services [U.S. DHHS]. (2004). *Mental health response to mass violence and terrorism: A training manual*. DHHS Pub. No. SMA 3959. Rockville, MD: Center for Mental Health Services, Substance Abuse and Mental Health Services Administration.

U.S. Department of Health and Human Services, Substance Abuse and Mental Health Services Administration, Center for Mental Health Services. (2005, July/August). Consensus on recovery achieved. *Mental Health Transformation Trends: A Periodic Briefing, 1*(3), 4.

van Sluytman, L. G. (2013). *Micro aggressions. Encyclopedia of Social Work Online*. New York, NY: Oxford University Press. doi:10.1093/acrefore/9780199975839.013.987.

Walsh, F. (2003). Family resilience: A framework for clinical practice. *Family Process, 42*(1), 1–18.

Walsh, J. (2013). *The recovery philosophy and direct social work practice*. Chicago, IL: Lyceum.

Watson, P. J., Brymer, M. J., & Bonanno, G. A. (2011). Postdisaster psychological intervention since 9/11. *American Psychologist, 66*(6), 482–494.

Wegman, H. L., & Stetler, C. (2009). A meta-analytic review of the effects of childhood abuse on medical outcomes in adulthood. *Psychosomatic Medicine, 71*(8), 805–812.

Weiss, T., & Berger, R. (Eds.). (2010). *Posttraumatic growth and culturally competent practice: Lessons learned from around the world*. Hoboken, NJ: Wiley.

# Chapter 2
# Rights-Based Approach to Working with Torture Survivors

> Bataar[1], a young homosexual Mongolian student, was beaten and detained by police officers as he was leaving a party given by his gay friends one night. Held in a cell for over a month, police officers gang-raped him multiple times while other police officers looked on and taunted him for being gay. The officers forced him to crawl on all fours like a dog and lick their boots daily. He was locked in a pen with menacing dogs. Officers threatened that they would force Bataar to engage in sex acts with the dogs, telling him he was not human. On several occasions, an officer held open Bataar's mouth and urinated into it, forcing him to drink the urine. The police threatened to kill Bataar if they ever found him attending any gay event in the future. Before they released Bataar, an officer forced him to sign a document renouncing his homosexuality. Before Bataar's detention he had obtained a student visa to study in the United States. He left Mongolia for the United States within days of his release, fearful for his safety.

Who could Bataar turn to for help or justice in Mongolia when he was tortured at the hands of police officers? Does torture also take place in prisons and other places of detention in the United States? What would you want to know about Bataar's experience and the context in Mongolia that would inform your work with him? If Bataar came to your attention in the United States, what avenues for rights-based clinical social work engagement and intervention might you have (assuming that Bataar was interested in working with a social worker)? What rights-based core principles would guide your work with Bataar?

The torture that Bataar was subjected to by authorities in his country is unfortunately not an isolated or rare incident. This chapter starts by defining torture and identifying some of the recent definitional controversies and key contextual factors. The prime targets of torture, prevalence estimates, and common sequelae are discussed and the problem of US exceptionalism is explored. Torture is framed as a human rights violation and relevant international human rights mechanisms and tools

[1] The names and other identifying information in all case material have been changed to protect confidentiality, and aspects of each case are a composite from more than one person.



S. M. Berthold, *Human Rights-Based Approaches to Clinical Social Work*,
SpringerBriefs in Rights-Based Approaches to Social Work, DOI 10.1007/978-3-319-08560-9_2

are identified. Core principles of a rights-based approach to clinical and forensic social work practice with survivors of state-sponsored[2] torture within a US context are described and promoted in this chapter. Discussion of the United States' use of torture is included, while drawing predominantly on cases of asylum-seeking[3] survivors in the United States who were tortured prior to coming to the United States. Key roles for clinical social workers related to the implementation of the United Nations' Convention Against Torture and Other Cruel, Inhuman or Degrading Treatment or Punishment (UNCAT) are explored. The chapter concludes with discussion of the importance of combating impunity and suggested class activities and resources.

## Definitional and Contextual Issues

### *Definition of Torture*

Torture was a sanctioned part of many legal proceedings in much of Europe from the mid-fourteenth century to the end of the eighteenth century, including being used by the Inquisition in heresy cases (Skoll, 2008). By the early twenty-first century torture had generally become publically unacceptable while flourishing in secret (Amnesty International, 2014; Nowak, 2012). Article 1 of the UNCAT, adopted in 1984, defines torture as follows:

> ... 'torture' means any act by which severe pain or suffering, whether physical or mental, is intentionally inflicted on a person for such purposes as obtaining from him or a third person information or a confession, punishing him for an act he or a third person has committed or is suspected of having committed, or intimidating or coercing him or a third person, or for any reason based on discrimination of any kind, when such pain or suffering is inflicted by or at the instigation of or with the consent or acquiescence of a public official or other person acting in an official capacity. It does not include pain or suffering arising only from, inherent in or incidental to lawful sanctions. (UN General Assembly, 1984, Article 1.1)

This UNCAT definition is the most commonly used definition for torture worldwide. The US definition of torture adopted in the Torture Victims Relief Act (18 U.S.C. 2340(1) 1998) is more narrow than that of UNCAT, despite the fact that the United States is a signatory to the UNCAT:

---

[2] While the term torture has been used by some to describe violent acts inflicted during domestic violence, child abuse, and other atrocities, the focus of this chapter will be on torture when the perpetrator is a governmental/state authority and/or when the authorities cannot or will not protect an individual from torture at the hands of others in keeping with the United Nations' definition (UN General Assembly, 1984, Article 1.1).

[3] Asylum seekers must establish that they have been persecuted by the authorities in their country based on at least one of five grounds: political opinion, religious beliefs or practices, nationality, race, or membership in a social group. Information about who is eligible to apply for asylum in the United States can be found at: http://www.uscis.gov/faq-page/asylum-eligibility-and-applications-faq. For more information see the US Citizenship and Immigration Services' (USCIS) website at: www.uscis.gov/humanitarian/refugees-asylum/asylum.

> 'torture' means an act committed by a person acting under the color of law specifically intended to inflict severe physical or mental pain or suffering (other than pain or suffering incidental to lawful sanctions) upon another person within his custody or lawful control. (18 U.S.C. 2340(1) 1998)

The way the United States defines what constitutes severe physical or mental pain has been contentious (Basoglu, Livanou, & Crnobaric, 2007). The US definition of torture and its use of torture have faced intense criticism within the United States and abroad, including by some high ranking US military and other officials; leading torture treatment clinicians, researchers, attorneys, and human rights groups; and the UN Committee Against Torture (Amnesty International, 2006; Basoglu et al., 2007; Davis, 2012; Luban & Shue, 2012). A key concern relates to the United States' efforts to distinguish psychological from physical torture, thus weakening legal protections against the former.

## *Who is Targeted for Torture*

While some are targeted for torture due to their political beliefs and/or activities in opposition to those in power, others are tortured due to their nationality, race, religious beliefs or practices (including being agnostic or atheist), and/or membership in a social group (e.g., lesbian, gay, bisexual, transgender, queer/questioning (LGBTQ)). Others may be tortured due to mistaken identity (e.g., for their imputed political or religious identity or activities, no matter if in error). These individuals may happen to live near an area with heavy rebel activity and the government forces assume (incorrectly) that they are aligned with or supporting the rebels. Some of those who manage to survive torture flee their homelands seeking safety.

In the United States, prisoners are particularly vulnerable to torture and cruel, inhuman or degrading treatment or punishment (CIDT). Prisoners most targeted for sexual violence by officials and other prisoners are: youth in juvenile and adult facilities; transgender and gay detainees or those perceived to be gender variant or gay; immigration detainees; and first-time, nonviolent offenders (Stop Prisoner Rape, 2006). Practices such as excessive strip searches, solitary confinement, the shackling of women prisoners during childbirth, and interrogation methods used by some guards are notable violations (ACLU, 2012; Human Rights Watch/ACLU, 2012). Persons in psychiatric hospitals, nursing homes, and children in congregate care are similarly at risk for chemical restraint when it is not medically appropriate or necessary (Kisken, 2013; Penturf, 2013). It is hard to determine the prevalence of torture and CIDT when those victimized are kept largely hidden from public view with poor access and oversight.

## *Estimates of the Prevalence of Torture Worldwide*

Amnesty International estimates that 112 countries worldwide engaged in the practice of torture of their citizens in 2012 (Amnesty International, 2013). Roughly two-thirds of all governments worldwide sanction torture (Engstrom & Okomura, 2004), including the United States, despite the universal condemnation of the practice of torture (Hajjar, 2012). The United Nations Special Rapporteur on torture and other cruel, inhuman, or degrading treatment or punishment has stated that at least half the countries in the world are engaging in torture or mistreatment at any moment (Méndez & Wentworth, 2011). Reports of torture in Syria are making headlines at the time of this writing, a glaring example of the limitations of existing international efforts to prevent and prohibit torture. Many instances of torture, however, occur outside of the limelight. Conservative estimates are that between 10 and 30 % (300,000–900,000) of the 3 million refugees who came to the United States since 1975 from many countries were torture survivors (Modvig & Jaranson, 2004), and that the percentage among asylum seekers is likely greater (Burnett & Peel, 2001). At the same time, it is difficult to estimate the numbers of individuals from other populations in the United States who have been tortured and subjected to CIDT. These would include children and adults that are kept in solitary confinement and vulnerable persons chemically restrained in the United States in order to subdue and control them more easily.

## *US Exceptionalism and US State-Sponsored Torture*

> Chris, a 27-year-old American man was convicted of aggravated murder and sentenced to death. In the supermax[4] prison where he has been held for the past five years, Chris is confined to his small cell with a solid steel door 23 hours per day. Even during the several hours of exercise time he is allowed per week, he has minimal contact with other humans, limited to guards shackling and handcuffing him and taking him to a cage where he exercises alone. He has been beaten and raped by several of the guards. Strip searches are routine whenever he goes in or out of his cell to the infirmary or to meet with his lawyer. Chris became psychotic during his first year in the supermax, with frightening visual hallucinations of tigers and other wild animals in his cell. He continues to talk to himself and believes that Jesus and Satan are spying on him through the electronic surveillance equipment in his cell. He has tried to kill himself twice at the supermax.

The US government often points to torture and other human rights violations committed by state actors outside of the United States while failing to examine its own actions through a human rights lens. The contradiction is glaring. The United States ratified the International Covenant on Civil and Political Rights (ICCPR) in 1992 and the UNCAT in 1994 and thus has obligations to adhere to the commitments it made not to torture or inflict CIDT or punishment. Notably, however, at the time of this writing the United States has not signed or ratified the 2002 Optional Protocol to the CAT (OPCAT, a treaty that supplements the 1984 CAT) and therefore, is not subject to international inspection of conditions of detention such as the prison where Chris is held. The United States provides asylum to individuals who fled from other countries after being tortured by their governments (recognizing torture as a severe

[4] Supermax prisons are supermaximum security prisons, or control units, that have the highest level of security. The conditions amount to long-term solitary confinement.

form of persecution) and yet engages in torture itself. Such double standards related to human rights and not engaging fully with the international dialogue related to human rights law have been identified as hallmarks of exceptionalism related to human rights (Ignatieff, 2005). The United States has failed to sign or ratify some major human rights documents and has not fulfilled its duties and obligations in regards to some of the human rights treaties it has ratified. Hertel and Libal (2011) warn of the dangers associated with engaging in such US exceptionalism.

The United States' use of solitary confinement with minors (Grassian, 2006; Human Rights Watch/American Civil Liberties Union, 2012) and the torture of enemy combatants and suspected terrorists (Hajjar, 2012; Mayer, 2009) are striking examples of the US Government's violation of human rights through torture (UN Committee Against Torture, 2006). The former chief prosecutor for the military commissions at Guantanamo Bay, Cuba, Retired Air Force Col. Morris Davis, publically condemned the US use of torture in an op-ed in the *Los Angeles Times*, stressing that torture is always illegal (Davis, 2012). The UNCAT, ratified by the United States, prohibits torture unconditionally, such that "No exceptional circumstances whatsoever, whether a state of war or a threat of war, internal political instability or any other public emergency, may be invoked as a justification of torture" (UN General Assembly, 1984, Article 1). Many organizations (and some legislators) have also denounced the United States' involvement in torture, including the National Association of Social Workers, the National Religious Campaign Against Torture, the National Consortium of Torture Treatment Programs and its member centers, Human Rights First, and Amnesty International, calling for such things as accountability, the release of the Senate Intelligence Committee's report on torture and for a federal truth commission to investigate the use of torture by the United States post-9/11 (Gosztola, 2014; Keller & Granski, 2013; Leahy, 2009; NASW, 2006). The United Nations' Special Rapporteur on Torture and Committee on Torture have repeatedly condemned the US criminal justice system for use of such measures as lengthy solitary confinement and capital punishment (Gilligan & Lee, 2013; Interim Report of the Special Rapporteur, 2011; Méndez, 2012). Solitary confinement, ostensibly employed for the protection of minors held in adult facilities, and long-term segregation in supermax prisons can lead to psychosis and other severe psychiatric harm in a relatively short time and has been identified as a type of torture (Grassian, 2006; HRW/ACLU, 2012).

The UN Human Rights Committee (2014) expressed a number of concerns about the human rights record of the United States regarding torture in its *Concluding Observations on the Fourth Periodic Report of the United States of America*. Among these were: the United States continues to maintain that the ICCPR does not apply to individuals under its jurisdiction who are being held outside its territory; the limited legal reach of the ICCPR and lack of its full implementation at local levels in the United States; the conditions of detention, including the use of solitary confinement; the extensive use of nonconsensual psychiatric treatment; the extremely limited number of individuals held accountable for past acts of torture, CIDT, and enhanced interrogation; and the absence of comprehensive legislation in the United States criminalizing torture in all its forms, including mental forms of torture.

## *Common Sequelae of Torture: Psychological Distress, Poor Health, and Resilience*

It is important for clinical social workers to understand the range of possible impacts of torture on individuals as this information can be used to guide clinical assessment and intervention. As in the case of Bataar described at the outset of this chapter, torture often leaves one feeling demoralized, dehumanized, and humiliated on top of struggling with other common physical, psychological, social, and spiritual sequelae (Kinzie et al., 2008; Ortiz, 2001). A meta-analysis of epidemiological studies of torture survivors and refugees in the United States and their home countries found high rates of mental health problems (Steel et al., 2009). Similarly high rates of mental health problems were found in a systematic review of studies of refugees resettled in Western countries (Fazel, Wheeler, & Danesh, 2005). The most common psychiatric conditions diagnosed in refugees are depression, posttraumatic stress disorder (PTSD), comorbid PTSD and depression, psychotic disorders, and anxiety conditions such as phobias and panic (Kinzie, Jaranson, & Kroupin, 2007; Marshall, Schell, Elliot, Berthold, & Chun, 2005; Steel et al., 2009). Often, neither depression nor PTSD captures the range of distress. Complex presentations may include shame, mistrust, conversion, somatic symptoms, unexplained pain, feeling of permanent damage, dissociation, sexual problems, self-blame, guilt, and/or low self-esteem (Quiroga & Jaranson, 2005). Some survivors may also engage in tension reduction behaviors (e.g., substance use, self-injurious behaviors, other forms of externalizing anxiety reduction strategies; Briere & Scott, 2012). These same clinical conditions and symptoms are commonly found in US born individuals who are tortured and/or subjected to CIDT or punishment as well (Grassian, 2006; HRW/ACLU, 2012). Torture survivors may experience a chronic fluctuating course of posttraumatic symptoms, with periods of exacerbations typically triggered by things that remind them of their torture and periods of remission (Kinzie, 2011). Some torture survivors may benefit from long-term treatment (Boehnlein & Kinzie, 2011; Dube, Felitti, Dong, Giles, & Anda, 2003; Kinzie, 2001, 2011; Marshall et al., 2005).

A growing body of epidemiologic research has found an association between exposure to trauma, mental and adverse physical health outcomes, and premature death in veteran, torture, refugee and other populations (Boscarino, 2004; Coughlin, 2012; Schnurr & Green, 2004; Wagner et al., 2013). Trauma exposure and PTSD have been found to be associated with various health conditions such as cardiovascular disease, musculoskeletal conditions, diabetes, gastrointestinal disease, chronic fatigue syndrome, fibromyalgia, and other health conditions. Particularly robust is the evidence linking exposure to psychological trauma and cardiovascular disease across a variety of populations and stressors (Boscarino, 2004).

Torture often affects survivors' capacity to trust others and form interpersonal bonds, retain a sense of identity, maintain faith in a system of justice, and sustain a sense of existential meaning and hope (Briere & Scott, 2012; Costanzo, Gerrity, & Lykes, 2007; Ortiz, 2001). Torture among refugees and incarcerated youth and adults in the United States is associated with high rates of suicidality (Grassian, 2006;

Human Rights Watch/American Civil Liberties Union, 2012), especially when PTSD is present (Ferrada-Noli, Asberg, Ormstad, Lundin, & Sundbom, 1998). Detention of torture survivors who are seeking asylum has been found to be detrimental for their physical and mental health and to put them at risk for suicide (Keller et al., 2003; PHR and Bellevue/NYU, 2003; Silove, Steel, & Mollica, 2001). This is consistent with the experience of torture treatment specialists who also find that the risk of suicide for survivors seeking asylum is high around asylum hearings when they fear that they may be deported.

## *Stressors Related to Applying for Asylum and Ongoing Lack of Safety*

Asylum law is complex and the stakes of not succeeding in obtaining asylum or another form of legal relief are high. Survivors often live in fear of the dangers associated with being deported back to the country where they were tortured and are typically still seen as a threat to the powers that be. Some torture survivors have been blacklisted and fear that they would be picked up by the authorities at the airport when they first arrive back in their homeland, detained again, and tortured. Many were threatened with death or subjected to mock execution as part of their previous torture and often fear that the authorities would murder them if they returned home.

The asylum process is typically a very retraumatizing and stressful experience, with survivors being required to write and testify in tremendous details about experiences that they have been desperately trying to forget and avoid, including sexual torture and other experiences that are considered deeply stigmatizing and shameful in their culture (Berthold & Gray, 2011; Gangsei & Deutsch, 2007; Herlihy & Turner, 2009). Survivors may experience the legal system as their adversary rather than advocate (Martinez & Fabri, 1992).

Most specialists (and survivors themselves) agree that safety is the most essential ingredient necessary in order for a torture survivor to recover and flourish (Fabri, 2001; Gangsei & Deutsch, 2007; Ortiz, 2001). Obtaining asylum can be an important step toward gaining increased safety. Even in exile, however, one cannot be assured of a safe and trauma-free life. Survivors of torture have been trafficked, subjected to community violence, been diagnosed with cancer and other serious health problems, and experienced other traumas after fleeing their homelands seeking safety. There have been documented reports of perpetrators of torture and other human rights violations from other countries living in the United States and other countries where survivors have fled.[5]

[5] The Center for Justice and Accountability (CJA), cofounded by a clinical social worker (Gerald Gray), has successfully prosecuted some of these perpetrators in the United States (see CJA website for details: http://www.cja.org/). Social workers and other trauma clinicians have contributed

## *Impact on Family and Community*

The impact of state-sponsored torture typically affects not only the torture survivor himself or herself, but also his or her family members and community (Berthold, 2013b; Ortiz, 2001). Increased marital and/or intergenerational conflict, compromised family or parental functioning, reduced tolerance for the expression of emotional distress, and increased pressure on children to be successful are all possible in the aftermath of torture (Center for Victims of Torture, 2005). Family members, friends, and associates have told many survivors who fled to the United States that their perpetrators have continued to look for them after they left their country. Quite a few of the survivors treated by torture treatment specialists have had loved ones back home (including their children, spouses, siblings, elderly parents, other relatives, and associates) harmed by the authorities who were looking for them. This harm included being interrogated about the whereabouts of the torture survivor who fled and/or threatened, tortured, disappeared,[6] murdered, or forced into hiding. One of the common aims of state-sponsored torture is to instill fear in society and silence the opposition (Berthold, 2013b; Quiroga & Jaranson, 2005). Social withdrawal and increased distrust in authority figures and others is common. Some survivors and their loved ones may no longer know if they can trust their friends and associates. Indeed, the survivor may have been apprehended by his or her torturers as a result of someone close to them revealing his or her identity and/or whereabouts under the duress of torture. Social networks, typically a keen source of practical, social, and emotional support, may constrict in the aftermath of torture.

## *Resilience and Strengths*

Not all survivors of torture suffer from PTSD or other mental health conditions. Some are highly resilient, possessing significant strengths (Guskovict, 2012; Moio, 2008). Often conceptualized as a defense mechanism, resilience enables individuals to effectively adapt and thrive when faced with adversity or trauma (Bonanno, 2004; Masten & Obradovic, 2008). Some research indicates that the most prevalent outcome of potentially traumatic events (PTEs) may not be psychopathology,

---

to fighting impunity by providing forensic assessment, testimony, and psychological support to survivor witnesses during the preparation and litigation phases of these cases.

[6] A "disappeared" person is one who has been abducted by the authorities or a rebel, guerilla, or militia group that the authorities cannot or will not protect them from. Family members, friends, and associates of the disappeared person are unable to locate him or her. There may be no news of the person for months or years. Occasionally, the disappeared person may reappear alive or as a corpse, often with evidence that he or she has been abused or tortured. Eventually, if they are not found, it is usually assumed that the disappeared person has been murdered. In such cases, the uncertainty about the disappeared person's fate or lack of bodily remains can be agonizing for the loved one(s) left behind.

but rather resilience and a stable trajectory of healthy functioning (Bonanno, Westphal, & Mancini, 2011). Research with torture survivors has identified a number of factors that appear to be protective or mitigate the harmful impact of their torture, including: the presence of strong support (Basoglu et al., 1994b; Moio, 2008), spirituality (Holtz, 1998), firm commitment to a cause (Basoglu et al., 1997), and advance preparation for one's torture (Basoglu, Paker, Ozmen, Tasdemir, & Sahin, 1994a). A survivor may be highly resilient and functional in some areas of their lives, while still struggling with symptoms of psychological distress and/or challenges functioning in other areas. Being a survivor of torture or other human rights violations does not define who a person is. It is only one part of his or her life experience.

## Relevant Human Rights Mechanisms and Tools

A number of human rights mechanisms and tools are relevant to the problem of torture. The Universal Declaration of Human Rights (UDHR), adopted by the United Nations in 1948, was the first comprehensive international human rights document (UN General Assembly, 1948). Article 5 of the UDHR explicitly bans torture and cruel, inhuman, or degrading treatment or punishment for all persons. Torture is a clear violation of the basic rights all persons possess simply because they are human. Torture is typically conducted in such a manner as to strip the targeted individual of all of his or her control, freedom, dignity, and rights.

In addition to the UDHR, other human rights treaties and laws are relevant to torture. Common Article 3 of the Geneva Conventions, for example, prohibits the murder, torture, cruel, humiliating, or degrading treatment of detainees from non-international conflicts (International Committee of the Red Cross, 1949). The UNCAT (UN General Assembly, 1984) prohibits torture absolutely and furthermore bars states from returning anyone to a country if there is a substantial likelihood that she or he may be tortured there. Under the Illegal Immigration Reform and Immigrant Responsibility Act (1996), an individual has the right to a credible fear screening by a US Customs and Immigration Services Asylum Officer when he or she enters the United States if they are subject to expedited removal.[7] The purpose of this screening is to establish if the individual has a credible fear of being tortured or persecuted if the United States returns the individual to his to her home country.

Children have not been spared from torture, despite strong prohibitions against this practice. Among the many rights ensured by the United Nations Convention on the Rights of the Child (OHCHR, 1989), Article 37 prohibits children from being subjected to torture, cruel, inhuman, and degrading treatment including capital punishment and life without possibility of parole. General Comment 14 (OHCHR, 2013)

---

[7] Problems with the credible fear process were reported during a recent Congressional hearing in the United States (Noferi, 2014). Some torture survivors have been denied a credible fear hearing and deported back to their homeland where their lives were in danger (Chideya, 2005).

stresses that children should be respected as rights holders and that children have the right to have their best interests given primary consideration. Article 12 of the CRC articulates children's rights to have their voices heard. Violence by guards/staff against incarcerated youth (and adults) and shackling during childbirth have been identified as violations of CAT (ACLU, 2012; Human Rights Watch/ACLU, 2006; National Religious Campaign Against Torture, n.d.). Although the United States has not ratified the CRC as of the time of this writing, social workers can still use the CRC to guide their work. Rights-based clinical social workers can play a significant role in facilitating and ensuring that the voices of the children they work with, including those who are incarcerated, are heard and that the children are not tortured.

Many of the rights contained in the ICCPR (UN General Assembly, 1966) are commonly denied to torture survivors, including the absolute right: to be free from torture and other CIDT or punishment; to be free from slavery and servitude; not to be subjected to prolonged arbitrary detention; to freedom from systematic racial discrimination; and recognition as a person before the law (habeas corpus). In addition, the ICCPR includes the following *non-derogable* rights relevant to torture survivors that cannot be revoked or suspended, even during a national or public state of emergency (OHCHR, 2001): the right to life; the prohibition against taking hostages, abductions, or unacknowledged detention; and freedom of thought, conscience and religion. The ICCPR also provides people with the right to participate in politics and public life and the freedom of assembly and association, rights that are often not provided to torture survivors.

## Clinical Interventions, Application of Core Principles of a Rights-Based Approach, and Forensic Issues

### *Contexts in Which Social Workers may Encounter Torture Survivors*

Clinical social workers in the United States may more routinely come across torture in populations other than asylum seekers (unless they work with a specialty torture treatment program). For example, they may encounter torture and CIDT or punishment in the context of their work in prisons or detention centers (e.g., solitary confinement, the shackling of women prisoners during childbirth; Human Rights Watch/American Civil Liberties Union, 2006, 2012; Lewis, 2012), corporeal punishment of youth in schools (Murphy & Vagins, 2012), and indiscriminate use of chemical restraint in psychiatric or nursing home facilities as well as in child residential, foster care, and juvenile justice facilities (Kisken, 2013; Penturf, 2013). Although some of these practices are frequently not framed or perceived by the United States as torture, they are by others. Whether one calls such treatment CIDT or torture, both are condemned and prohibited by the CAT that the United States has ratified and is obligated to uphold.

## *Core Principles of a Rights-Based Approach Applied*

The act of torture strips a person of their rights, including the right to self-determine what happens to their physical and psychological integrity. This underscores why a rights-based approach that supports the survivor's self-determination and ability to reclaim their role as protagonist in their own life (Barbera, 2014) is so essential to their healing process. A rights-based approach to clinical practice with torture survivors is structured to be disparate in all ways to what they experienced during torture to support the reclaiming of their humanity and agency (Fabri, 2001; Ortiz, 2001). Torturers often utilize torture methods that are designed to destroy the victim's sense of humanity and worth. For Bataar, the young Mongolian man from the case example at the beginning of this chapter, it was vital that his social worker treated him with respect and upheld his fundamental dignity and humanity. While these practice behaviors are essential for professional and ethical social work practice with any person, tortured or not, they are particularly crucial when the nature of the trauma violated the most basic concepts of what it means to be human. These are important ingredients in an overall approach to counteract the dehumanizing treatment survivors experienced at the hands of their torturer(s).

As mentioned in Chapter 1, it is particularly important not to rush through the process of obtaining a torture survivor's signed consent for services (or signing of other documents) given that the act of signing a document as part of their torture is a fairly common experience for many survivors (e.g., Bataar, in the opening vignette, was forced to sign a document denouncing his identity as a gay man). Some survivors are forced under the duress of torture to sign a false confession or a blank piece of paper before their torturers will release them, and are told that the authorities will fill in his or her alleged "crimes" later. This was the case for "John" (a pseudonym), locked for months in a so-called "safe house," sodomized and beaten by multiple soldiers each day, accused of being a dissident.

As part of the trauma, those subjected to torture are often told by the perpetrator(s) that, if they survive, nobody will believe them (Gangsei & Deutsch, 2007), that there is no point in telling anyone, and that, if they do, they (or their loved ones or associates) will be tortured or killed. These threats, along with the common posttraumatic stress response of avoidance of things that remind the survivor of the trauma, contribute to many survivors not feeling safe or able to tell their social worker or others about their torture. Survivors and their family members frequently live with shame and fear of further persecution, feelings that also reinforce their remaining silent about the torture. It can be impossible to find the words to express or explain one's traumatic experiences (Dalenberg, 2000) in any language. They may worry that, even if they did reveal their experience of torture, the clinician would not believe or truly understand what happened or will think less of them (given the intense shame and stigma associated with many of the methods of torture; Fabri, 2001). Indeed, it can be hard or frightening for a clinician to know what humans are capable of doing to one another and confront evil (Northwood, 2003; the impact of this work on clinical social workers will be discussed in detail in Chapter 5 of this book).

Given this reality and the negative impact of human-perpetrated torture on relationships, social workers providing clinical services to torture survivors must attend deeply to building a safe and trusting therapeutic relationship. In the absence of a trusting relationship, the process of healing may be negatively affected (Fabri, 2001; Kanninen, Salo, & Punamaki, 2000). Employing strong basic clinical skills (e.g., active listening, validating that what the person went through was real, and demonstrating trustworthiness over time) can be valuable mechanisms of healing. Demonstrating one's commitment to upholding the survivor's right to confidentiality, a foreign concept for some, by checking with the survivor each time and gaining their consent before communicating with others involved in their case to coordinate services reinforces that one is trustworthy and responsive. A survivor recently told his social worker, after being granted asylum after 6 years of court appearances and multiple bouts of suicidal ideation, that regaining faith in humans again through his relationship with the social worker helped him the most in his recovery. "You cared about me and didn't give up. Nobody has ever done that before. You stuck with me over all these years," the survivor explained, adding, "You remained hopeful when I was hopeless. That helped me to keep going" (Anonymous survivor, personal communication, March 4, 2014).

## *Recommendations for Clinicians Consonant with a Rights-Based Approach from a Survivor*

Ortiz (2001), an American Ursuline nun abducted and tortured in 1989 by members of the US backed Guatemalan military for her work with indigenous peoples, describes what it feels like to be a survivor of torture and to receive services from a clinician, emphasizing what is and what is not helpful. While noting that suicide is a very real concern for some survivors of torture, Ortiz describes how frightening and retraumatizing forced hospitalization can be (recreating the feeling of detention during one's torture). She recommends that it be avoided when possible. Ortiz (2001) provides insight that for some torture survivors, "suicide would be granting our perpetrators the satisfaction of knowing that they were successful in destroying us completely. Instead, for us, survival is our ultimate act of defiance" (p. 21). She urges practitioners to focus more heavily on the resilience found in survivors, honor their cultural beliefs and approaches to healing, recognize transitional survival strategies (rather than just labeling them as pathological), be nonjudgmental, and give survivors control over their own decisions and their path toward recovery.

Ortiz urges clinicians to be cautious not to misdiagnose, something more likely if the clinician does not understand the experience of torture or take adequate time to create a therapeutic environment conducive to the survivor feeling safe to reveal details of his or her experiences. Ortiz (2001) recounts the experience of a woman misdiagnosed with an eating disorder that explained that her problem with eating was not a control issue as the psychiatrist posited. Her problem with eating was because she would start to choke when she tried to swallow food, flooded with memories of being raped and forced to swallow the semen (and sometimes urine) of her torturers. Another survivor, labeled as depressed, acknowledges that of course his heart was very sad after witnessing his neighbors murdering each other and being forced to flee and leave loved ones behind. For this survivor, and many others, deep sadness was normal and to be expected, rather than a sickness or mental illness. Misdiagnosis can lead to inappropriate treatment and further abuses and deprivation of rights, leaving the survivor to feel labeled, dehumanized, and inferior, much like the way they were treated by their torturers.

## *Narrative Exposure Therapy (NET) and Self-Trauma Model (STM): Consistent with Rights-Based Approach*

Two models of treatment, Narrative Exposure Therapy (NET) and the Self-Trauma Model (STM), will be briefly discussed as examples of being consonant with a rights-based practice and appropriate for work with torture survivors and other survivors of human rights violations. NET was developed for the short-term treatment of individuals who are experiencing PTSD as a result of massive violations of their human rights (Schauer, Neuner, & Elbert, 2005). It draws on Trauma-Focused Cognitive Behavioral Therapy (TF-CBT; Cohen, Mannarino, & Deblinger, 2006) and Testimony Therapy developed to treat Chilean torture survivors (Cienfuegos & Monelli, 1983). Among the many strengths of this therapeutic approach from a human rights perspective, is that NET does not medicalize the problem of posttraumatic stress or stigmatize the individual who is suffering. The problem is defined as a political and social one outside the individual (Schauer et al. 2005). Survivors create narratives of their lives, including their traumas, which can be very therapeutic. These narratives can also be helpful in documenting human rights violations and hence, are politically and socially meaningful (Bichescu, Neuner, Schauer, & Elbert, 2007). In addition, paraprofessional counselors have been trained to use NET with refugees and torture survivors in refugee camps and other resource poor community-based locations, making it more accessible in some ways than many of the trauma-informed therapies. Rights-based clinical social work practitioners are urged to use treatment approaches that are supported by the evidence for use with the populations they work with. McPherson (2012) reviewed eight randomized control trials of NET for the treatment of PTSD in diverse populations. McPherson (2012) and Robjant and Fazel (2010) independently found preliminary evidence for the effectiveness of NET for reducing PTSD in survivors of torture and mass violence.

Briere's STM incorporates knowledge about complex trauma and draws from cognitive behavioral therapy, metacognitive awareness, psychodynamic therapy, affect regulation training, and mindfulness (Briere, 2002; Briere & Scott, 2012). STM is primarily a model that guides the clinician in conceptualizing and intervening in any severe trauma, rather than a substitute for torture-specific methodologies (Briere, 2010). It attends to a number of sociocultural issues in a way that is well suited to work with torture survivors and others who are marginalized and oppressed (Briere & Lanktree, 2011). Briere (2010) has identified some of the issues particularly relevant to torture survivors that STM can address, including: extreme posttraumatic stress, especially hyperarousal and reexperiencing; memories that are easily triggerable; trust issues; low self-esteem, helplessness, and other cognitive consequences of the torture; and the sense of isolation associated with their unspeakable memories. While working with a survivor to process his or her posttraumatic stress, STM also focuses on reinstating or developing the survivor's *self-capacities* in the areas of affect regulation, relatedness, and identity. STM allows for flexibility and is attentive to individual differences, and as such, is consonant with a rights-based approach in the sense of not imposing one path toward recovery or a strictly structured, manualized approach to treatment. The processing of traumatic memories is conducted gradually and carefully, utilizing titrated exposure, and ensuring that the survivor is prepared and has a relatively solid sense of stability and safety before beginning the trauma work. Some survivors need to strengthen their affect regulation skills first, before they can safely process their trauma. In addition, trauma processing in the STM is conducted within the *therapeutic window*, striving for a balance between not overwhelming the survivor while ensuring that the processing and exposure to traumatic memories is sufficiently therapeutically challenging so as to avoid chronic posttraumatic outcomes (Briere, 2010). Avoidance behaviors, labeled by some non-rights-based practitioners as maladaptive and signs of "resistance," are a hallmark of posttraumatic stress for many survivors. These behaviors may block the processing of one's traumatic experience(s). STM reframes avoidance as the survivor's effort to titrate their exposure. For a rights-based practitioner utilizing STM, the survivor's "emotional pain associated with traumatic events is slowly metabolized in the context of non-overwhelming, safe, and empathically-attuned discussions of the past" (Briere, 2010, p. 5).

## *Forensic Social Work with Torture Survivors Seeking Asylum*

Social workers have a long history of close collaboration with attorneys and other providers in serving torture survivors seeking asylum. Social workers and other clinicians have much to contribute forensically to the asylum cases of survivors of torture (Berthold, 2013a), contributions that also promote the realization of some of their human rights. Perhaps most notably, when a survivor is granted asylum or another form of legal relief such as Withholding of Removal or relief under the Convention Against Torture,[8] they no longer live in fear of being deported and they have their right to live in peace and security or, in some cases, to live at all safeguarded.

In addition to providing crisis intervention, short-term and longer-term therapeutic services to survivors, clinical social workers can conduct forensic psychosocial

[8] Information about these forms of relief can be obtained from the USCIS website: www.uscis.gov

assessments to objectively document whether there is any psychological evidence consistent with an experience of torture. This takes place within the context of a fuller psychosocial evaluation of the survivor's mental health, functioning, and experiences over their lifetime (Gangsei & Deutsch, 2007; Jacobs, Evans, & Patsalides, 2001). Depending on their findings, social workers also may provide psychosocial affidavits to be used as evidence in the survivor's asylum interviews and/or immigration court proceedings[9]. Social workers also sometimes testify as expert witnesses or treating clinicians in immigration court, providing their expert opinion regarding the asylum applicant's mental status and presentation in court, impact of torture and other persecution, how mental health symptoms and culture relate to the applicant's credibility or delay in applying for asylum, whether the applicant appears to be malingering or not, and the likely impact of deportation on the applicant's psychological health (Meffert, Musalo, McNiel, & Binder, 2010). They may also provide valuable testimony regarding the impact of trauma on memory that may support a favorable credibility finding (Einhorn & Berthold, in press; Herlihy & Turner, 2013).

## *Making Forensic Assessment a Therapeutic Process*

Seeking remedy for torture through the asylum system has many weaknesses and there is a relative lack of formal supports in the United States for survivors until and unless they are able to obtain legal status. Depending on where in the United States the survivor lives, it may take years for the survivor to have his or her asylum case resolved[10] (TRAC Immigration, 2014), particularly if he or she or the government appeals the decision of the immigration judge. Some survivors obtain asylum within a year of applying. This is more common if they do not need to appear in immigration court. Having objective corroborating evidence from a clinical social worker at the beginning may help make a difference, supporting a positive resolution of the case at the asylum interview stage so that the applicant never has to go to immigration court. When a torture survivor has to prepare to testify multiple times, only to have the case continued, they are at risk for decompensating psychologically in the weeks leading up to each hearing (i.e., intensified nightmares and flashbacks, increased hopelessness and suicidal ideation, and the emergence of psychotic symptoms). Given how distressing it typically is for torture survivors to have to disclose and testify about their traumatic experiences (Gangsei & Deutsch, 2007), social workers have a vital role to play in preparing survivors psychologically to be able to work successfully

[9] The USCIS website is a good source for continually updated information about the different stages of the asylum process and related policies (www.uscis.gov/humanitarian/refugees-asylum/asylum).

[10] The Transactional Records Access Clearinghouse (TRAC) Immigration (2014) indicated that there were 328,094 immigration cases pending in FY2014 in the United States.

with their attorney and to be able to testify effectively about their experiences under sometimes intense cross-examination (Meffert et al., 2010). Social workers can provide valuable psychological support through the process.

Gangsei and Deutsch (2007) provide guidance and recommend strategies to facilitate making the psychosocial assessment in the context of an asylum proceeding as therapeutic as possible, while safeguarding the rights of the survivor. They point to many possible emotional benefits of a forensic assessment conducted in a therapeutic fashion for the survivor/asylum seeker, including: enabling the survivor to understand that it is essential for them to tell what happened to them and its impact; elucidating for the survivor the link between his or her past torture and current emotional distress; and assisting the survivor to heal from his or her experiences of humiliation, marginalization, distrust, and fear while developing emotional and cognitive control (see also van der Ver & van Waning, 2004). Ultimately, a key benefit of the evaluation may be to provide corroborating evidence that may support a grant of asylum. Gangsei and Deutsch (2007) elaborate:

> the traumas and emotional wounds of torture occur in an interpersonal context. An attitude of respect can help to heal the wound of humiliation. Taking the survivor's emotional and physical comfort seriously can help to heal the wound of degradation. Information about the process, reliability in appointment times and consistent follow-through can help to heal the wound of mistrust. Also careful attentive listening can demonstrate that fellow human beings do care about the survivor's suffering. (p. 85)

In these and other ways, a forensic psychosocial assessment can contribute to safeguarding and realizing the rights of survivors, treating them with respect and dignity throughout.

## *Clinical Support for Survivor Advocates and Activists*

Survivors of torture play prominent and valuable roles in advocacy campaigns to fight against impunity, promote the prevention of torture worldwide, expose human rights violations, advocate for the reform of immigration and detention policies, and fight for justice and the rights of all targeted for state persecution. The Torture Abolition and Survivors Support Coalition (TASSC) International is a very active organization in the United States by and for torture survivors that engages in such work. Many survivors were tortured because of their political and other activism, religious beliefs, and advocacy efforts. Reconnecting or remaining connected with one's activism or beliefs has been found to be protective (Basoglu et al., 1997).

Putting a human face on the atrocity of torture can be a powerful strategy in advocacy campaigns. Many nonprofits and advocacy groups seek to have survivors as spokespeople for their cause. As mentioned elsewhere, many survivors of torture are strong and resilient people, yet some survivors who initially feel comfortable and prepared to speak publically about torture find that when the time comes, the experience is more than they can handle emotionally. Engaging in these campaigns and/or testifying against one's perpetrators are not positive experiences for all, and may put a survivor at risk for revictimization (Martinez & Fabri, 1992). Many have found that their intrusive or other symptoms have intensified after speaking publically, an experience that some anticipate and are willing to accept in order to further their cause. For others, however, the negatives outweigh any possible benefits. Social workers should keep in mind that torture survivors might feel an obligation to give back to an agency that has helped them. A rights-based social worker can help to ensure that a survivor's right to privacy and self-determination are protected, and that they are not unduly pressured into participating if they do not want or feel able to. Social workers may support the survivor in anticipating possible challenging moments and developing strategies to address them if they arise. They may provide clinical support and accompaniment throughout these opportunities for survivors to engage in social justice projects that are meaningful and can promote healing and restore a sense of connection with one's identity and with others (Marton, Berthold & Libal, 2013). It should always be up to the individual to make a decision that is right for them, without coercion, no matter how subtle.

## Implementation of CAT: Important Roles for Clinical Social Workers

Using the CAT General Comment[11] No. 3 (UN Committee Against Torture, 2012), various key roles for clinical social workers will be identified relevant to the implementation of CAT. This is meant to supplement the core rights-based approach described in Chapter 1 of this book.

### *Redress and Compensation*

Article 14 of CAT holds States accountable for ensuring that "the victim of an act of torture obtains redress and has an enforceable right to fair and adequate compensation, including the means for as full rehabilitation as possible" (UN Committee Against Torture, 2012, para. 1). The General Comment acknowledges that, although the Committee Against Torture of the United Nations uses the term *victim*, that those who have experienced torture may prefer to be referred to as *survivor.*[12] Further, survivors have a right to be recognized as survivors and are entitled to compensation and rehabilitation even when their perpetrators have "not been identified, apprehended, prosecuted or convicted" (UN Committee Against Torture, 2012, para. 3).

[11] General Comments are published on thematic issues by the human rights treaty bodies (in this case, the Committee Against Torture) to clarify how the treaty body interprets the content of various human rights provisions.

[12] As survivor Sr. Diana Ortiz writes, "To call us victims is to validate the image our torturers tried to mold us into and leave us—weak, subjugated, helpless. We are not victims. We are survivors" (Ortiz, 2001, p. 15).

## *Avoiding Retraumatization*

Survivors are often retraumatized when they are placed in a situation where they have to try to prove that they have been tortured in the absence of being able to identify their perpetrators. Frequently, the torturers blindfold their targets, mask themselves or use other means to hide their identities from their victims. These realities can take a very heavy toll psychologically on the survivor, and clinical social workers can provide valuable psychological support and treatment as well as evidence to support the survivor's claims of torture. In addition, clinical social workers may contribute to the determination of what full and effective redress, reparations, and restitution called for by CAT would mean for a given survivor through an individualized and holistic assessment (UN Committee Against Torture, 2012, para. 11).

The UN Committee Against Torture also stresses that is it important to involve the victim of torture in the redress process, a process that has as its goal the restoration of the victim's dignity (UN Committee Against Torture, 2012). When a survivor of torture is called to take part in an administrative or legal proceeding that seeks the provision of reparation and justice, they have a right to protection aimed at avoiding retraumatization, including procedures to protect those who have faced gender-based violence and protocols to treat sensitively those who are particularly vulnerable, such as those who were tortured due to their gender identity or sexual orientation (UN Committee Against Torture, 2012). If called to testify and/or provide evidence through other means during investigations, the survivor typically must revisit in great detail some of the most terrifying, painful, and shameful events of their lives—events that most have been trying to forget and go to great lengths to avoid thinking or talking about (Berthold & Gray, 2011; Herlihy & Turner, 2013). The process of being interviewed by an asylum officer or cross-examined in immigration court or a tribunal may also trigger memories of being interrogated as part of their torture. Clinical social workers have a valuable role to play in preparing survivors psychologically to be able to effectively participate in the redress process without sustaining further lasting harm as well as advocating for protocols to be put in place to minimize retraumatization during the proceedings (e.g., allowing rape survivors to testify behind a partition or using a one-way closed circuit television[13]).

## *Full and Public Disclosure of the Truth*

The CAT calls for the "full and public disclosure of the truth" (UN Committee Against Torture, 2012, para. 16) related to the torture, while recognizing that the well-being, safety, and interests of the survivor and other affected individuals (i.e., family members, persons who intervened, witnesses) must be safeguarded. Clinical

[13] See Ciorciari and Heindel (2011) for further discussion of these issues drawing on examples from the International Criminal Court (ICC) and International Criminal Tribunal for Rwanda (ICTR).

social workers can assess the impact on the survivor and their family of having sexual torture made public, for example, and provide evidence of this impact in an effort to protect the rights and well-being of the survivor. In many of the cultures where sexual torture of women takes place, the survivor is shunned and stigmatized, and the shame and stigma extends to her relatives. A married woman's spouse may leave her if it is known that she has been raped, and an unmarried girl or woman who has been sexually tortured and her unmarried female relatives may no longer be considered marriageable. The survivor may be killed in an *honor killing* (Leatherman, 2011). Such realities can have long-lasting and multilayered effects on the well-being of the survivor, leaving her in lifelong poverty, marginalized, and oppressed. Revelations of sexual torture of males can have extreme consequences as well, particularly given the common taboo of acknowledging that this takes place coupled with the societal and cultural expectations of masculinity in many parts of the world (Ortiz, 2001). Survivors of sexual torture may not be ready or able psychologically to reveal the whole truth or anything about what happened to them (Bogner, Herlihy, & Brewin, 2007; Bogner, Brewin, & Herlihy, 2009; Herlihy & Turner, 2009). Some may not have enough self-regulation skills, may experience significant dissociation and may need trauma-informed treatment before they may be able to talk about their sexual trauma, even with a clinician (Briere, 2002, 2010).

## As Full Rehabilitation as Possible

Some survivors may feel some measure of validation of the harm they have sustained by receiving redress, reparations, or restitution. No matter what compensation may be provided to a survivor of torture (monetary and/or other), however, survivors may well feel that it cannot truly compensate them for what they have endured. Social workers can provide psychotherapy aimed at this and other common existential issues faced by survivors as a result of their torture (Ortiz, 2001; Yalom, 1980). Therapy is centrally about promoting the person's human dignity, health, and well-being, all of which are intrinsically connected to human rights. Clinicians also support survivors' right to bodily integrity and freedom from torture.

CAT identifies the right of torture survivors for "as full rehabilitation as possible" (UN Committee Against Torture, 2012, para. 11). The International Rehabilitation Council for Torture Victims (IRCT, 2013) has defined the following components as essential in any effort to realize the right to rehabilitation from torture: services must be state-funded, victim-centered, multifaceted, and linked to national education and health systems. Clinical social workers can be part of teams that contribute to holistic rehabilitation in keeping with the recommendations of the IRCT. Social workers are trained to identify and build on the strengths and resilience of those they serve, delivered within the context of a trusting and confidential therapeutic relationship that seeks to minimize the retraumatization of the survivor. This approach to rehabilitation is one that the CAT identifies as of utmost importance (UN Committee Against Torture, 2012). These services work to restore a sense of dignity. Survivors have the right to choose their service provider and should be provided with effective services and have their outcomes measured (UN Committee Against Torture, 2012), something that rights-based clinical social workers routinely assess through benchmarks and the evaluation of indicators of success.

Clinically, it is typically recommended to proceed at the trauma survivor's own pace when doing trauma work, facilitating their revisiting and recounting the trauma over time, and making sure that they have sufficient coping ability to regulate their emotional distress (Briere, 2002; Briere & Scott, 2012; Fabri, 2011; Quiroga & Jaranson, 2005). For some survivors with less effective self-regulatory skills, severe psychopathology and lower functioning, it may be contraindicated to do trauma work (Briere & Scott, 2012). By the time a clinical social worker starts to work with an asylum seeker there may not be much time before their assessment report would need to be filed in court or with an asylum officer, putting pressure on them to have the survivor tell them about their torture and its impact before the survivor may be psychologically prepared or capable of doing so. Social workers operating from a rights perspective will prioritize the survivor's well-being over an arbitrary court filing date. They may advocate for a continuance (to postpone the court hearing) and support it with a letter to the court documenting the mental health or health reasons why the survivor is not able to proceed with the hearing at that time. The decision of whether to advocate in this way should only be done in close consultation with the survivor themselves and the survivor's attorney, as there can be negative impacts of continuances as well.

## *Training*

Clinical social workers can also make a difference by collaborating in the training of military, security forces, law enforcement personnel, and legal and health professionals called for by the UN Committee Against Torture (2012). Clinical social workers experienced in serving torture survivors are well equipped to conduct training recommended by the Committee related to the needs of survivors and vulnerable marginalized populations at risk for torture as well as about the psychological portions of the *Istanbul Protocol.* This protocol is a UN document that provides international guidelines to be used by governments and human rights organizations regarding documenting the medical and psychological evidence and consequences of torture (UN Office of the High Commissioner for Human Rights, 2004). The Istanbul Protocol also addresses relevant ethical codes, international legal standards, and investigation standards and principles.

## Conclusion

Rights-based clinical social workers have many avenues available to them for making significant contributions to safeguard and facilitate the realization of the rights of those who have been subjected to torture and/or cruel, inhuman, or degrading treatment or punishment. The rights-based approach described in this chapter is relevant not only for working with asylum seekers who fled their homelands after experiencing state-sponsored torture, it is also applicable to work with many populations frequently served by clinical social workers in the United States such as those who are incarcerated, in mental health or nursing home facilities, or children in congregate care. Core rights-based principles to guide clinical social work with torture survivors as well as two treatment models that are consonant with this approach to practice with this population were introduced in this chapter.

In addition to providing treatment, clinical social workers can be involved in a number of other ways that support survivors' rights. They can provide testimony in individual asylum applicant's cases regarding compelling psychological or other reasons that an exception to the one-year bar[14] should be made by the adjudicator so that the merits of the person's asylum case can be heard (Musalo & Rice, 2008). Their first-hand knowledge of the problems faced by asylum seekers from their clinical work with survivors can be incorporated into larger advocacy campaigns for immigration reform (e.g., eliminating the one-year bar for filing asylum applications within one's first year in the United States; easing constraints on processing family reunification; shortening the time it takes to have cases adjudicated).

Not everyone needs or wants psychotherapy. For many torture survivors, psychotherapy is a foreign concept, one that may be distant from their indigenous approaches to healing after trauma and incomprehensible (Fabri, 2001). In some societies, seeing a mental health professional (if one exists) is stigmatizing and generally reserved for persons who are chronically and severely mentally ill. Many survivors may be resilient and functioning well. They may gain strength, healing, and transformation through taking collective action or through ritual or the arts (Aristizabal & Lefer, 2010). Torture survivors and human rights defenders around the world have utilized creative methods in the struggle for human rights, including: theater of the oppressed depictions of torture; symbolic funeral march to the gates of Fort Benning in Columbus, Georgia as part of the annual Vigil to Close the School of the Americas[15] (a military training school that trained Latin American soldiers and

[14] A provision of the Illegal Immigration Reform and Immigrant Responsibility Act (1996) codified by the Immigration and Nationality Act, the one-year bar makes any individual who seeks asylum in the United States ineligible for asylum unless they apply within 1 year of arrival (8 U.S.C. § 1158(a)(2)(B)). Exceptions to this rule exist, allowing a waiver for those applicants who successfully demonstrate materially changed circumstances affecting their eligibility or extraordinary circumstances that made it impossible for them to apply within their first year in the United States (see Musalo & Rice, 2008).

[15] The School of the Americas (SOA) was renamed the Western Hemisphere Institute for Security Cooperation (WHINSEC) in 2000/2001.

security officers to torture and commit other human rights abuses); exposing perpetrators of human rights violations in Egypt using Flickr (Piggipedia, created by an Egyptian blogger in 2008); and Turkish protesters symbolically standing silently at locations where government atrocities took place to protest and memorialize the abuse (Aristizabal & Lefer, 2010; New Tactics in Human Rights, n.d.). An innovative project, New Tactics in Human Rights (n.d.), connects these activists through regional meetings, on-line forums and dialogues, and through social media. In doing so, opportunities to learn from one another and collaborate are fostered and a virtual and expanded support network is developed to combat isolation and enhance collective action. Clinical social workers have much to learn from these activists as they broaden their vision of pathways to healing and transformation after torture consistent with a rights-based approach to practice.

Most perpetrators of state-sponsored torture are never brought to justice. This is the problem of impunity, a reality that thwarts some survivors' quest for justice, realization of their right to redress and compensation, and healing. Rare exceptions can be found in the small number of high level perpetrators prosecuted by such bodies as the International Criminal Court (ICC), the International Criminal Tribunal for the former Yugoslavia (ICTY), the International Criminal Tribunal for Rwanda (ICTR), the Center for Justice and Accountability (CJA), and the States tried by the Inter-American Human Rights Court and the European Court of Human Rights. Although the United States had a key role in the development of the ICC, it has refused to officially recognize or join the ICC. By not joining the ICC, US political and military leaders could not be held accountable to the uniform international standard of justice unlike participating States. This is another example of US exceptionalism.

The UN Committee Against Torture recognizes that survivors often cannot bring their perpetrators to justice in their homeland. Further, the Committee holds that States are obligated to prosecute or extradite torturers found in their territory and commends States who provide civil remedies for survivors tortured in other countries (UN Committee Against Torture, 2012, para. 22). Social workers can and do work with survivors and attorneys to fight against the impunity of perpetrators. Providing clinical support so that torture survivors are able to testify in immigration proceedings or in legal proceedings against the perpetrator is one way that clinical social workers can contribute to the fight against impunity. Providing objective forensic evidence of the human rights violations in expert witness reports and testimony may be quite valuable. Obtaining asylum involves recognition by a powerful government that those who tortured them persecuted them and, by so doing, violated their rights. Some survivors may experience this as a measure of justice, albeit it cannot compare to what it would mean to be able to bring their perpetrator(s) to justice. Despite the limitations and roadblocks to justice, rights-based clinical social workers can contribute to the realization of rights of torture survivors in a number of meaningful ways as well as collaborate with survivors and other human rights' activists in the campaign to prevent torture.

## Suggested Activities/Resources

*Case Discussion* Have students read the following vignette of a torture survivor (Claude) and engage in discussion in small groups, reflecting on the discussion questions provided.

> Claude (a pseudonym) was tortured in his native country by members of a Special Forces unit of the military due to his support of a political opposition party. His torturers hung him from the ceiling each day as he was subjected to beatings and interrogations. When Claude continually refused to provide the information they wanted, the names and whereabouts of his fellow party members, several officers forced him to watch as they gang raped his wife. After 6 months, Claude was released after signing a false confession. His torturers threatened to find him and kill him if he continued his opposition work. Claude fled his country immediately after he was released, crossing the border to a neighboring country and making his way to the United States. He did not say goodbye to his wife and children, as he feared being picked up and tortured again or killed by the military if he went home. Claude called his wife once he arrived in the United States to let her know he was safe. He is disturbed by frequent nightmares of his torture and images of seeing his wife raped. His calls to his wife have become more infrequent.
>
> Claude connected with a group of fellow exiled party members in the United States and members of the group helped him to find a place to stay and secure a job as an accountant. Claude reports that he was an accountant back home and that it is meaningful for him to be able to work in his profession and send money home to support his family. He is functioning well at work, where he is able to keep busy and productively focused on activities far removed from his torture. It is when he has free time that he struggles. Claude complains that he is flooded with memories of his torture and his wife's rape when he is not at work. At those times he cannot get the sound of his wife screaming out of his head, and he frequently feels overpowered by a sense of helplessness and shame that reminds him of his sense of impotence as he watched his wife being raped.
>
> The asylum officer who interviewed Claude referred him to immigration court as the officer found inconsistencies between his verbal and written accounts. His asylum case has been continued several times as the immigration judge assigned to hear his case had other older "priority" cases that took precedence. Four years after arriving in the United States, he still has yet to have the merits of his case heard in court. He and his wife have been arguing. Claude's wife tells him that she does not understand how it could possibly be taking so long to resolve his case and accuses Claude of not wanting to sponsor her and their children. When he last spoke to his wife, Claude was devastated to learn that his oldest son was abducted and killed by members of the military who were hunting for Claude.

### Discussion Questions: The Case of Claude

1. What human rights violations are present in Claude's case?
2. Which human rights instruments help you to understand the case from a rights-based perspective?
3. How would you approach your work with Claude drawing on the core principles of a rights-based approach presented in this chapter?
4. What might be key roles that a clinical social worker could perform in implementing CAT in the case of Claude?

***YouTube and Internet resources*** for classroom viewing and discussion:

- *Atlas of Torture:* For an interactive map depicting the prevalence of torture worldwide click on: http://www.univie.ac.at/bimtor/countrymap. This resource provides news and background information regarding torture and ill-treatment. It includes a search tool that enables one to search for facts about torture for particular countries.
- *Well Founded Fear (47 min.)*: a 2000 documentary about the US asylum process by directors Shari Robertson and Michael Camerini. Excerpts of interviews of asylum applicants by asylum officers are included. Retrieved from http://vimeo.com/46242686
- *Caring for a torture survivor* (a free online course from Boston Center for Health and Human Rights). Retrieved from http://survivors-ebook.bcrhhr.com/swf/book.swf. This course includes YouTube excerpts of a clinical/forensic interview of a torture survivor, retrieved from https://www.youtube.com/watch?v=qdQvXHlC_sc&feature=youtu.be and https://www.youtube.com/watch?v=95MGmWsoMzc
- *The Healing Club* – a short documentary on YouTube about the work of the Program for Torture Victims and its services for survivors of torture in Los Angeles, California. Retrieved from http://www.youtube.com/watch?v=Ovzd3zKxEsw
- Hector Aristizabal's *Imaginaction* website: http://imaginaction.org/get-involved/the-blessing-next-to-the-wound. Includes a series of videos regarding the role of imagination and Theatre of the Oppressed techniques in the struggle for human rights, information about Hector's play *Nightwind* regarding his own torture in Columbia (http://imaginaction.org/performances), and a link to Hector's book: *The Blessing Next to the Wound: A Story of Art, Activism, and Transformation.*

***Resources*** (selected)

*U.S. and International Torture Treatment Providers:*

- National Consortium of Torture Treatment Programs (NCTTP): http://www.ncttp.org/
- International Rehabilitation Council for Torture Victims (IRCT): www.irct.org
- Torture Abolition and Survivors Support Coalition (TASSC) International: http://www.tassc.org

*Resources for providers and survivors:*

- HealTorture.org (www.healtorture.org): an on-line resource site for survivors of torture and providers who serve them. The website is funded by the US Department of Health and Human Services, Administration for Children and Families, Office of Refugee Resettlement and is a project of the Center for Victims of Torture.
- Office of Refugee Resettlement's Services for Survivor of Torture website: http://www.acf.hhs.gov/programs/orr/resource/services-for-survivors-of-torture
- New Tactics in Human Rights' website: www.newtactics.org
- Just Detention International (http://www.justdetention.org/) and Stop Prisoner Rape (*spr.igc.org*) are human rights organizations working to combat the problem of rape in prison.

- Links to manuals regarding forensic assessment of torture survivors:
  1. Istanbul Protocol: http://phrtoolkits.org/toolkits/istanbul-protocol-model-medical-curriculum/module-2-istanbul-protocol-standards-for-medical-documentation-of-torture-and-medical-ethics/the-istanbul-protocol/the-istanbul-protocol-2/
  2. Istanbul Protocol Model Medical Curriculum: https://sites.google.com/a/effective-medical-physiciansforhumanrights.org/model-curriculum-on-the-documentation-of-torture-and-ill-treatment/
  3. Examining Asylum Seekers manual: http://physiciansforhumanrights.org/library/reports/examining-asylum-seekers-manual-2012.html

## References

American Civil Liberties Union [ACLU]. (2012). ACLU briefing paper: The shackling of pregnant women & girls in U.S. prisons, jails & youth detention centers. ACLU Reproductive Freedom project—ACLU National Prison Project. Retrieved from www.aclu.org/prisoners-rights/women-prison+&cd=2&hl=en&ct=clnk&gl=us&client=firefox-a.

Amnesty International. (2006, May 19). *UN Committee Against Torture condemns US detention policies, calls for change*. London: Amnesty International. AI Index: AMR 51/079/2006. Retrieved from http://www.amnesty.org/en/library/asset/AMR51/079/2006/en/b14f64b5-d42d-11dd-8743-d305bea2b2c7/amr510792006en.html.

Amnesty International. (2013). *Amnesty International report 2013: The state of the world's human rights*. London, UK: Author.

Amnesty International. (2014, May 13). *Torture in 2014: 30 years of broken promises*. London, UK: Author. Retreived from http://www.amnesty.org/en/library/info/ACT40/004/2014/en.

Aristizabal, H., & Lefer, D. (2010). *The blessing next to the wound: A story of art, activism, and transformation*. New York, UK: Lantern Books.

Barbera, R. (2014). Learning by doing: Integrating social & economic justice and human rights into social work practice. In K. R. Libal, S. M. Berthold, R. L. Thomas, & L. M. Healy (Eds.), *Advancing human rights in social work education*. Alexandria, VA: Council on Social Work Education.

Basoglu, M., Paker, M., Ozmen, E., Tasdemir, O., & Sahin, D. (1994a). Factors related to long-term traumatic stress responses in survivors of torture in Turkey. *Journal of the American Medical Association, 272*(5), 357–363.

Basoglu, M., Paker, M., Paker, O., Ozmen, E., Marks, I., Incesu, C., & Sarimurat, N. (1994b). Psychological effects of torture: A comparison of tortured with nontortured political activists in Turkey. *American Journal of Psychiatry, 151*(1), 76–81.

Basoglu, M., Mineka, S., Paker, M., Aker, T., Livanou, M., & Gok, S. (1997). Psychological preparedness for trauma as a protective factor in survivors of torture. *Psychological Medicine, 27*(6), 1421–1433.

Basoglu, M., Livanou, M., & Crnobaric, C. (2007). Torture versus other cruel, inhuman & degrading treatment: Is the distinction real or apparent? *Archives of General Psychiatry, 64*, 277–285.

Berthold, S. M. (2013a). Medical and psychological evidence of trauma in asylum cases. In S. K. Brown & F. D. Beam (Eds.), *Encyclopedia of migration*. SpringerReference.com. Retrieved from http://www.springerreference.com/docs/html/chapterdbid/349344.html.

Berthold, S. M. (2013b). Torture. *Encyclopedia of social work online*. New York, NY: Oxford University Press. doi:10.1093/acrefore/9780199975839.013.1057.

Berthold, S. M., & Gray, G. (2011). Post-traumatic stress reactions and secondary trauma effects at tribunals: The ECCC example. In B. Van Schaack, D. Reicherter, & Y. Chhang (Eds.), *Cambodia's hidden scars: Trauma psychology in the wake of the Khmer Rouge* (pp. 92–120). Phnom Penh, Cambodia: Documentation Center of Cambodia.

Bichescu, D., Neuner, F., Schauer, M., & Elbert, T. (2007). Narrative exposure therapy for political imprisonment-related chronic posttraumatic stress disorder and depression. *Behaviour Research and Therapy, 45,* 2212–2220.

Boehnlein, J. K., & Kinzie, J. D. (2011). The effect of the Khmer Rouge on the mental health of Cambodia and Cambodians. In B. Van Schaack, D. Reicherter, & Y. Chhang (Eds.), *Cambodia's hidden scars: Trauma psychology in the wake of the Khmer Rouge* (pp. 33–45). Phnom Penh, Cambodia: Documentation Center of Cambodia.

Bogner, D., Herlihy, J., & Brewin, C. R. (2007). Impact of sexual violence on disclosure in Home Office interviews. *British Journal of Psychiatry, 191,* 75–81.

Bogner, D., Brewin, C., & Herlihy, J. (2009). Refugees' experiences of Home Office interviews: A qualitative study on the disclosure of sensitive personal information. *Journal of Ethnic and Migration Studies, 36,* 519.

Bonanno, G. A. (2004). Loss, trauma, and human resilience: Have we underestimated the human capacity to thrive after extremely aversive events? *American Psychologist, 59,* 20–28.

Bonanno, G. A., Westphal, M., & Mancini, A. D. (2011). Resilience to loss and potential trauma. *Annual Review of Clinical Psychology, 7,* 511–535. doi:10.1146/annurev-clinpsy-032210-104526.

Boscarino, J. A. (2004). Posttraumatic stress disorder and physical illness: Results from clinical and epidemiologic studies. *Annals of the New York Academy of Sciences, 1032,* 141–153.

Briere, J. (2002). Treating adult survivors of severe childhood abuse and neglect: Further development of an integrative model. In J. E. B. Myers, L. Berliner, J. Briere, C. T. Hendrix, T. Reid, & C. Jenny (Eds.), *The APSAC handbook on child maltreatment* (2nd ed., pp. 175–202). Newbury Park, CA: Sage.

Briere, J. (2010, July 1). *A summary of self-trauma model applications for severe trauma: Treating the torture survivor.* Supplementary material for a webinar presentation to the Advanced Clinicians Peer Consultation Group of the National Consortium of Torture Treatment Programs. Los Angeles, CA: Author.

Briere, J., & Lanktree, C. B. (2011). *Treating complex trauma in adolescents and young adults.* Thousand Oaks, CA: Sage.

Briere, J., & Scott, C. (2012). *Principles of trauma therapy: A guide to symptoms, evaluation and treatment* (2nd ed.). Thousand Oaks, CA: Sage.

Burnett, A., & Peel, M. (2001). Asylum seekers and refugees in Britain: The health of survivors of torture and organized violence. *British Medical Journal, 322*(7286), 606–609.

Center for Victims of Torture (2005). *Healing the hurt: A guide for developing services for torture survivors.* A project of the National Capacity Building Project. St. Paul, MN: Author. Retrieved from www.HealTorture.org.

Chideya, F. (2005, May 3). U.S. settles with Kenyan asylum seeker. *NPR.* Retrieved from http://www.npr.org/templates/story/story.php?storyId=4628618.

Cienfuegos, A. J., & Monelli, C. (1983). The testimony of political repression as therapeutic instrument. *American Journal of Orthopsychiatry, 53,* 43–51.

Ciorciari, J. D., & Heindel, A. (2011). Trauma in the courtroom. In B. Van Schaack, D. Reicherter, & Y. Chhang (Eds.), *Cambodia's hidden scars: Trauma psychology in the wake of the Khmer Rouge* (pp. 121–147). Phnom Penh, Cambodia: Documentation Center of Cambodia.

Cohen, J. A., Mannarino, A. P., & Deblinger, E. (2006). *Treating trauma and traumatic grief in children and adolescents.* New York, NY: Guilford Press.

Costanzo, M., Gerrity, E., & Lykes, M. B. (2007). Psychologists and the use of torture in interrogations. *Analyses of Social Issues and Public Policy, 7*(1), 7–20.

Coughlin, S. S. (Ed.), (2012). *Post-traumatic stress disorder and chronic health conditions.* Washington, DC: American Public Health Association.

Dalenberg, C. (2000). Speaking trauma: The inadequacy of language in trauma treatment. In C. Dalenberg (Ed.), *Countertransference and the treatment of trauma* (pp. 57–84). Washington, DC: American Psychological Association.

Davis, M. D. (2012, July 30). Consign Bush's 'torture memos' to history: How should we mark the 10th anniversary of the effort by the Bush administration to justify torture? By ensuring it never happens again. Op-Ed in *Los Angeles Times*. Retrieved from http://www.latimes.com/news/opinion/commentary/la-oe-davis-torture-memos-bybee–20120730%2C0%2C6058023.story.

Dube, S. R., Felitti, V. J., Dong, M., Giles, W. H., & Anda, R. F. (2003). The impact of adverse childhood experiences on health problems: Evidence from four birth cohorts dating back to 1990. *Preventive Medicine, 37*(3), 268–277.

Einhorn, B. J., & Berthold, S. M. (in press). Reconstructing Babel: Bridging cultural dissonance between asylum seekers and asylum adjudicators. In B. N. Lawrance & G. Ruffer (Eds.), *Adjudicating refugee and asylum status: The role of witness, expertise, and testimony*. Cambridge, UK: Cambridge University Press.

Engstrom, D. W., & Okomura, A. (2004). A plague of our time: Torture, human rights, and social work. *Families in Society, 85,* 291–300.

Fabri, M. R. (2001). Reconstructing safety: Adjustments to the therapeutic frame in the treatment of survivors of political torture. *Professional Psychology: Research and Practice, 32*(5), 452–457.

Fabri, M. R. (2011). Best, promising and emerging practices in the treatment of trauma: What can we apply in our work with torture survivors? *Torture, 21*(1), 27–38.

Fazel, M., Wheeler, J., & Danesh, J. (2005). Prevalence of serious mental disorder in 7000 refugees resettled in western countries: A systematic review. *Lancet, 365*(9467), 1309–1314.

Ferrada-Noli, M., Asberg, M., Ormstad, K., Lundin, T., & Sundbom, E. (1998). Suicidal behavior after severe trauma. Part 1: PTSD diagnoses, psychiatric comorbidity, and assessments of suicidal behavior. *Journal of Traumatic Stress, 11*(1), 103–112.

Gangsei, D., & Deutsch, A. C. (2007). Psychological evaluation of asylum seekers as a therapeutic process. *Torture: Journal on Rehabilitation of Torture Victims and Prevention of Torture, 17*(2), 79–87.

Gilligan, J., & Lee, B. (2013, September 5). Report to the New York city board of correction. Retrieved from http://solitarywatch.com/wp-content/uploads/2013/11/Gilligan-Report.-Final.pdf.

Gosztola, K. (2014, March 11). The CIA, Senate Intelligence Committee & the culture of impunity for torture. *The Dissenter.* Retrieved from http://dissenter.firedoglake.com/2014/03/11/the-cia-senate-intelligence-committee-the- culture-of-impunity-for-torture/.

Grassian, S. (2006). Psychiatric effects of solitary confinement. *Journal of Law and Policy, 22,* 325–383.

Guskovict, K. (2012, August 8). Identifying and reinforcing resiliency in torture survivors. Webinar sponsored by the National Partnership for Community Training, a program of the Florida Center for Survivors of Torture. Retrieved from http://gulfcoastjewishfamilyandcommunityservices.org/refugee/2012/07/12/webinar-on-identifying-and-reinforcing-resiliency-in-torture-survivors/#more-1201609.

Hajjar, L. (2012). *Torture: A sociology of violence and human rights.* New York, NY: Routledge.

Herlihy, J., & Turner, S. (2009). The psychology of seeking protection. *International Journal of Refugee Law, 21*(2), 171–192.

Herlihy, J., & Turner, S. (2013). What do we know so far about emotion and refugee law? *Northern Ireland Legal Quarterly, 64*(1), 47–62.

Hertel, S., & Libal, K. (2011). *Human rights in the United States: Beyond exceptionalism.* New York, NY: Cambridge University Press.

Holtz, T. (1998). Refugee trauma versus torture trauma: A retrospective controlled cohort study of Tibetan refugees. *Journal of Nervous and Mental Disease, 186*(1), 24–34.

Human Rights Watch/American Civil Liberties Union. (2006). *Custody and control: Conditions of confinement in New York's Juvenile Prisons for Girls.* New York, NY: Human Rights Watch.

Human Rights Watch. (2010). *My so-called emancipation: From foster care to homelessness for California youth*. New York, NY: Human Rights Watch.

Human Rights Watch/American Civil Liberties Union. (2012). *Growing up locked down: Youth in solitary confinement in jails and prisons across the United States*. New York, NY: Human Rights Watch.

Ignatieff, M. (2005). *American exceptionalism and human rights*. Princeton, NJ: Princeton University Press.

Illegal Immigration Reform and Immigrant Responsibility Act, Pub. L. No. 104–208, Div. C, § 604(a), 110 Stat. 3009–690 (1996).

Immigration and Nationality Act of 1952, Pub. L. No. 82–414, 8 U.S.C. § 1158(a)(2)(B). Interim Report of the Special Rapporteur of the Human Rights Council on Torture and Other Cruel, Inhuman or Degrading Treatment or Punishment, delivered to the General Assembly, U.N. Doc. A/66/268 (Aug. 5, 2011).

International Committee of the Red Cross (ICRC). (1949). Geneva Convention Relative to the Treatment of Prisoners of War (Third Geneva Convention), 75 UNTS 135. Retrieved from http://www.refworld.org/docid/3ae6b36c8.html. Accessed 12 Aug 1949.

International Rehabilitation Council for Torture Victims [IRCT]. (2013). IRCT defines way forward to realise the right to rehabilitation. *World Medical Journal, 59*(6), 234.

Jacobs, U., Evans, E. B., & Patsalides, B. (2001). Principles of documenting psychological evidence of torture. Part I & II. *Torture, 11*(3), 85–89 and *11*(4), 100–102.

Kanninen, K., Salo, J., & Punamaki, R.-L. (2000). Attachment patterns and working alliance in trauma therapy for victims of political violence. *Psychotherapy Research, 10*(4), 435–449.

Keller, A. S., & Granski, M. (2013, December 16). A U.S. truth commission. Op-ed letter to the *New York Times*. Retrieved from http://www.nytimes.com/2013/12/17/opinion/a-us-truth-commission.html?_r=0.

Keller, A. S., Rosenfeld, B., Trinh-Shevrin, C., Meserve, C., Sachs, E., Singer. E., … & Ford, D. (2003). Mental health of detained asylum seekers. *Lancet, 362*(9397), 1721–1723.

Kinzie, J. D. (2001). Psychotherapy for massively traumatized refugee: The therapist variable. *American Journal of Psychotherapy, 55*(4), 475–490.

Kinzie, J. D. (2011). Guidelines for psychiatric care of torture survivors. *Torture, 21*(1), 18–26.

Kinzie, J. D., Jaranson, J. M., & Kroupin, G. V. (2007). Diagnosis and treatment of mental illness. In P. F. Walker & E. D. Barnett (Eds.), *Immigrant medicine* (pp. 639–651). Philadelphia, PA: Saunders Elsevier.

Kinzie, J. D., Riley, C., McFarland, B., Hayes, M., Boehnlein, J., Leung, P., & Adams, G. (2008). High prevalence rates of diabetes and hypertension among refugee psychiatric patients. *Journal of Nervous & Mental Disease, 196*(2), 108–112.

Kisken, T. (2013, March 7). Local nursing homes leading movement to reduce chemical restraints. *Ventura County Star*. Retrieved from http://www.vcstar.com/news/2013/mar/07/local-nursing-homes-leading-movement-to-reduce/.

Leahy, P. (2009, February 12). A truth commission to investigate Bush-Cheney administration abuses. *Huffington Post*. Retrieved from http://www.huffingtonpost.com/sen-patrick-leahy/a-truth-commission-to-inv_b_166461.html.

Leatherman, J. L. (2011). *Sexual violence and armed conflict*. Cambridge: Polity Press.

Lewis, M. (2012, April 12). Standing up against sexual assault by the state. [Web log comment]. Retrieved from https://www.aclu.org/blog/prisoners-rights-womens-rights/standing-against-sexual-assault-state.

Luban, D., & Shue, H. (2012). Mental torture: A critique of erasures in U.S. law. *Georgetown Law Journal, 100*, 823–863.

Marshall, G. N., Schell, T. L., Elliot, M. N., Berthold, S. M., & Chun, C.-A. (2005). Mental health of Cambodian refugees 2 decades after resettlement in the United States. *Journal of the American Medical Association, 294*(5), 571–579.

Martinez, A., & Fabri. M. (1992). The dilemma of revictimization. *Torture, 2*, 47–48.

Marton, M., Berthold, S. M., & Libal, K. (2013, November). *Working cross-professionally on social justice advocacy projects in refugee services*. Presented at the 28th Annual Midwest Clinical Conference: Harnessing the Storm: Responses to the "New Normal". Interprofessional Center for Counseling and Legal Services at the University of St. Thomas School of Law, Minneapolis, MN.

Masten, A. S., & Obradović, J. (2008). Disaster preparation and recovery: Lessons from research on resilience in human development. *Ecology and Society, 13*(1), 9. Retrieved from http://www.ecologyandsociety.org/vol13/iss1/art9/.

Mayer, J. (2009). *The dark side: The inside story of how the war on terror turned into a war on American ideals*. New York, NY: Anchor Books.

McPherson, J. (2012). Does Narrative Exposure Therapy reduce PTSD in survivors of mass violence? *Research on Social Work Practice, 22*(1), 29–42.

Meffert, S. M., Musalo, K., McNiel, D. E., & Binder, R. L. (2010). The role of mental health professionals in political asylum processing. *The Journal of the American Academy of Psychiatry and the Law, 38*(4), 479–489.

Méndez, J. E. (2012). The death penalty and the absolute prohibition of torture and cruel, inhuman, and degrading treatment or punishment. *Human Rights Brief, 20*(1), 2–6.

Méndez, J. E., & Wentworth, M. (2011). *Taking a stand: The evolution of human rights*. New York, NY: Palgrave Macmillan.

Modvig, J., & Jaranson, J. (2004). A global perspective of torture, political violence, and health. In J. P. Wilson & B. Drozdek (Eds.), *Broken spirits: The treatment of PTSD in asylum seekers and refugees with PTSD* (pp. 33–52). New York, NY: Brunner-Routledge Press.

Moio, J.A. (2008). *Resiliency and recovery: An exploration of meaning and personal agency for women survivors of state sponsored torture* (Doctoral dissertation). Available from Dissertations and Theses database. (UMI No. 3346914).

Murphy, L. W., & Vagins, D. J. (2012, December 12). *Written statement of the American Civil Liberties Union for a hearing on "Ending the School-to-Prison Pipeline."* Submitted to the Senate Judiciary Subcommittee on the Constitution, Civil Rights and Human Rights. Washington, DC: ACLU Washington Legislative Office. Retrieved from https://www.aclu.org/files/assets/aclu_statement_for_sjc_subcomm_hearing_on_the_school_to_prison_pipeline_12_2012.pdf.

Musalo, K., & Rice, M. (2008). The implementation of the one-year bar to asylum. *Hastings International and Comparative Law Review, 31,* 693–715.

NASW. (2006). *Oppose torture in any form*. Washington, DC: NASW. Retrieved from http://www.socialworkers.org/diversity/intl/092206b.asp.

National Religious Campaign Against Torture. (n.d.). Solitary confinement: Torture in an age of mass incarceration. Retrieved from http://www.truah.org/images/stories/hrs13-22-NRCAT.pdf.

New Tactics in Human Rights. (n.d.). Website. www.newtactics.org.

Noferi, M. (2014, January 14). Congressional hearings on asylum seekers facing U.S. expedited removal process. Center for Migration Studies (CMSNY). Retrieved from http://cmsny.org/2014/01/14/congressional-hearings-on-asylum-seekers-facing-u-s-expedited-removal-process/#ixzz2xN7m2OTZ.

Northwood, A. (2003). *Study group guide for psychotherapy with torture survivors*. Minneapolis, MN: Center for Victims of Torture.

Nowak, M. (2012). Keynote speech: Torture in the 21st century: Conclusions - six years as UN Special Rapporteur on Torture. In A. Dayif, K. Hesketh, & J. Rice (Eds.), *On Torture* (pp. 21–30). Jerusalem, Israel: Adalah - The Legal Center for Arab Minority Rights in Israel, Physicians for Human Rights - Isreael, and Al Mezan Center for Human Rights in Gaza.

Office of the High Commissioner for Human Rights (OHCHR). (1989). *Convention on the Rights of the Child*. Retrieved from http://www.ohchr.org/EN/ProfessionalInterest/Pages/CRC.aspx.

Office of the High Commissioner for Human Rights (OHCHR). (2001). CCPR General Comment No. 29: Article 4: Derogations during a State of Emergency. Adopted at the Seventy-second Session of the Human Rights Committee. CCPR/C/21/Rev.1/Add.11. Accessed 31 Aug 2001.

Office of the High Commissioner for Human Rights (OHCHR). (2013). General Comment No. 14: On the right of the child to have his or her best interests taken as a primary consideration Retrieved from http://tbinternet.ohchr.org/_layouts/treatybodyexternal/Download.aspx?symbolno=CRC%2fC%2fGC%2f14_&Lang=en.

Ortiz, D. (2001). The survivors' perspective: Voices from the center. In E. Gerrity, T. M. Keane, & F. Tuma (Eds.), *The mental health consequences of torture*. The plenum series on stress and coping (pp. 13–64). New York, NY: Klewer Academic/Plenum Publishers.

Penturf, S. (2013, October 17). Should the state of Texas be allowed to do this to children? *The Liberty Blog*. [Web log comment]. Retrieved from www.aclutx.org/blog/%3Fp%3D2051+&cd=1&hl=en&ct=clnk&gl=us&client=firefox-a.

Physicians for Human Rights and the Bellevue/NYU Program for Survivors of Torture (PHR & Bellevue/NYU). (2003). *From persecution to prison: The health consequences of detention for asylum seekers*. Boston, MA: Authors.

Quiroga, J., & Jaranson, J. M. (2005). Politically-motivated torture and its survivors: A desk study review of the literature. *Torture, 15*(2–3), 1–111.

Robjant, K., & Fazel, M. (2010). The emerging evidence for narrative exposure therapy: A review. *Clinical Psychology Review, 30,* 1030–1039.

Schauer, M., Neuner, F., & Elbert, T. (2005). *Narrative exposure therapy: A short-term intervention for traumatic stress disorders after war, terror and torture*. Gottingen, Germany: Hogrefe & Huber.

Schnurr, P. P., & Green, B. L. (Eds.). (2004). *Trauma and health: Physical health consequences of extreme stress*. Washington, DC: American Psychological Association.

Silove, D., Steel, Z., & Mollica, R. F. (2001). Detention of asylum seekers: Assault on health, human rights, and social development. *Lancet, 357,* 1436–1437.

Skoll, G. R. (2008). Torture and the fifth amendment: Torture, the global war on terror, and the constitutional values. *Criminal Justice Review, 33*(1), 29–47. doi:10.1177/0734016808315585.

Steel, Z., Chey, T., Silove, D., Marnane, C., Bryant, R. A., & van Ommeren, M. (2009). Association of torture and other potentially traumatic events with mental health outcomes among populations exposed to mass conflict and displacement: A systematic review and meta-analysis. *Journal of the American Medical Association, 302*(5), 537–549.

Stop Prisoner Rape (2006). In the shadows: Sexual violence in U.S. detention facilities. A shadow report to the U.N. Committee Against Torture. Retrieved from http://spr.igc.org/.

Torture Victims Relief Act of 1998, P.L. 105–320, 18 U.S.C. § 2340(1) (1998).

Transactional Records Access Clearinghouse (TRAC) Immigration. (2014). Immigration Court Backlog Tool: Pending Cases and Length of Wait in Immigration Courts. Retrieved from http://trac.syr.edu/phptools/immigration/court_backlog/.

UN Committee Against Torture (CAT). (2006). UN Committee against Torture: Conclusions and Recommendations, United States of America, CAT/C/USA/CO/2. Retrieved from http://www.refworld.org/docid/453776c60.html. Accessed 25 July 2006

UN Committee Against Torture. (2012, November 19). General Comment No. 3 of the Committee against Torture. Convention against Torture and other Cruel, Inhuman or Degrading Treatment or Punishment, CAT/C/GC/3, Geneva: United Nations. Retrieved from http://www2.ohchr.org/english/bodies/cat/docs/GC/CAT-C-GC-3_en.pdf.

UN General Assembly. (1948). Universal Declaration of Human Rights, 217 A (III). Retrieved from http://www.unhcr.org/refworld/docid/3ae6b3712c.html. Accessed 10 Dec 1948.

UN General Assembly. (1966). International Covenant on Civil and Political Rights, United Nations, Treaty Series, vol. 999, p. 171. Retrieved from http://www.refworld.org/docid/3ae6b3aa0.html. Accessed 16 December 1966.

UN General Assembly. (1984). Convention against Torture and Other Cruel, Inhuman or Degrading Treatment or Punishment, United Nations, Treaty Series, vol. 1465, p. 85. Retrieved from http://www.refworld.org/docid/3ae6b3a94.html. Accessed 10 Dec 1984.

UN Human Rights Committee (HRC). (2014). Concluding Observations on the Fourth Periodic Report of the United States of America, CCPR/C/USA/CO/4. Retrieved from http://www.refworld.org/docid/5374afcd4.html. Accessed 23 April 2014.

UN Office of the High Commissioner for Human Rights (OHCHR). (2004). Manual on the Effective Investigation and Documentation of Torture and Other Cruel, Inhuman or Degrading Treatment or Punishment (Istanbul Protocol), HR/P/PT/8/Rev.1. Retrieved from http://www.refworld.org/docid/4638aca62.html.

van der Veer, G., & van Waning, A. (2004). Creating a safe therapeutic sanctuary. In J. P. Wilson & B. Drozdek (Eds.), *Broken spirits: The treatment of traumatized asylum seekers, refugees, war and torture victims* (pp. 187–219). New York, NY: Brunner-Routledge.

Wagner, J., Burke, G., Kuoch, T., Scully, M., Armeli, S., & Rajan, T. V. (2013). Trauma, healthcare access, and health outcomes among Southeast Asian refugees in Connecticut. *Journal of Immigrant and Minority Health, 15*(6), 1065–1072.

Yalom, I. (1980). *Existential psychotherapy*. New York, NY: Basic Books.

# Chapter 3
# Rights-Based Clinical Practice with Survivors of Human Trafficking

Chun Hei,[1] a woman in her early twenties from South Korea, was trafficked to the United States. She was locked in a room with other young women in a rundown hotel. Her passport was taken away and she was not allowed to communicate with the outside world. She was not even allowed to call her parents to tell them she had arrived in the United States. She felt stripped of control over basic aspects of her life. Each afternoon, a muscular armed man escorted her to another building where she was forced to have sex with multiple men until the early morning hours. In the early days when she protested, she was beaten or injected with drugs to subdue her. Chun Hei learned that protesting was pointless. She was never given the money she made and was provided with only minimal food and provocative clothing to wear. She was denied access to healthcare and contraceptives and some of the men refused to wear condoms. When her boss discovered that she was pregnant, he forced her to have an abortion despite her protests. Although Chun Hei loathed the idea of having the child of one of her "Johns," she believed that abortion was a sin. She was forced to resume her sexual "hospitality" services a few days after her abortion. One of Chun Hei's Johns ("Mike," a pseudonym) became quite attached to her, eventually helping her to escape from her traffickers and to live with him in another nearby city. Chun Hei felt very dependent on Mike and feared going out on her own as she believed that she might encounter those who had held her who she believed were looking for her. Over time, Chun Hei and Mike began to argue and she felt increasingly controlled and disrespected by Mike. Chun Hei began to injure herself by burning her arm with cigarette butts, cutting her belly with a razor blade, or slamming her head into the wall until she experienced relief. These were strategies she had engaged in off and on, starting as a teen in South Korea, at times when she felt particularly anxious and vulnerable. One night, Chun Hei ended up in the emergency room after Mike called the ambulance when he found her drunk and with a rope tied around her neck. Chun Hei had tried to hang herself after one of her fights with Mike.

Which of Chun Hei's rights were violated? What human rights mechanisms might provide relevant guidance to a clinical social worker in this case? Does a person have to be transported across international borders like Chun Hei to be considered trafficked? How might you approach your work with Chun Hei from a rights perspective if you were a hospital social worker and met her in the emergency room? What rights-based principles would inform your clinical work with Chun Hei if she chose to engage in therapy with you after leaving the hospital? Given the information you

[1] The names and other identifying information in all case material in this chapter have been changed to protect confidentiality, and aspects of each case are a composite from more than one person.



S. M. Berthold, *Human Rights-Based Approaches to Clinical Social Work*,
SpringerBriefs in Rights-Based Approaches to Social Work, DOI 10.1007/978-3-319-08560-9_3

have about Chun Hei, what key clinical issues might be important to address in your early work with her? What else would you want to know to inform your approach?

Chun Hei, a contract slave,[2] is one of the millions of persons worldwide who have been exploited and severely traumatized through human trafficking. Human trafficking is a clear human rights violation, one that is illegal everywhere, yet is prosperous and flourishing. At its core, human trafficking is about the abuse of power, exploitation for financial gain, domination, and control. This criminal industry is estimated to make billions in profits each year for traffickers off of the enslavement and suffering of others (Belser, 2005). Fundamentally, human trafficking deprives people of their basic human rights. The impact on the health and well-being of the trafficked individuals, their family, and society is profound.

Clinical social workers may well encounter survivors of domestic or international human trafficking in a number of settings such as child welfare, hospitals, outpatient health or mental health clinics, homeless or domestic violence shelters, and substance abuse programs. These clinicians are often well placed to identify those subjected to trafficking, intervene and support their recovery of rights and well-being. Social workers must be equipped to identify those affected by trafficking and dispelled of common myths. Identifying those subjected to human trafficking, however, is not enough. Survivors have a right to have their voices heard and respected in their process of recovery and in any legal responses.

Adopting a human rights-based approach can enhance the therapeutic quality of clinical social work with survivors and provide an opportunity for countering some of the deleterious effects of their trafficking experiences. This chapter focuses on explicating the important roles that rights-based clinical social workers can and do play in working with survivors of domestic and international human trafficking. The problem of human trafficking is defined and contextual issues and common sequelae are described. Trafficked persons are identified as rights holders and relevant human rights mechanisms and tools are noted. Core principles for the clinical and forensic assessment and treatment of survivors of trafficking are illustrated consonant with a rights-based approach. Examples of macro efforts to address trafficking are introduced and the role of clinical social workers in effectively spanning micro and macro practice with this population is described. Suggested class activities and resources are provided at the end of the chapter.

## Definitional and Contextual Issues

### *Definition of Human Trafficking*

The United Nations has defined trafficking in persons as:

[2] A contract slave typically signs an employment contract for a guaranteed job in a distant location, only to find themselves coerced (sometimes with violence) into working without pay. In some cases, the contracts are used to claim legitimacy and hide the fact that slavery is occurring (Bales, 2007).

> The recruitment, transportation, transfer, harboring, or receipt of persons, by means of the threat or use of force or other forms of coercion, abduction, fraud, deception, the abuse of power, or of a position of vulnerability or giving or receiving of payments or benefits to achieve the consent of a person having control over another person, for the purpose of exploitation. Exploitation shall include, at a minimum, the exploitation of the prostitution of others or other forms of sexual exploitation, forced labor or services, slavery or practices similar to slavery, and servitude or the removal of organs (Article 3, para. (a) of the Protocol to Prevent, Suppress and Punish Trafficking in Persons, UN General Assembly, 2000c).

Article 5 of this protocol requires that states adopt domestic legislation to criminalize human trafficking, acting as an accomplice or organizing others to engage in trafficking, and attempts to traffic persons.

In 2000, the United States passed legislation in keeping with international standards to protect victims of human trafficking. This legislation has been reauthorized several times, including in March 2013 (Trafficking Victims Protection Reauthorization Act, 2013a, P.L. 113–4). Under the Victims of Trafficking and Violence Protection Act of 2000 (P.L. 106–386) (known as the TVPA), "severe forms of trafficking in persons" is defined as:

a. sex trafficking in which a commercial sex act is induced by force, fraud, or coercion, *or* in which the person induced to perform such an act has not attained 18 years of age; or
b. the recruitment, harboring, transportation, provision, or obtaining of a person for labor or services through the use of force, fraud, or coercion for the purpose of subjection to involuntary servitude, peonage, debt bondage, or slavery (Sec. 103, 8).

The definition of trafficking does not require that a victim has been physically moved from one place to another. Further, the coercion involved does not have to be overt, physical, or extreme. It may be subtle and psychological in nature (Trafficking Victims Protection Reauthorization Act, 2013b, 18 U.S.C. § 1581).

At its core, in both the US and UN definitions, human trafficking is about violence against others and the use of deceptive and coercive methods in order to exploit and enslave them. Some prefer to use the term slavery over human trafficking as it provides historical context, does not connote crossing international borders, and emphasizes the human suffering involved (Androff, 2010)—names matter. The TVPA and the Palermo Protocol[3] use various terms to describe trafficking in persons including slavery, involuntary servitude, forced labor, and debt bondage (USDOS, 2013a). Rights-based social workers should be attentive to and respectful of the terms survivors use to describe themselves and their experiences rather than imposing their own conceptualizations on survivors.

---

[3] The Protocol to Prevent, Suppress and Punish Trafficking in Persons, especially Women and Children (known as the Palermo Protocol) was one of three protocols adopted by the United Nations in 2000 (and entered into force on 25 December 2003). These protocols supplemented the 2000 Palermo Convention (Convention against Transnational Organized Crime).

## *Understanding the Contexts in Which Human Trafficking Occurs*

Misconceptions and myths about human trafficking abound. Social workers must educate themselves about the wide range of contexts in which human trafficking may occur. It is vital to understand, for example, that people may be considered trafficking victims regardless of whether they were born into a state of servitude, were transported to the exploitative situation, previously consented to work for a trafficker, or participated in a crime as a direct result of being trafficked (USDOS, 2013a, p. 31). Social workers also need to know that the problem is not confined to sex trafficking (DeStefano, 2007). It is not all international in nature. The International Labour Organization reported in 2012 that the majority of victims were trafficked within the borders of their own country and that at any point in time, 3 out of every 1000 persons worldwide are subjected to forced labor (International Labour Organization, 2012). US citizens were reported to be victims in 41% of the sex trafficking cases and 20% of the labor trafficking cases reported in the United States between 2008 and 2012 (Polaris Project, 2013a). Not all traffickers are members of large organized crime groups. Trafficking does not only affect women and girls. Men, boys, and transgender individuals are also trafficked. At the time of this writing, there is an unprecedented number of unaccompanied minors from Mexico and Central America entering the United States. Some unaccompanied minors have fled from family abuse, gang violence, or other forms of exploitation and, without family or other protection in transit or exile, have been particularly vulnerable to traffickers.

## *Scope and Form of the Problem Worldwide and in the United States*

Human trafficking has a wide transnational reach and, after drug smuggling, is considered the second largest organized criminal industry worldwide (ATEST, 2014). Reliable prevalence estimates of human trafficking are challenging or impossible to obtain. The methodologies utilized to estimate this problem have lacked sufficient rigor and the problem itself is inherently hidden given its underground criminal nature (Stransky & Finkelhor, 2008). Recent estimates show that 27 million men, women, and children are subjected to human trafficking worldwide (Bales, 2007; USDOS, 2013a), of whom approximately 21 million have been trafficked into forced labor (International Labor Organization, 2012). Nearly all of these men, women, and children have lacked access to help and have had their rights violated on a daily basis, some for many years. Only an estimated 40,000 were identified as having been trafficked in 2012 (USDOS, 2013a). The United States is known to be a destination, transit, and source country for human trafficking (USDOS, 2013a). In the 5 years from 2008 to 2012, the National Human Trafficking Resource Center (NHTRC) hotline received reports about 9298 cases of human trafficking in the United States (Polaris Project, 2013a).

Trafficking, sometimes called modern-day slavery, takes many forms of which sexual trafficking is perhaps the most publicized. Forcing someone to do labor or provide services through physical and/or psychological violence is also trafficking. The Trafficking in Persons Report 2013, for example, identified human trafficking in many industries including: boys forced to engage in illegal drug production and transportation in Mexico and the UK; debt bondage of entire families in South Asia in rice mills, stone quarries, brick kilns, and in agriculture; males in Africa and South America trafficked in mining, logging, construction, and agriculture; and Burmese and Cambodian boys and men forced to work on fishing boats (USDOS, 2013a). Children who are forced or coerced into being child soldiers and used as combatants, messengers, spies, porters, cooks, guards, and/or servants, or forced to marry or have sex with the soldiers is another example of trafficking (USDOS, 2013a). The top industries where trafficking can be found in the United States are: domestic labor, food service/restaurants, peddling, and traveling sales for labor trafficking; and pimp-controlled prostitution, brothels, and escort/delivery services for sex trafficking (Polaris Project, 2013a).

## *Common Sequelae of Human Trafficking*

Being sold or coerced into forced labor or sexual slavery, with the ensuing loss of dignity and control over even the most basic aspects of one's life, is traumatic in and of itself. Layer on top of that the abuse and neglect that is common during the time under the control of the traffickers, and it is easy to see that the experience endangers the health and well-being of those who are trafficked. As with other types of human-perpetrated trauma (including torture and intimate partner violence discussed in Chapters 2 and 4 of this book), human trafficking has an impact across multiple domains of the lives of survivors (Hossain, Zimmerman, Abas, Light, & Watts, 2010; Oram, Stöckl, Busza, Howard, & Zimmerman, 2012; Zimmerman et al., 2008). Most of the research has been conducted with girls and women survivors of sex trafficking, so further study is needed to better understand the impact of trafficking on males, transgender survivors, and survivors of other types of trafficking. The specific reactions and manifestations of distress vary from one individual to another and depend, in part, on the nature of the trafficking, the meaning of the experiences for the survivor, as well as the survivor's intersectional position.

Survivors may struggle cognitively with difficulty concentrating, confusion, and memory disturbance. Common forms of physical distress include insomnia, chest or other pains, fatigue, or nausea. Persistent or recurrent episodes of feeling powerless, helpless, and trapped or without control are common. Most survivors experience, at least for a time, reliving their trafficking experiences in various forms (e.g., through intrusive traumatic memories, flashbacks, and nightmares) and avoidance of things that remind them of the trauma. Survivors may have prominent feelings of numbness, dissociative episodes, strong feelings of shame or worthlessness, or other forms of psychological distress. Many survivors grapple with hopelessness, suicidal ideation, and suicidal and self-injurious behavior. They may experience existential and/or spiritual distress such as questioning or loss of their faith or existential despair. Relational challenges are common, such as strained or conflictual interpersonal relationships, the breakdown of trust in others, and clinging or withdrawing behavior. Trafficking survivors have high rates of post-traumatic stress disorder (PTSD) and depression, substance abuse problems, dissociative symptoms, somatic complaints, and panic attacks. While less common, some experience psychotic symptoms. Social workers should understand that symptoms of distress may appear to be of a psychotic nature but may be more accurately understood as a posttraumatic response (Briere & Scott, 2012). Sometimes, notable changes in personality may occur. Child victims have had portions of their childhoods stolen and, having been trafficked at important developmental stages, may well experience disruption of healthy developmental trajectories.

Trafficked persons also commonly experience physical health problems. These may include chronic pain or broken bones, concussions, burns, or other injuries as a result of beatings or other physical abuse. They may experience malnutrition due to neglect and insufficient or non-nutritious food. They are often overworked and become chronically exhausted. Their traffickers typically deprive them of access to routine or urgent medical care. Those who are trafficked for sex are placed at risk for contracting various sexually transmitted diseases, developing reproductive health problems, and being killed.

Trafficking takes a toll on the family system as well. In some cases, the family does not know what happened to the person. The person may be separated from family members for years or a lifetime. The trafficked person may live in fear of the traffickers themselves. Many traffickers threaten to harm (or kill) the targets or their loved ones if they do not cooperate. A person who is trafficked may blame him or herself for putting family members at risk, even if those family members were abusive to him or her. They may think, for example, that had he or she not run away, this never would have happened. Some survivors fear being shunned by the community or disowned if their loved ones find out that they were forced into prostitution or another form of sex trafficking. This happens in some societies. Instances of honor killing for those who have been trafficked for sex have also been reported (AlZoubi, 2011). In other cases, an immediate or extended family member sold the person into trafficking. The contextual possibilities are many, with a complex array of effects that may develop for trafficked persons.

## Trafficking As a Human Rights Problem and Relevant Human Rights Mechanisms/Tools

### *Trafficked Persons as Rights Holders*

Joy Ngozi Ezeilo, the UN Special Rapporteur on Trafficking in Persons (2011), has made it clear that trafficked persons are rights holders who are entitled to effective remedies for the rights violations they have endured. Instead, they are often perceived and treated as instruments to assist in criminal investigations and prosecutions (Craggs and Martins 2010 as cited in UN Special Rapporteur on Trafficking in Persons (2011), para. 52). Ezeilo indicates that survivors of trafficking rarely receive compensation. "At worst, many trafficked persons are wrongly identified as irregular migrants, detained and deported before they have an opportunity to even consider seeking remedies" (UN Special Rapporteur on Trafficking in Persons, 2011, para. 61).

The remedies received by trafficked persons are often not holistic in nature but ad hoc and aimed to further the goals of the criminal investigation (e.g., temporary residence permits and recovery assistance conditional on the survivor cooperating with law enforcement). Linking the provision of services to the willingness or capability of survivors to cooperate with law enforcement goes against fundamental human rights principles related to trafficking (Office of the High Commissioner for Human Rights, 2010).

Ezeilo recommends that States should make improvements to the system of identification of trafficked persons, provide enhanced access to information and free legal and interpretation services, and provide temporary or permanent residence permits when the survivor is not able to return to his/her country of origin safely "or a return would not otherwise be in the best interests of the trafficked person for reasons related to his or her personal circumstances, such as the loss of citizenship or cultural and social identity in the country of origin" (UN Special Rapporteur on Trafficking in Persons, 2011, para. 76). The special rapporteur also advised States to consider the asylum claims of trafficked persons when there is risk of retaliation or reprisal from the traffickers. Additionally, the special rapporteur recommended unconditional medical, psychological, social, and legal services required to recover (UN Special Rapporteur on Trafficking in Persons, 2011, para. 66). These recommended services, however, appear to be limited to the first 90 days after the individual is identified as a victim of trafficking. Given the nature of the experience of trafficking and its serious impact (discussed later in this chapter), 90 days is often insufficient for recovery to take place. Rights-based social workers should advocate for more comprehensive and longer-term services. It is notable that the special rapporteur also stressed that many States disproportionately provide services to adult women from foreign countries that are trafficked for sex, rather than to survivors of internal/domestic or other forms of trafficking. Social workers should advocate for ensuring that everyone's rights are respected and services are provided equitably.

## *Relevant Human Rights Documents*

The United Nations and other international, regional, and sub-regional organizations have various mechanisms in place to combat human trafficking, a good summary of which can be found in the Trafficking in Persons Report 2014 (USDOS, 2014, pp. 428–429). This report, updated annually, also includes a listing of countries which are signatories and which have also ratified various anti-trafficking protocols. Key United Nations' Protocols relevant to human trafficking include:

- The Optional Protocols to the Convention on the Rights of the Child on: (1) the Sale of Children, Child Prostitution, and Child Pornography (UN General Assembly, 2000a)[4]; and (2) the Involvement of Children in Armed Conflicts (UN General Assembly, 2000b);
- Articles 34 and 35 of the Convention on the Rights of the Child (CRC) (UN General Assembly, 1989);
- Article 4 of the Universal Declaration of Human Rights (UN General Assembly, 1948);
- Article 8 of the International Covenant on Civil and Political Rights (UN General Assembly, 1966a);
- The 2000 United Nations Protocol to Prevent, Suppress, and Punish Trafficking in Persons, Especially Women and Children ("Palermo Protocol," supplementing the UN Convention against Transnational Organized Crime) (UN General Assembly, 2000c);
- Article 7 of the International Covenant on Economic, Social and Cultural Rights (UN General Assembly, 1966b); and
- Article 6 of the Convention on the Elimination of All Forms of Discrimination against Women (CEDAW) (UN General Assembly 1979).

## Clinical Interventions, Application of Core Principles of a Rights-Based Approach, and Roles in Legal Cases

There are many valuable roles that social workers operating from a rights-based approach can play in clinical work with survivors of human trafficking. Currently, there are a number of psychosocial services that are offered to survivors or those at risk of being trafficked. These services typically are focused on the rehabilitation or protection of survivors or on prevention of trafficking and often are run by non-governmental organizations (NGOs) (ILO, 2009; Van Hook, Gjermeri, & Haxhiymeri, 2006). Survivors may cooperate with police and other authorities, such as when survivors in the United States provide information to federal and local authorities to assist in the apprehension of the perpetrator(s) and testimony if the case is brought to trial. Survivors may benefit from psychological preparation and support during these legal processes (USDOS, 2014) and from addressing the impact of their trafficking experiences in therapy with a clinical social worker.

[4] The United States ratified this optional protocol in 2001. It is only one of three states, however, that have not ratified the Convention on the Rights of the Child (CRC) at the time of this writing (along with Somalia and South Sudan; see https://treaties.un.org/Pages/ViewDetails.aspx?src=TREATY&mtdsg_no=IV-11&chapter=4&lang=en).

## Core Principles of a Rights-Based Approach Applied

How can a clinical social worker providing therapy or other clinical interventions to survivors of trafficking operate from a rights-base? Clinical social workers working with this population should be steeped in cultural humility and trauma-informed approaches, and should be person-centered (as described in Chapter 1 of this book). Rights-based practitioners seek to gain a deep understanding of the survivor's experience and ensure that his or her freedom and agency are not further taken away. The words of one survivor make this point eloquently:

> My definition of freedom is deeper than most. For so long my freedom was nonexistent. My every move was watched, my every conversation was observed. My clothing and food portions and options were at the mercy of another. Living in fear and terror, I had no ability to make or understand decisions and my physical self seemed to belong to everyone but me.
> —Withelma "T" Ortiz Walker Pettigrew, Human Trafficking Survivor, Advocate, and Activist, 2012 (USDOS, 2013a, p. 46)

When providing clinical services to a survivor of human trafficking (similar to work with any population), it is always essential to explore his or her prior history and current life circumstances. It is not helpful to solely attend to the trafficking and its immediate impact, but to thoroughly assess and work with the person as a whole, taking into account his or her life history. The situations and contexts that led individuals to be at risk for being trafficked often were other human rights violations. For example, some may have been sold or lured into seemingly lucrative employment due to extreme poverty. Others, as in the case of Chun Lei from the opening vignette, were seeking to escape from child abuse. Traffickers have ensnared some youth in the United States who have run away from home, are homeless, or are in other vulnerable circumstances. Torture treatment specialists have also worked with individuals who, desperate to find any means of escaping their homeland where they had been tortured, were deceived and controlled by traffickers. These individuals' earlier life experiences have shaped their psychological make-up and may well contribute to their current vulnerabilities and/or resilience. The trafficking experience may trigger reminders of earlier traumas. A thorough clinical social worker may uncover additional rights violations and have the opportunity to address those with the person and support the realization of his or her rights or redress of past violations. In addition, such an approach provides an opportunity for working through the layers and complexities of the survivor's traumatic experiences.

## Rights-Based Therapy: The Example of Chun Hei

> Upon discharge from the hospital, Chun Hei was referred to an agency that specialized in providing clinical services to traumatized refugees and immigrants. Sarah, her clinical social worker, identified that she had been trafficked and connected her with adjunctive legal and case management services with a local nonprofit that served trafficking survivors. Chun Hei eventually moved into a shelter run by that nonprofit for other survivors of human

trafficking. After a number of therapy sessions with Sarah, Chun Hei shared that she had long been looking for a way to leave home in South Korea. For as long as she could remember, her father had been abusive to her. Chun Hei's father whipped her with his belt and called her "stupid" and a "worthless girl." Her father often compared her to her older brother, saying that she would "never amount to anything," even when she earned very high grades in school. By the time Chun Hei was 12, her father had lost his job and was drinking more and more heavily. He began to beat Chun Hei more frequently. Although she aspired to be a scientist, her father told her that it was too expensive to send Chun Hei to University, and that her family needed her to work to help support the family. One day Chun Hei's neighbor told her about an employment company that was recruiting people to go to work in the hospitality industry in the United States. She believed that this would be her chance to escape her abusive father, and she rushed to sign up, although the details were sketchy. Her father was eager for her to go, and reminded her of her responsibility to send money home to support the family. Once in the United States, Chun Hei quickly learned that she had been deceived.

Chun Hei developed very low self-esteem and confidence as a result of her extensive experience of child abuse. She did not believe herself to be capable or lovable. Chun Hei blamed herself for her experiences with her "employers" in the United States, calling herself "stupid" for choosing to work for someone who did not pay her, kept her locked up, and forced her to have sex with numerous men day after day. She often heard the sound of her father's voice, internalized from years of psychological and physical abuse, impressing upon her that she deserved to be abused. She had let her family down by failing to be able to send money home to support them—one of the final things her father had impressed upon her before she left South Korea.

When Sarah first started to work with her, Chun Hei did not conceptualize her "employers" as traffickers nor did she see herself as someone who was entitled to any rights. One of the early tasks in therapy was for Chun Hei to begin to understand that she had been trafficked—this was necessary before it was possible for Chun Hei to grasp and embrace the concept that she had a right not to be abused and trafficked. The brainwashing she had been subjected to by her traffickers contributed to Chun Hei's not identifying herself as a survivor of trafficking. Her traffickers had told Chun Hei many times, while she was in an exhausted and vulnerable state, that she chose to come to the United States on a contract, was obligated to fulfill her contract, and had no hope for a different future. Her traffickers also impressed upon her that the police were her enemy and would deport her if she tried to go to them for help. They portrayed themselves as her protectors and the only people who cared about her. The messages she had received that she was worthless throughout her childhood from her abusive father appeared to have laid the foundation for her traffickers' brainwashing to work.

Chun Hei struggled for a long time when she had choices to make or was presented with options, finding it very difficult to know what she wanted, having had her right to self-determination and agency stripped away from her as a young child. For example, she went back and forth multiple times between whether to continue to live with Mike (her former "John") or at the shelter. She also had a hard time deciding upon what services she wanted and did not want. Her first session with Sarah was conducted with an interpreter. Ultimately, after several sessions with the interpreter, Chun Hei requested to continue her therapy sessions in English. Although she was not fluent in English, she did not trust any interpreter to: (a) not be connected to traffickers; (b) keep confidentiality (she feared word might get back to her parents about her experiences); and/or (c) not to judge her, given the strong cultural and religious prohibitions against prostitution in her society. Chun Hei's assertiveness was a good sign—showing her emerging sense of empowerment and that she believed she was entitled to have her wishes taken into consideration and that she did not have to accept what someone else imposed on her. Sarah and Chun Hei continued their sessions in English. Although Chun Hei struggled at times to find the words in English to express herself, she and Sarah managed to communicate fairly well. One benefit of not working with an interpreter was that this facilitated Chun Hei's growing confidence in her ability to express and speak for herself.

Part of the work Sarah did with Chun Hei was ensuring and advocating for her right not only to healthcare, including contraceptives and STD testing previously denied to her, but also to having care delivered in an environment that felt safe to her. When her case manager from the shelter brought her to a gynecologist for a checkup, Chun Hei was afraid to tell the case manager that she did not feel safe with the doctor as his appearance resembled the male doctor her traffickers brought her to when they forced her to have an abortion. Contributing to her distress was the fact that the doctor's office was located in one of the areas where she frequently had been forced to go to service her Johns. Furthermore, Chun Hei felt ashamed and humiliated when this OB-GYN appeared shocked and horrified when taking her sexual history. In therapy with Sarah, her concerns eventually came out. Driven by a trauma-informed and rights-based foundation to her practice, Sarah supported Chun Hei in asserting her right to choice in providers and importantly, where the office was located. Chun Hei ultimately decided that she wanted to transfer her care to a female OB-GYN, one who worked closely with Sarah with similarly traumatized individuals, had a warm and empathic demeanor, supported her right to make her own decisions about her health care and life choices, and did not make her feel judged.

During the early phase of therapy, Chun Hei wanted someone else to make decisions for her. She felt overwhelmed when faced with making a decision and flooded with self-doubt. She feared she was making the wrong decision and would have to pay severe consequences, consumed with intense anxiety and the belief that she was a "bad" person. Throughout her life, Chun Hei's father and later her traffickers had made virtually all of her decisions for her. One of the only big decisions she had made for herself, choosing to sign a contract to work in the United States, had brought her more pain. At the time that Chun Hei started therapy, Mike had taken on the role of decision maker in her life. This marked a time when her non-suicidal self-injurious (NSSI)[5] behaviors escalated. At times Chun Hei felt so numb that cutting or burning herself was the only way she felt anything, including feeling alive. She preferred to

[5] Non-suicidal self-injury (NSSI) refers to the destruction of one's own body tissues without the intent of killing oneself (Klonsky & Muehlenkamp, 2007). The behavior is intentional and is not socially sanctioned.

feel physical pain to feeling emotional pain or nothing. She had learned to dissociate as a child as a way to protect herself from the ongoing abuse from her father. This skill had served her well during the time she was trafficked and forced to provide sexual “hospitality” services, offering her some small measure of protection. She could not control whether she was forced to sleep with numerous men or not. Chun Hei engaged in injuring herself in part, it appeared, because this was one of the only things that she felt she had any control over; that, and whether or not she committed suicide.

Recognizing that Chun Hei had not developed alternative (more adaptive) strategies for self-soothing and regulating her intense affect other than to self-injure, Sarah made it a priority to work with Chun Hei to build adaptive strategies and support her practice of them when she felt anxious and vulnerable. Chun Hei’s awareness of her emotions and the factors that triggered her to self-injure increased over time, and she gained a deeper understanding of the function her self-injurious behavior served in her life. One of her priorities in therapy became to learn other ways to get her needs met and, in doing so, reduce her urge to hurt herself. Consistent with a rights-based approach and the literature[6] on treatment of those who self-injure (Gonzales & Bergstrom, 2013; Nixon & Heath, 2008), Sarah adopted a stance of accepting Chun Hei’s self-harming behavior without condoning it, monitoring her suicidality,[7] developing a safety plan (Stanley & Brown, 2012), and working with her toward replacing her self-injurious behavior with more healthy coping strategies at a pace she could tolerate. Sarah encouraged and reinforced Chun Hei’s behavior of openly sharing her self-injurious episodes in therapy, not judging or blaming her. If Sarah had criticized Chun Hei for hurting herself or tried to force her to give up her long-time self-injurious coping strategies, it is likely that it would not have worked. Chun Hei was used to getting that reaction from her parents and Mike. For years, injuring herself was one of the only things she felt she had control over in her life and, given the reactions she received from others when they discovered what she had done, she was adept at hiding these behaviors from others.

Attention to safeguarding and maximizing Chun Hei’s rights was made when developing a safety plan with her. For example, Sarah ensured that Chun Hei was in control over designating who would be notified in the event of an emergency. The safety plan consisted of empowering Chun Hei with a written list of early warning signs, coping strategies, ways of making her environment safer (including not keeping alcohol in her home), and sources of support that she could use to prevent

[6] Further research is needed to examine which interventions are most effective for individuals who engage in NSSI (Gonzales & Bergstrom, 2013; Nock, 2010).

[7] Similar to many of those who self-injure, Chun Hei did not have suicidal thoughts or intent at the times she engaged in injuring herself (Nock, 2010). She did have suicidal thoughts and a history of multiple suicide attempts, however, these were separate from her self-injurious episodes. Addressing Chun Hei’s self-injurious behavior was a top priority, since NSSI may inadvertently result in suicide (such as when the person cuts deeper than he or she intended) and is associated with a greater risk for developing a suicide plan compared to those who do not self-injure (Whitlock & Knox, 2007).

a suicide attempt or de-escalate a suicidal crisis. This was part of the longer term work in therapy focused on supporting Chun Hei in reclaiming her rights over her own body and her own agency in making decisions for herself.

Given her history of multiple suicide attempts and self-injurious behavior, Chun Hei was referred to a psychiatrist for evaluation. Her right to accessing mental health care included her right to refuse medication or treatment altogether. After a trial on several different types of medication, Chun Hei decided not to continue with psychotropic medication given the unwanted side effects she was experiencing. Gradually, Chun Hei stopped hurting herself and drinking alcohol once she had experienced relief and success in reducing her feelings of anxiety and vulnerability through other means. In doing so, Chun Hei was able to experience herself as a capable person with power and agency for one of the first times in her life. Chun Hei began to think seriously about her future.

## *Legal Avenues/Prosecuting Perpetrators: Roles for Clinical Social Workers*

> Chun Hei believed that it was not an option to return to South Korea as she felt that she had brought shame to herself and her family for engaging in "sexual hospitality work." She feared that her parents would never accept her back if they knew what she had done, or that her father would abuse her further. With the support of her legal team, she came to believe that her only viable option (other than suicide, a choice she was still at times actively considering) was to cooperate with the US Federal Authorities in their efforts to apprehend and prosecute her traffickers. By cooperating she would become eligible for a T visa[8] and would be allowed to stay in the United States. Chun Hei was retraumatized by the process of being interviewed by the authorities about her traffickers and what they had subjected her to. Ultimately, the authorities could not get enough evidence to bring her traffickers to trial, but Chun Hei was still able to obtain a T visa giving her legal status in the United States as she had cooperated fully. As she began to feel stronger and safer, Chun Hei decided to move to a different city away from the scene of her trafficking experiences. She obtained a scholarship and returned to school to pursue her childhood dream of being a scientist.

Trafficking is a prevalent crime worldwide but can be difficult to prosecute (Jones, Engstrom, Hilliard, & Diaz, 2007). Impunity for the traffickers is a huge problem. Traffickers often claim that the victim consented and voluntarily sought to work for them. The significant psychological distress experienced by many survivors, including their anxiety and fear related to the safety of family members back home whom the perpetrators have often threatened to harm or kill if the victim goes to the authorities, may make them feel unable to cooperate with an investigation or prosecution (Shigekane, 2007).

[8] Victims of human trafficking may be eligible for T Nonimmigrant Status (T visa). A T visa allows a survivor of trafficking to remain in the United States to assist authorities in an investigation or prosecution of the traffickers and provides a route toward permanent residency in the United States. More information can be obtained from the USCIS website at: www.uscis.gov/humanitarian/victims-human-trafficking-other-crimes/victims-human-trafficking-t-nonimmigrant-status.

Social workers can play a meaningful role in providing clinical support to trafficking survivors as they make a decision regarding whether or not to cooperate with the federal authorities that are investigating and trying to prosecute their traffickers. Of course, social workers need to stay within their scope of practice at all times and make sure not to offer legal advice. In Chun Hei's case, and other similar cases, Sarah collaborated closely with the attorneys involved who were specialized in representing survivors of trafficking. In addition to psychologically supporting these survivors, Sarah was able to assist the attorneys at times when they struggled with interviewing the highly traumatized and distraught survivors.

Undocumented survivors of trafficking, such as Chun Hei in the vignette example above, often fear the stigma and consequences they may face if they are deported. They may feel, as Chun Hei did, that they have no option but to cooperate with law enforcement authorities in the investigation and prosecution of their traffickers in order to qualify for legal status in the United States through a T visa.[9] Typically, the process of cooperating with the authorities can be exceedingly retraumatizing, as the survivors must go through the events of their trauma over and over again in great detail under intense questioning (USDOS, 2014). If they end up testifying in civil or criminal proceedings against their trafficker(s), they must do so in close proximity to those who inflicted great harm on them and be open to vigorous cross-examination and scrutiny of their credibility. Sarah had to hospitalize Liliya (a pseudonym), one of the other survivors of trafficking she worked with, as she became highly suicidal during the several weeks long civil trial against her traffickers. Her traffickers smirked and glared at Liliya during her testimony. Liliya won her case. The legal proceedings were a retraumatizing yet ultimately empowering process for Liliya. Clinical practitioners can work to ensure that the survivor's rights are protected, that they are able to make an informed choice rather than be coerced into cooperating with the authorities, prepare them psychologically for their work with authorities and their testimony, and provide clinical support throughout the proceedings.[10]

Undocumented trafficking survivors also may be eligible for asylum in the United States, however, a grant of asylum is left to the discretion of the adjudicator (Aschenbrenner, 2012). Knight (2007) analyzed US asylum cases where human trafficking was at least part of the basis for a claim of persecution and concluded that the United States did not provide protection to many who had experienced the serious harm of trafficking. One of the common reasons given for denial of these cases has been the

[9] Victims of trafficking in the United States may also be eligible for other forms of relief such as Continued Presence (USICE, 2010), allowing them to remain temporarily in the United States during an ongoing investigation into the trafficking. Victims of qualifying crimes who cooperate with law enforcement may be eligible for a U visa (USICE, 2014).

[10] It is important to know that those under the age of 18 are not required to cooperate with the authorities, including in order to obtain a T visa (Victims of Trafficking and Violence Prevention Act 2000, Pub L. No. 106–386 § 107(c)(1), 114 Stat. 1464 (2000)). It is also possible for adults to seek a waiver of the requirement of cooperating with law enforcement in order to obtain a T visa if they have documented significant psychological or physical impairment that makes the survivor unable to cooperate (VAWA, 2005, Section 801(a)(3)).

failure of the applicant to make a clear nexus (or link) between their persecution and at least one of the five protected grounds required for a grant of asylum.[11] In addition, despite the evidence that State actors often condone or facilitate (and thus fail to protect the victim) or are directly involved in the act of trafficking, some adjudicators do not grant asylum (Knight, 2007; Piotrowicz, 2008; UNHCR, 2006). Many of these cases do not have the benefit of expert witness testimony related to the psychosocial evidence. Sarah and other clinical social workers have conducted forensic assessments and testified as expert witnesses in the asylum cases of trafficking survivors. This can be another route to helping to protect and further the rights of survivors. In addition to clinical and forensic interventions, structural, policy, law enforcement, and other macro efforts to combat trafficking are essential.

## Macro Efforts to Combat Trafficking: Relevance to Clinical Social Workers

Governments, intergovernmental organizations, and non-profit and human rights organizations worldwide have increasingly engaged in coordinated and enhanced efforts to combat the problem of human trafficking, some of which will be briefly mentioned here. Clinical social workers need to be aware of these efforts for several reasons. Human trafficking violates the social work code of ethics and universal human rights (Androff, 2010). At the core of the mission of the social work profession is serving vulnerable populations and advocating for social justice and human rights (Libal et al., 2014). The wide-scale scope and covert nature of human trafficking is likely to continue to produce millions of victims in the absence of coordinated global macro efforts across key sectors, including among clinicians working on the ground with survivors of trafficking. Clinical knowledge of the population gained by social workers contributes in making them valuable members of human trafficking task forces and collaborators in shaping advocacy and policy efforts.

On a different note, engaging in advocacy or other macro initiatives can contribute to the clinical social worker's own self-care. In the absence of connecting with others in a meaningful way, clinical social workers that work with trafficking survivors may be more at risk of vicarious trauma and, in turn, of having a negative impact on those they work with (a topic covered in Chapter 5 of this book). Becoming connected to a larger social justice and human rights movement combating human trafficking may be healthy not just for the social worker but also for the trafficking survivors they serve. That being said, some survivors will benefit from having clinical support if they choose to share their experiences publically, due to the potentially retraumatizing effect that it has on some.

[11] Of the five protected grounds (political opinion, religion, race, nationality, or membership in a social group), political opinion or social group membership are typically the most relevant for victims of trafficking (Knight, 2007).

Androff (2010) recommends a variety of policy options to eradicate trafficking and modern-day slavery including: "the implementation and enforcement of existing laws and treaties, changing economic structures, improving social services, harnessing the powers of the media and other institutions of civil society, and ensuring the prevention of new cases. Both the supply and demand side of slavery requires attention" (p. 219). Human rights organizations have implemented creative campaigns, engaging private hotel companies and other industries where trafficking is prominent to build supportive corporate, legal, and cultural standards to eradicate trafficking (see http://ecpatusa.org/wp/ and http://www.endslaveryandtrafficking.org/).

Under federal law, minors who have been induced to engage in commercial sex acts are recognized as victims of severe trafficking (Trafficking Victims Protection Act, 22 U.S.C. 7102). Many state laws had historically been in conflict with this. Recently, increased efforts have been made to ensure that trafficked individuals are identified as such and not prosecuted as criminals. In 2010, the Texas Supreme Court made a landmark ruling in *Matter of B. W.* (2010) that children involved in prostitution are victims rather than criminals. The United States also works to reunite families affected by human trafficking through the Return, Reintegration, and Family Reunification Program for Victims of Trafficking (USDOS, 2013b).

Anti-trafficking criminal legislation has been enacted in all states in the United States and all but one territory (Polaris Project, 2013b; USDOS, 2013a). "Safe Harbor" laws are an example of such efforts (End Child Prostitution and Trafficking-USA (ECPAT-USA), 2014). A person-centered approach is at the heart of safe harbor laws that require training for law enforcement and other first responders regarding the identification[12] of victims of trafficking and strategies to assist them. The development of collaborative interdisciplinary statewide systems of care is promoted. Children are no longer subject to prosecution for prostitution under safe harbor laws, and penalties for buyers and traffickers are increased. In 2008, New York enacted the Safe Harbor for Exploited Children Act, the first of its kind. Other states have followed suit, passing similar bills and galvanizing a movement advocating for similar laws in other states. In 2013 alone, there was quite a bit of legislative development to combat human trafficking, including child trafficking. Notably, the Trafficking Victims Protection Act (TVPA) (P.L. 113–4) was reauthorized in March 2013 as part of the reauthorization of VAWA (Violence Against Women Reauthorization Act of 2013, 2013). VAWA P.L. 113–4 renewed federal funding and protection for those subjected to human trafficking, including funding for the first time for victims who are domestic minors, and expanded the jurisdiction of law enforcement to fight and prosecute US citizens engaged in sex tourism abroad. The Strengthening the Child Welfare Response to Human Trafficking Act of 2013 (H.R. 1732 and S. 1823) was reintroduced in Congress. If passed, this legislation would extend protection from trafficking to the child welfare system as it has been recognized that youth in the child welfare system are at high risk for being trafficked (USDOS, 2013a). A new innovative

[12] Training includes strategies to identify those who present as fearful, show signs of abuse, or appear to be under the control of others (USDOS, 2013a).

"focus country" approach is being recommended by The Alliance to End Slavery and Trafficking (ATEST), an alliance of prominent human rights organizations in the United States working against the problem of human trafficking domestically and internationally (ATEST, 2014). This approach involves the implementation of comprehensive prevention, prosecution, protection, and reintegration strategies. These macro efforts are notable and much needed given the scope and complexity of the problem of human trafficking. This is one of many issues to which clinical social workers can make valuable contributions in both micro and macro areas of practice.

## Conclusion

Human trafficking is a worldwide phenomenon that violates human rights and has devastating effects on trafficked individuals, their families, societies, and the world at large. In the words of Secretary of State John Kerry:

> Here and around the world, trafficking in persons destroys lives. It threatens communities. It creates instability. It undermines the rule of law. And it is a horrendous assault on our most dearly held values of freedom and basic human dignity. We, along with every nation, bear the responsibility to confront modern slavery by punishing traffickers and helping survivors get their lives back on track.
> —Secretary of State John F. Kerry White House Forum to Combat Human Trafficking, 2013 (USDOS, 2013a, p. 23).

Those who are already in marginalized or otherwise vulnerable positions in society appear to be most at risk for being trafficked. Given the complexity and scope of the problem of human trafficking, any effective response must involve a coordinated and interdisciplinary approach. Clinical social workers, particularly those who operate from a strong human rights base, have much to contribute to this effort.

Clinical social workers utilize their psychotherapeutic training and skills to support the healing process of those who are trafficked. In addition, social workers provide valuable clinical support to survivors who may engage with law enforcement in the frequently retraumatizing process of investigation and prosecution of those who trafficked them. Forensic psychosocial assessments conducted by clinical social workers may yield findings that are relevant to asylum applications or testimony in court cases against the traffickers. Much work remains to be done to combat human trafficking and fulfill the rights of those who are trafficked. Some of the current macro efforts to address this problem were highlighted in this chapter. Front line clinicians often develop important knowledge and passion about the issues that make them valuable assets on teams engaged in advocacy and policy work in this arena. Human trafficking is a great example of a realm of practice where clinical social workers can make a significant difference by engaging in both micro and macro practice. Throughout, firm grounding in the core principles of a rights-based approach is essential to promote healing and ensure that the voices of those affected by human trafficking are heard and that their rights are safeguarded and realized.

## Suggested Activities/Resources

*Case Discussion* Have students read the following case vignette and engage in discussion in small groups, reflecting on the discussion questions provided.

> During the summer after graduating from high school, "Josh" (a pseudonym) was approached by a recruiter who told him he could travel around the country and make $350 a week selling magazines and cleaning products. This was appealing to Josh who often lamented that he had never been outside of his small town in the Midwest of the United States and was eager to expand his horizons. Josh joined a crew traveling in a van from state to state. The leaders charged excessive fees for food, lodging, and transportation. Forced to work long hours each day, 7 days a week, Josh found that he still was only earning $200 a week. Even so, the leaders kept his money and other valuables, including his driver's license and cell phone, in their safe and did not allow him access to them. The leaders claimed that this was for Josh's own good in order to prevent thefts. When Josh asked to use some of his money to buy medicine for his headaches, one of the leaders beat him. He was told that he did not have any money as he had failed to meet his sales quotas. When Josh protested, the leader threatened to kidnap his sister and force her into prostitution. The threats escalated and the crew leaders started to deny Josh's access to food when he did not make his quota of sales, and eventually to force him to recruit other young men. Normally kept under close surveillance by the leaders, Josh managed to run away one day when the leader was not looking. He came to a shelter where you work.

Discussion Questions: The Case of Josh

1. What human rights violations appear to be present in the case of Josh?
2. Has Josh been trafficked? Why or why not?
3. How do the core principles of a rights-based approach to clinical social work presented in this chapter help us to understand Josh's case from a rights-based perspective?
4. What human rights instrument(s) may be particularly relevant to your work with Josh? Discuss which principles apply and how.
5. How would you work with Josh from a rights-based perspective? In what way(s) might this differ from a more traditional needs-based social work approach?

*Additional Classroom Activity*

- MTV's Backstory (thebackstory.mtv.com): A creative interactive video project by MTV that takes viewers through the backstory of how various victims of trafficking were coerced or lured into situations of trafficking. Viewers are prompted to read excerpts from books, gain more information from anti-trafficking groups, and sign petitions. It is an engaging platform to introduce students to the topic.

*Resources (Selected)*

- National Human Trafficking Resource Center (NHTRC) 24/7 Hotline: 1-888-373-7888 or text "Help" or "Info" to BeFree (233733). The NHTRC is a national, toll-free hotline that answers calls and texts from anywhere in the country, 24 hours a day, 7 days a week, every day of the year. Individuals can call to report a tip or to be connected with anti-trafficking services or technical assistance in their area. It is operated by the non-governmental non-profit organization Polaris Project. For more information visit: http://www.polarisproject.org/what-we-do/national-human-trafficking-hotline/the-nhtrc/overview.

- US Department of Justice—The Trafficking in Persons and Worker Exploitation Task Force Complaint Line to report suspected cases: 1-888-428-7581.
- US State Department Office to Monitor and Combat Trafficking in Persons: see http://www.state.gov/j/tip/ (includes such things as unconventional approaches to combat modern slavery and a wealth of other information and links).
- The US State Department's annual Trafficking in Persons Report (TIP) contains extensive information about human trafficking in the United States and around the world and the efforts to combat it. It also includes a list of relevant human rights mechanisms, identifying which States are signatories and which have ratified each. The TIP 2014 report can be accessed at: http://www.state.gov/j/tip/rls/tiprpt/2014/index.htm.
- End Child Prostitution and Trafficking—USA (ECPAT-USA) (http://ecpatusa.org): ECPAT-USA works to protect sexually exploited children in the United States from criminalization. Examples of resources available through ECPACT-USA:
  - Video: "What I Have Been Through Is Not Who I Am" (a documentary that seeks to raise awareness of commercially sexually exploited children) http://www.youtube.com/watch?v=BmmRTjoL3R0
  - Online training program for hotel employees: "The Role of Hospitality in Preventing and Reacting to Child Trafficking."
- Alliance to End Slavery and Trafficking (ATEST) (http://www.endslaveryandtrafficking.org/): ATEST is an alliance of 11 US-based human rights organizations that have anti-slavery programs in the United States and in other parts of the world. Member organizations collaborate in the fight against human trafficking and modern-day slavery.
- US Department of Justice—Human Trafficking Prosecution Unit (http://www.justice.gov/crt/about/crm/htpu.php): This website provides information on victim/witness rights as well as about the Victim Witness Coordinator who can assist trafficked persons to navigate the federal legal system.
- US Department of Health and Human Services resources:
  - US Department of Health and Human Services (2012, May). *Services available to victims of human trafficking: A resource guide for social service providers.* Washington, DC: US Department of Health and Human Services
  - For information on human trafficking and the HHS Anti-trafficking in Persons Program, visit www.acf.hhs.gov/trafficking.
- Minnesota Center Against Violence and Abuse's (MINCAVA) electronic clearinghouse (on trafficking): http://www.mincava.umn.edu/categories/935.

## References


Alliance to End Slavery & Trafficking (ATEST). (2014, Feb). *Recommendations for a trafficking in persons focus country approach*. Washington, DC: ATEST.

AlZoubi, M. (2011, Nov). Human trafficking: A Muslim issue. *Chicago Crescent*. Retrieved from http://www.chicagocrescent.com/crescent/newsDetail2010.php?newsID=20725.

Androff, D. K. (2010). The problem of contemporary slavery: An international human rights challenge for social work. *International Social Work, 54*(2), 209–222.

Aschenbrenner, K. (2012). Discretionary (in)justice: The exercise of discretion in claims for asylum. *University of Michigan Journal of Law Reform, 45*, 595–633.

Bales, K. (2007). *Ending slavery: How we free today's slaves*. Berkeley, CA: University of California Press.

Belser, P. (2005). *Forced labour and human trafficking: Estimating the profits. Working paper 42*. Geneva, Switzerland: International Labour Office.

Briere, J., & Scott, C. (2012). *Principles of trauma therapy: A guide to symptoms, evaluation and treatment* (2nd ed.). Thousand Oaks, CA: Sage.

DeStefano, A. (2007). *The war on human trafficking: US policy assessed*. New Brunswick, NJ: Rutgers University Press.

End Child Prostitution and Trafficking-USA (ECPAT-USA). (2014). Safe harbor. Retrieved from http://ecpatusa.org/wp/what-we-do/helping-children-in-america/safe-harbor/.

Gonzales, A. H., & Bergstrom, L. (2013). Adolescent non-suicidal self-injury (NSSI) interventions. *Journal of Child and Adolescent Psychiatric Nursing, 26*, 124–130.

Hossain, M., Zimmerman, C., Abas, M., Light, M., & Watts, C. (2010). The relationship of trauma to mental disorders among trafficked and sexually exploited girls and women. *American Journal of Public Health, 100*(12), 2442–2449.

International Labor Organization [ILO]. (2009). *Training manual to fight trafficking in children for labour, sexual, and other forms of exploitation: Textbook 2—advocacy against child trafficking at policy and outreach levels*. Geneva, Switzerland: ILO.

International Labour Organization [ILO]. (2012). ILO 2012 global estimate of forced labour. Executive summary. Retrieved from http://www.ilo.org/global/topics/forced-labour/publications/WCMS_181953/lang-en/index.htm.

Jones, L., Engstrom, D., Hilliard, T., & Diaz, M. (2007). Globalization and human trafficking. *Journal of Sociology and Social Welfare, 34*(2), 107–122.

Klonsky, E. D., & Muehlenkamp, J. J. (2007). Self-injury: A research review for the practitioner. *Journal of Clinical Psychology, 63*(11), 1045–1056.

Knight, S. (2007). Asylum from trafficking: A failure of protection. *Immigration Briefings, 7*(7), 1–22.

Libal, K. R., Berthold, S. M., Thomas, R. L., & Healy, L. M. (Eds.). (2014). *Advancing human rights in social work education*. Alexandria, VA: CSWE Press.

*Matter of B. W.* (2010, June 18). NO. 08-1044 (Supreme Court of Texas on petition). Retrieved from http://www.supreme.courts.state.tx.us/historical/2010/jun/081044.pdf.

Nixon, M. K., & Heath, N. L. (Eds.). (2008). *Self-injury in youth: The essential guide to assessment and intervention*. Florence, KY: Routledge.

Nock, M. K. (2010). Self-injury. *Annual Review of Clinical Psychology, 6*, 339–363.

Office of the High Commissioner for Human Rights [OHCHR]. (2010). *Principles and guidelines on human rights and human trafficking, commentary*. Geneva, Switzerland: OHCHR.

Oram, S., Stöckl, H., Busza, J., Howard, L. M., & Zimmerman, C. (2012). Prevalence and risk of violence and the physical, mental, and sexual health problems associated with human trafficking: Systematic review. *PLoS Medicine, 9*(5), e1001224. doi:10.1371/journal.pmed.1001224.

Piotrowicz, R. (2008). The UNHCR's guidelines on human trafficking. *International Journal of Refugee Law, 20*(2), 242–252.

Polaris Project. (2013a). Human trafficking trends in the United States: National human trafficking resource center 2007–2012. Retrieved from http://www.polarisproject.org/resources/hotline-statistics/human-trafficking-trends-in-the-united-states.

Polaris Project. (2013b). 2013 state ratings on human trafficking laws. Retrieved from http://www.polarisproject.org/what-we-do/policy-advocacy/national-policy/state-ratings-on-human-trafficking-laws/2013-state-ratings-on-human-trafficking-laws.

Shigekane, R. (2007). Rehabilitation and community integration of trafficking survivors in the United States. *Human Rights Quarterly, 29,* 112–136.

Stanley, B., & Brown, G. K. (2012). Safety planning intervention: A brief intervention to mitigate suicide risk. *Cognitive and Behavioral Practice, 19*(2), 256–264.

Stransky, M., & Finkelhor, D. (2008). How many juveniles are involved in prostitution in the U.S.? Retrieved from http://www.unh.edu/ccrc/prostitution/Juvenile_Prostitution_factsheet.pdf.

Trafficking Victims Protection Reauthorization Act of 2013. (2013a). P.L. 113-4. 22 U.S.C. § 7102.

Trafficking Victims Protection Reauthorization Act of 2013. (2013b). P.L. 113-4. 18 U.S.C. § 1581.

UN General Assembly. (1948). Universal Declaration of Human Rights, 10 December 1948, 217 A (III). Retrieved from http://www.unhcr.org/refworld/docid/3ae6b3712c.html.

UN General Assembly. (1966a). International Covenant on Civil and Political Rights, 16 December 1966, United Nations, Treaty Series, vol. 999, p. 171. Retrieved from http://www.unhcr.org/refworld/docid/3ae6b3aa0.html.

UN General Assembly. (1966b). International Covenant on Economic, Social and Cultural Rights, 16 December 1966, United Nations, Treaty Series, vol. 993, p. 3. Retrieved from http://www.unhcr.org/refworld/docid/3ae6b36c0.html.

UN General Assembly. (1979). Convention on the Elimination of all Forms of Discrimination against Women, 18 December 1979, United Nations, Treaty Series, vol. 1249, p. 13. Retrieved from http://www.refworld.org/docid/3ae6b3970.html.

UN General Assembly. (1989). Convention on the Rights of the Child, 20 November 1989, United Nations, Treaty Series, vol. 1577, p. 3. Retrieved from http://www.refworld.org/docid/3ae6b38f0.html.

UN General Assembly. (2000a). Optional Protocol to the Convention on the Rights of the Child on the Sale of Children, Child Prostitution and Child Pornography, 25 May 2000, A/RES/54/263. Retrieved from http://www.unhcr.org/refworld/docid/3ae6b38bc.html.

UN General Assembly. (2000b). Optional Protocol to the Convention on the Rights of the Child on the Involvement of Children in Armed Conflict, 25 May 2000. Retrieved from http://www.refworld.org/docid/47fdfb180.html.

UN General Assembly. (2000c). Protocol to Prevent, Suppress and Punish Trafficking in Persons, Especially Women and Children, supplementing the United Nations Convention against Transnational Organized Crime. 15 November 2000. Retrieved from http://www.unhcr.org/refworld/docid/4720706c0.html.

UN High Commissioner for Refugees (UNHCR). (2006). Guidelines on international protection No. 7: The Application of Article 1A(2) of the 1951 Convention and/or 1967 Protocol Relating to the Status of Refugees to Victims of Trafficking and Persons at Risk of Being Trafficked, 7 April 2006, HCR/GIP/06/07. Retrieved from http://www.refworld.org/docid/443679fa4.html.

UN Special Rapporteur on Trafficking in Persons. (2011, April 13). Report of the special rapporteur on trafficking in persons, especially women and children, Joy Ngozi Ezeilo. Retrieved from http://www2.ohchr.org/english/bodies/hrcouncil/docs/17session/A-HRC-17-35.pdf.

U.S. Department of State (USDOS). (2013a). Trafficking in persons report 2013. Retrieved from http://www.state.gov/j/tip/rls/tiprpt/2013/.

U.S. Department of State (USDOS). (2013b). President's interagency task force. Progress in combating trafficking in persons: The U.S. government response to modern slavery. Retrieved from http://www.state.gov/j/tip/rls/reports/2013/207198.htm.

U.S. Department of State (USDOS). (2014). Trafficking in persons report 2014. Retrieved from http://www.state.gov/j/tip/rls/tiprpt/2014/index.htm.

U.S. Immigration and Customs Enforcement (USICE). (2010). Continued presence: Temporary immigration status of victims of trafficking. Retrieved from www.ice.gov/doclib/human-trafficking/pdf/continued-presence.pdf.

U.S. Immigration and Customs Enforcement (USICE). (2014). Victims of criminal activity: U nonimmigrant status. Retrieved from www.uscis.gov/humanitarian/victims-human-trafficking-other-crimes/victims-criminal-activity-u-nonimmigrant-status/victims-criminal-activity-u-nonimmigrant-status.

Van Hook, M., Gjermeri, E., & Haxhiymeri, E. (2006). Sexual trafficking of women: Tragic proportions and attempted solutions in Albania. *International Social Work, 49*(1), 29–40.

Victims of Trafficking and Violence Protection Act of 2000. (2000, Oct 28). 114 STAT. 1464 Public Law 106–386.

Violence Against Women and Department of Justice Reauthorization Act of 2005 [VAWA]. (2005). 119 STAT. 2960 Public Law 109–162.

Violence Against Women Reauthorization Act of 2013. (2013). 127 STAT. 54 Public Law 113–4.

Whitlock, J., & Knox, K. L. (2007). The relationship between self-injurious behavior and suicide in a young adult population. *Archives of Pediatrics and Adolescent Medicine, 161*(7), 634–640.

Zimmerman, C., Hossain, M., Yun, K., Gajdadziev, V., Guzun, N., Tchomarova, M., & Watts, C. (2008). The health of trafficked women: A survey of women entering posttrafficking services in Europe. *American Journal of Public Health, 98,* 55–59.

# Chapter 4
# Intimate Partner Violence and a Rights-Based Approach to Healing

Claire[1], a 32-year-old African American lesbian biologist, entered treatment with a clinical social worker as she was experiencing frequent troubling memories of her abuse as a child. These memories had intensified after she and her partner Helen adopted a daughter 1 year earlier. After several months of treatment, Claire revealed to her social worker that Helen had left her after a particularly bad argument during which Claire had punched Helen multiple times in the back. Claire was remorseful, recalling how it reminded her of seeing her father beat her mother on many occasions when she was young. She recounted that this was not the first time she had punched Helen. "I never wanted to grow up to be like my dad," Claire pronounced to her social worker.

What rights issues may be particularly relevant in this case? What would your reaction be upon learning that Claire had punched Helen? How would you approach working with Claire? How would a rights-based approach inform your strategy? Where would you start? How might you balance and attend to issues of safety and rights in your work? What other information would you want to know to guide your work with Claire?

Intimate partner violence (IPV)[2] is a worldwide problem with serious consequences for individuals, families, and societies. IPV can result in death and, for those who survive, serious injuries. The consequences can span physical, mental, social, cultural, and spiritual domains (Black et al., 2011; WHO, 2013a). This chapter applies principles from a rights-based approach to clinical practice to work with those who have experienced IPV. The problem of IPV is defined and framed within the context of human rights and selected prevalence data are summarized. Space constraints do not allow for comprehensive attention to the full range of types of IPV cases. The experiences of several special populations affected by IPV are highlighted (i.e., children and families; heterosexual male and lesbian, gay, bisexual, transgender, and queer/questioning (LGBTQ) survivors; and undocumented survivors). Relevant human rights mechanisms and tools are described, and selected core principles and foundational considerations for clinical social workers working

[1] The names and other identifying information in all case material in this chapter have been changed to protect confidentiality, and aspects of each case are a composite from more than one person.

[2] IPV is a form of gender-based violence (GBV), and is sometimes referred to as domestic violence (DV) or battering. Much of the UN literature uses the term GBV.

 
S. M. Berthold, *Human Rights-Based Approaches to Clinical Social Work*,
SpringerBriefs in Rights-Based Approaches to Social Work, DOI 10.1007/978-3-319-08560-9_4

with IPV survivors are discussed. Rights-based recommendations and several key challenges for clinical practice with this population are presented. Often, social work practitioners and society at large think of trauma survivors (or "victims") as being distinct from perpetrators. The reality is often more complex and nuanced, with some survivors of trauma having also perpetrated violence against others at some time in their life. A human rights-based approach facilitates effective and ethical practice with both perpetrators and survivors of IPV. Attention to work with perpetrators (a commonly underexamined topic) is explored in this chapter, highlighting the value of conducting a holistic assessment and working with the complexities presented from a rights-based framework including with those perpetrators who may have been mandated to receive services (Rooney, 2009; UN Special Rapporteur on Violence Against Women, 2013). Restorative justice approaches are described and discussed as an alternative model to addressing the problem of IPV. The chapter ends with suggested class activities and selected resources.

## Definitional and Contextual Issues

### *Defining Intimate Partner Violence*

The United Nations (UN) Committee on the Elimination of Discrimination Against Women[3] (1992; hereafter referred to as the CEDAW Committee) did not originally explicitly address violence against women as discrimination or a human rights concern. Over time, violence against women came to be identified as a serious form of discrimination, a human rights concern for which states were to be held accountable. The Declaration on the Elimination of Violence Against Women (DEVAW; UN General Assembly, 1993), adopted by the UN General Assembly in 1993, was based on the CEDAW Committee's General Recommendation 19 (UN CEDAW, 1992). DEVAW defined violence against women as follows:

> ... the term "violence against women" means any act of gender-based violence that results in, or is likely to result in, physical, sexual or psychological harm or suffering to women, including threats of such acts, coercion or arbitrary deprivation of liberty, whether occurring in public or in private life. (UN General Assembly, 1993, Article 1)

---

[3] The CEDAW Committee is the body that monitors the implementation of the Convention on the Elimination of All Forms of Discrimination against Women (CEDAW) (Retrieved from http://www.ohchr.org/en/hrbodies/cedaw/pages/cedawindex.aspx). The CEDAW Committee is composed of an international group of 23 independent women's rights experts. State parties to the CEDAW must submit reports regularly to the CEDAW Committee regarding their implementation of the rights of the CEDAW Convention, and the CEDAW Committee develops concluding observations addressed to the state that include any concerns and recommendations the Committee may have. In addition, States may choose to ratify the Optional Protocol to the Convention (UN General Assembly, 1999). If they do, the CEDAW Committee is mandated to: (1) receive complaints of violations of those rights that are protected by the CEDAW Convention by States that have ratified the Optional Protocol; and (2) make inquiries about claims of systematic or grave violations of the rights of women.

Article 2 of DEVAW specifies physical, sexual, and/or psychological IPV as a possible form of violence against women.

## *Prevalence of Intimate Partner Violence*

There is an ample literature regarding the high prevalence of IPV and the host of negative associated consequences (Black et al., 2011; WHO, 2013b). The World Health Organization (WHO) considers IPV to be an epidemic (WHO, 2013a). The prevalence of IPV worldwide is alarming: approximately one-third (30%) of all women in the world who have been in an intimate relationship have been subjected to sexual and/or physical violence by their partner; the rate is 38% in some parts of the world (i.e., Southeast Asia); and approximately 38% of murdered women worldwide were killed by their intimate partners (WHO, 2013a).

In the United States, IPV is also a significant yet preventable problem that violates the human rights of its immediate target and other family members. The 2010 National Intimate Partner and Sexual Violence Survey (NISVS) was conducted with a nationally representative sample of 16,507 noninstitutionalized English and/or Spanish-speaking adult women and men in the United States. Results from the NISVS indicated that 35.6% of women and 28.5% of men in the United States had been subjected to physical violence, rape, and/or stalking by an intimate partner during their lifetime (Black et al., 2011). Not everyone is equally at risk for experiencing IPV. Compared to the overall sample in the 2010 NISVS (Black et al., 2011), young women and racial and ethnic minority men and women are disproportionately at risk. Black et al. (2011) comment that the higher rates in these sub-groups may be influenced in part due to significant stressors and social determinants of health including low income and relatively limited access to community resources, services, and education. These indicators are also signs of discrimination and disproportionality. These statistics point to widespread structural failures on the part of states to protect its citizens and other residents (McDowell, Libal, & Brown, 2012). Nonprofits and US officials who work with survivors of IPV and human trafficking understand that often survivors experience both types of violence, and that being subjected to IPV and/or threats of IPV has made some individuals at risk for being trafficked domestically or internationally (Freedom Network, 2012; Kelley, 2013).

## *Special Populations of Concern*

IPV is a widespread problem that affects individuals from diverse backgrounds. Attention will be given below to the phenomenon of IPV in several special populations of concern (i.e., children and families; heterosexual male and LGBTQ survivors; and undocumented survivors). This is not meant to be a comprehensive examination of IPV, given space constraints, but rather to be illustrative of some examples of the scope of the problem.

## *Impact on Children and Other Family Members*

Rights-based clinical social workers need to proactively be alert for the impact of IPV not only on the immediate target but also on others in the household and family, including children who may witness the violence or in situations where there is co-occurring IPV and child abuse (Appel & Holde, 1998; Bragg, 2003). Children also have a right to have their voices heard, and have their best interests protected (see the Convention on the Rights of the Child (UN General Assembly, 1989)). Children and other family members are at risk of being psychologically affected by witnessing IPV in their homes. Their rights to safety and security of person and to the highest standard attainable of mental health are often violated in the process. For those who first experience IPV at an early age, the impact can continue across their lifespan. Guidelines on best practices for screening, assessing, and protecting children in situations of IPV have been developed by the Children's Bureau at the Office on Child Abuse and Neglect (Bragg, 2003).

## *Heterosexual Male Victims and IPV Within LGBTQ Relationships*

The perpetrators of IPV are typically portrayed as heterosexual men and guidelines for providers often focus on women-centered care (WHO, 2013b). While existing evidence suggests that the majority of those who inflict violence on their intimate partners are heterosexual males, insufficient attention has been paid to the very real phenomenon that some women and LGBTQ individuals also perpetrate violence against those close to them (see NCAVP, 2013). It may be particularly difficult for heterosexual male or LGBTQ survivors to come forward to report IPV or seek assistance, feeling marginalized, stereotyped, and in some cases revictimized (NCAVP, 2013; Public Health Agency of Canada, 2009). Rights-based practitioners should be vigilant that they do not make assumptions or stereotype the heterosexual male and LGBTQ people they work with in this (or any other) regard (or any other persons for that matter).

Undeniably, advocates for women's rights in the United States won an important battle in passing the Violence Against Women Act (VAWA)[4] (and its subsequent reauthorizations) as part of a larger campaign to promote and protect the rights and well-being of women, a historically oppressed population. Social workers should

[4] The VAWA was first passed in the United States in 1994, and became the first federal legislation in the United States to designate sexual assault and domestic violence as crimes. VAWA provided federal resources to communities to address this type of violence. The provision of legal assistance was added in the 2000 reauthorization, and dating violence and stalking were added to the list of crimes. The 2005 reauthorization added attention to prevention, funding for rape crisis programs, linguistically and culturally specific services, and housing protections for survivors.

remember that, despite the name of the law protecting victims of IPV, (heterosexual) women are not the only victims of such crimes. A variety of genders/sexes are targeted by IPV and, although women still disproportionately suffer, VAWA also provides protection to men subjected to IPV (National Task Force to End Sexual and Domestic Violence Against Women, 2006). Despite its advances, VAWA was not fully in keeping with all human rights principles. For example, it was not implemented equitably, such that male IPV survivors reported a harder time accessing and qualifying for services (Stop Abusive and Violent Environments, 2010).

A major improvement from a rights perspective came with the 2013 reauthorization of VAWA that closed many of the justice and service gaps. An *Inclusion Mandate* was added banning discrimination of any person in the United States "on the basis of actual or perceived race, color, religion, national origin, sex, gender identity (as defined in paragraph 249(c)(4) of title 18, United States Code), sexual orientation, or disability" (VAWA, 2013, p. 8). Various provisions in the law were designed to stop discriminatory practices and make all programs and services funded in whole or in part by VAWA or the Office on Violence Against Women *inclusive* (e.g., Sect. 3, 13 A regarding civil rights and non-discrimination[5]*)*. The 2013 VAWA legislation also used gender-neutral terms in most of its provisions (e.g., "victims" instead of "women").

IPV in the context of intimate LGBTQ partnerships is often unrecognized and subject to considerable false assumptions, underreporting, denial by LGBTQ and non-LGBTQ individuals, and lack of appropriate shelters and other services (NCAVP, 2013). Researchers have uncovered a number of reasons that may lead LGBTQ survivors not to report IPV, including: homophobia; biphobia; transphobia; anti-HIV bias (both societal and internalized); concern that their safety will be further compromised if they report; fears that LGBTQ and HIV-affected communities may censure them; and insufficient knowledge by providers and responders about IPV in LGBTQ and HIV-affected communities (Davidson & Duke, 2009; Stotzer, 2009). Sizeable numbers of LGBTQ survivors reported misconduct by police officers in 2012 including: profiling, record rates of deportation, and being arrested when they reported IPV (NCAVP, 2013). Police are charged with protecting and serving the public, not with abusing them. The survivors had gone to the police for help after having their rights violated by their intimate partner.

The misconduct found by the National Coalition of Anti-Violence Programs (NCAVP, 2013) includes human rights violations against, among other things, the right to equal protection under the law. The NCVAP (2013) recommends that LGBTQ-specific service providers are needed in every state to address these barriers to care. A rights-based clinical social worker would go a step further, and frame it as a right, stressing that social workers and other practitioners and first responders, including law enforcement, must develop the knowledge base and attitudes to serve LGBTQ survivors without prejudice or discrimination. Such an approach is in

[5] An exception is made if sex-specific programming or sex segregation is deemed to be essential. In such cases, comparable services must be provided for those who are not eligible.

conformance with social work professional ethics (NASW, 1999), laws against hate crimes, and human rights.

## The Case of Undocumented Survivors of IPV

Undocumented individuals who are in the United States and have suffered IPV at the hands of their US-citizen- or permanent-resident spouses may be eligible for immigration relief through the VAWA (Violence Against Women Reauthorization Act of 2013, 2013). This would allow them to remain legally in the United States. In addition, some US immigration judges have granted asylum in cases where state actors were found to be accountable for failing to protect individuals from persecution in the form of IPV; however, the rulings are not consistent across judges, resulting in arbitrary and contradictory decisions and the lack of protection for many (Bookey, 2013; Musalo, 2010).

Clinical social workers potentially have much to contribute to VAWA cases and asylum cases that are based on IPV in much the same way as discussed in relation to torture cases in Chapter 2 of this book. Applying for relief under an act named to protect women may reinforce shame and stigma in a man abused by his female spouse who may already feel ashamed that a woman abused him, even more so if the meaning of such an experience detracts from his sense of masculinity valued in his culture (Migliaccio, 2001; Public Health Agency of Canada, 2009). Men and other individuals who are less commonly recognized as victims of IPV (e.g., LGBTQ persons or intimate partners of law enforcement or clergy or others in respected or prominent positions in society) may be particularly prone to feeling shame and guilt (Bragg, 2003). Social workers need to ensure that these marginalized survivors have equal rights and that their dignity and worth as human beings are respected.

## Historical Challenges to Framing IPV as a Human Rights Issue

There have been a number of historical challenges to framing IPV as a human rights issue. One of these key challenges relates to holding states accountable for their actions and inactions that contribute to the existence of IPV (Bunch, 1990; UN Special Rapporteur on Violence Against Women, 2013). Many countries continue to maintain that IPV is a private matter, one that is outside the public realm such that the state cannot and should not intervene (Libal & Parekh, 2009). The perpetrator of the act(s) of IPV is typically not a state actor.

Violence inflicted within the context of intimate partnerships has also traditionally not been considered a human rights violation in some parts of the world due to cultural and social values and norms. Violence against women and wives is often viewed as normal and to be expected—often the woman is blamed (Krug, Mercy, Dahlberg, & Zwi, 2002; UN Special Rapporteur on Violence Against Women, 2002).

Most of the work on IPV has focused on violence against heterosexual women perpetrated by heterosexual men, although individuals of all gender identities and sexual orientations are at risk for IPV as well as those of all races, cultures, ages, faith communities, and socioeconomic status. Transgender survivors or those who are abused within homosexual relationships often occupy marginalized and oppressed positions in society already, putting them at further risk for IPV (NCAVP, 2013). The perpetration of IPV by women on their male partners is a relatively taboo subject in many societies, and the men often experience significant shame as a result (Migliaccio, 2001, 2002; Public Health Agency of Canada, 2009). All of these factors have hampered efforts to safeguard the rights of those affected by IPV.

## Human Rights Mechanisms and Tools

### *Framing IPV as a Human Rights Issue*

In recent years, significant advances have been made in the framing of IPV as a human rights issue. IPV has been recognized as a clear violation of the human rights of women that has a significant but preventable public health impact[6] (WHO, 2013a). The Secretary-General of the UN, Ban Ki-Moon, has come out strongly against violence against women in all its forms. "There is one universal truth, applicable to all countries, cultures and communities: violence against women is never acceptable, never excusable, never tolerable" (Ki-Moon, 2008, para. 20).

IPV violates the victim's right to security of person, his or her right to bodily integrity, and sometimes, his or her right to life—all of which are violations of the person's human rights (Libal & Parekh, 2009). Over the last several decades many national, regional, and international bodies have framed IPV as a human rights issue in the United States and internationally (Amnesty International, 2005; Beasley & Thomas, 1994; Hawkins & Humes, 2002; Morgaine, 2009; Roth, 1994). The International Women's Rights Action Watch Asia Pacific, Center for Domestic Violence Prevention in Uganda, Coalition on Violence against Women—Kenya, and Women for Women's Human Rights/New Ways in Turkey are examples of organizations using a human rights framework in their work against IPV (Morgaine, 2009). The UN has been quite clear on this point, declaring IPV a pervasive human rights problem (UN Special Rapporteur on Violence Against Women, 2011).

[6] The public health framing of IPV has been criticized by some as losing the focus on the integrity, dignity and worth of the individual. From a human rights perspective, it is important to not solely focus on collective consequences/public health, but also on the individual harms that the state can prevent.

## *International Treaties*

A number of international treaties are relevant to framing IPV as a human rights issue and advancing the rights of those targeted by IPV. These include the International Covenant on Civil and Political Rights (ICCPR; UN General Assembly, 1966) and the CEDAW (UN General Assembly, 1979). In the context of women survivors of IPV, these documents provide for the right for women to receive equal protection under the law, just compensation, and due diligence to investigate and hold accountable perpetrators and prevent violations (Morgaine, 2009). In addition, the UN's Special Rapporteur on Violence Against Women and various human rights organizations, governmental, and intergovernmental bodies have created an important body of knowledge on this issue, finding some states to be complicit in failing to respond to prevent or protect individuals from IPV. The UN's Special Rapporteur on Violence Against Women (2011) issued a report on its mission to the United States in 2011. The Special Rapporteur noted some advancement but also observed insufficient legislation and implementation of existing laws to substantively prevent violence against women or protect women from such violence. The report includes recommendations regarding: remedies for victims; addressing discrimination against women particularly vulnerable to being targeted for violence, such as minority, immigrant, and poor women in the United States; improving detention conditions for women; and further investigating violence and prosecuting those responsible for inflicting violence against military women.

## *Use of Human Rights Tools in Campaigns to Combat and Prevent IPV*

Human rights tools have been creatively employed to advance state action against IPV (American Civil Liberties Union, 2013; Ford Foundation, 2004; New Tactics in Human Rights, n.d.). One such tool is DEVAW. While it does not hold the same force or legal authority as a convention or a treaty, DEVAW does provide strong guidance, sets a strong standard that is used in the CEDAW Committee's work with individual complaints, and provides a foundation for the Special Rapporteur's work. DEVAW holds states accountable for violence against women if the state condones such violence in the home or community, such as when the state formally prohibits violence against women but tolerates it by not acting or not effectively acting to end it. In addition, states are held accountable if state actors perpetrate the violence. DEVAW takes a strong stand against viewing IPV as solely a family matter that should not be scrutinized and whose perpetrators should not be held accountable publically.

Article 3 of DEVAW outlines the various human rights that women are entitled to equally enjoy and have protected, including:

a. The right to life;
b. The right to equality;

c. The right to liberty and security of person;
d. The right to equal protection under the law;
e. The right to be free from all forms of discrimination;
f. The right to the highest standard attainable of physical and mental health;
g. The right to just and favorable conditions of work; and
h. The right not to be subjected to torture, or other cruel, inhuman or degrading treatment or punishment (UN General Assembly, 1993).

The existence of human rights tools related to IPV has lent support to various campaigns around the world. On the International Day for the Elimination of Violence against Women in November 2011, then UN Women executive director Michelle Bachelet outlined policies and called for governments to take responsibility for ending violence against women. Bachelet stated:

> Although equality between women and men is guaranteed in the Constitutions of 139 countries and territories, all too often women are denied justice and protection from violence. This failure does not stem from a lack of knowledge but rather a lack of investment and political will to meet women's needs and protect their fundamental rights. It is time for governments to take responsibility. (Anderson, 2011, para. 7)

In response to the UN Women's COMMIT initiative, the European Union and 61 countries had pledged to take concrete actions to end violence against girls and women by the end of 2013 (UN Women, n.d.). These actions included: ratifying international conventions, passing relevant laws, strengthening legal and policy prevention efforts, engaging in public education campaigns, and providing enhanced services such as free hotlines, safe houses, and legal aid at no cost to survivors. In addition, some countries made efforts to expand the number of women in front-line peacekeeping, law enforcement, and other services (UN Special Rapporteur on Violence Against Women, 2013).

## Clinical Work with IPV: Key Roles for Social Workers, Application of Core Principles of a Rights-Based Approach, and Recommendations and Challenges

### Key Roles for Rights-Based Social Workers

**Front-Line Workers** Clinical social workers frequently come into contact with individuals affected by IPV. Indeed, they may be the first persons to become aware of the violence and can play a critical role in engaging survivors and ensuring that they have access to intervention and that their rights are promoted in the process. The WHO (2013c) recommendations for clinicians who provide first-line support are in keeping with the human rights-based approach to clinical social work discussed in Chapter 1 of this book. These relate to addressing confidentiality and its limits in situations of mandatory reporting, safeguarding the privacy of survivors, working with the survivor to increase safety, and approaching IPV survivors with a supportive and nonjudgmental attitude, validating their experiences and reinforcing that IPV is never acceptable. In a meta-analysis of qualitative studies of women IPV survivors' experiences with healthcare providers, women who did not feel pressured to pursue charges, leave the perpetrator, reveal information, or make therapeutic progress at a faster pace than they felt ready for reported more positive experiences (Feder, Hutson, Ramsay, & Taket, 2006).

## *Members of Multisystem Coordinated Teams*

Interdisciplinary comprehensive and coordinated care for survivors of IPV is strongly recommended by the WHO (2013c) and is in keeping with a rights-based approach. This could be provided either in healthcare settings or comprehensive service centers that address the casework, psychological, health, and legal issues relevant to survivors. Clinical social workers can play important roles on these teams. Responses should be coordinated across system, community, and individual levels, have a lifespan approach, and involve prevention as well as assessment and treatment for those subjected to IPV and the perpetrators. A social work response that spans micro, mezzo, and macro practice is needed to address IPV (similar to what is needed with torture and human trafficking as seen in Chapters 2 and 3 in this book).

## *Advocacy and Support Roles for Social Workers*

Clinicians working with this population should not feel constrained to only work individually or in groups with survivors of IPV. The WHO guidelines (2013c) note evidence for support and empowerment services as well as advocacy. When the IPV is occurring in a context where violence within intimate partnerships is normalized and condoned and perpetrators act in an atmosphere of impunity such as in Turkey, it is not enough to focus entirely at the micro level (Amnesty International, 2004; Freedom House, 2014). By ratifying the Optional Protocol to the Women's Convention, Turkey has authorized the CEDAW Committee to consider individual and group complaints for individual and structural redress for violations of their rights under the Convention. Rights-based clinical social workers can become educated about the complaint mechanisms of UN Treaty Bodies available to those who are subjected to IPV and other human rights violations. They can connect those targeted by IPV with specialized advocates or attorneys to assist them in filing complaints (Prasad, 2014) and, as appropriate, provide psychosocial evidence of their abuse. Complaint mechanisms have been used successfully to hold states accountable for protecting survivors of severe IPV.

## *Training for Police and Others in the Criminal Justice System*

Improved training for those within the criminal justice system is recommended (Black et al., 2011). This is vital to the effort to combat impunity for perpetrators. Enhanced and strengthened data, and monitoring and evaluation systems are also required. Clinical social workers can play several important roles in response to the problem of police misconduct and a "culture" of lack of responsiveness or understanding toward survivors who report IPV. Social workers can collaborate with survivors of IPV to conduct training for law enforcement and serve as evaluators and consultants to guide effective changes in the system.

Social workers are well equipped to participate in comprehensive training (or retraining) for law enforcement and other personnel to prevent discrimination and other rights violations against survivors. Training should emphasize that everyone has the right to have equal access to law enforcement intervention, protective orders, shelters, and other services. Social workers can advocate for the inclusion of a diverse array of IPV survivors in all prevention efforts such as homicide and lethality assessments and community response models such as the one utilized by the Family Justice Center in Boston (NCAVP, 2013). In addition, documentation of the psychosocial evidence of police abuse by clinical social workers working closely with survivors may be valuable for use in disciplinary hearings and civil and criminal lawsuits.

## *Core Principles of a Rights-Based Approach Applied*

Rights-based clinical social workers must be trauma-informed and approach their work with cultural humility as discussed in depth in Chapter 1. These domains are foundational to working with survivors of IPV given the multifaceted contextual factors that may contribute to or complicate the healing of these survivors. These factors include, in part: prior traumas and violations of human rights, sociocultural factors, socioeconomic status, the presence or lack of a positive support system, the role of substances, and the history of marginalization and oppression.

Clinical social workers and others working with those who have (or may have) experienced IPV must have expertise about the experiences of IPV as well as expertise regarding and experience in providing trauma-informed and trauma-specific treatment of common mental health conditions associated with IPV, such as depression and posttraumatic stress disorder (PTSD). This is vital given the risk of unintended harm to the survivor from intervention (WHO, 2013a). As is true in working with any person, care must be taken to avoid medicalizing or adopting too narrow of a lens regarding what the consequences and appropriate steps may be for any survivor. For example, it should not be assumed that the survivor necessarily wants to leave the relationship with the person who perpetrated IPV or that this is a viable option in the person's cultural context (Blagg, 2002). While there is a bias in some societies, including the United States, to remove the perpetrator of IPV from the home or to separate the perpetrator or victim, this is not the preferred course of action for some survivors and in other societies. Some persons who experience IPV prefer, for cultural and/or other reasons, to stay with their partner and seek ways to reduce harm and keep the family or relationship together. This is the case, for example, for some of those who participate in restorative justice programs that will be discussed later in this chapter.

A rights-based practitioner would approach their work with cultural humility and take the time to fully understand the experience from the person's point of view. He or she would ensure that the person has full control over selecting if they want treatment, and if so, what treatment or interventions they want and from whom. As discussed in depth in Chapter 1 of this book, this must be done with true informed consent. Rights-based clinical social workers must practice from a standpoint of cultural humility, recognizing that culture affects the way that survivors define and experience IPV and its effects, the types of stressors they experience, the decisions they make, their styles of coping and sources of support, how they respond to offers of assistance, how they present in treatment, and what services they may or may not deem to be welcomed or healing (Akinsulure-Smith, Chu, Keatley, & Rasmussen, 2013; Office for Victims of Crime, 2004; Warshaw & Brashler, 2009). Not only is this good practice, it is a must in order to further the human rights of survivors and ensure that they do not have services imposed on them that they do not want or were normed on other very different populations. The approach must be individually tailored, keeping in mind that what is appropriate may be a communal approach (perhaps including working with the couple, extended family, and/or others in the community) rather than one that works solely with the individual survivor. Promising outreach, advocacy, and intervention efforts being implemented throughout Indian country developed by and for various Indian tribes affected by IPV show examples of culturally responsive IPV services (Office for Victims of Crime, 2004). Treatment protocols that are developed in collaboration with advocates and survivors of IPV are supportive of a rights-based approach to practice, and give priority to ensuring that their voices are heard and right to self-determination is safeguarded.

Ultimately, promoting survivor self-determination and agency is vital to a rights-based approach to clinical social work with survivors of IPV. For some survivors, this may come in the form of individual agency. For others, collective action or agency may be most therapeutic and consonant with the expression of their rights, such as participating in the collaborative campaign that resulted in the recent successful reauthorization of VAWA (Violence Against Women Reauthorization Act of 2013, 2013). Another example of collective agency is the 2002 Human Rights Tribunal on Domestic Violence and Child Custody, symbolically and strategically held at the Massachusetts State House on Mother's Day (Morgaine, 2011; Ford Foundation, 2004). Female survivors of DV documented the severe human rights violations against women and the Massachusetts family court's failure to protect women and their children from battering in the context of child custody matters (Ford Foundation, 2004).

## *Rights-Based Recommendations and Challenges for Clinical Social Work Interventions*

### *Routine Screening: Controversy and Associated Challenges*

Routine clinical screening for IPV of all teens and adults seeking clinical social work services would lead to more identification of individuals who have experienced this kind of interpersonal violence. Not all relevant organizations and task forces, however, take the same stand on routine screening and many confine their focus to the screening of women (Moyer, 2013). The WHO does not recommend that clinicians screen all women in health care settings for IPV (Feder, Wathen, & MacMillan, 2013) given the lack of sufficient supporting evidence for the benefits (Taft et al., 2013) as well as a lack of evidence to suggest that such screening improves health outcomes or results in a lower incidence of IPV (Klevens et al., 2012; MacMillan et al., 2009). The WHO does advocate for clinicians to routinely assess those women who present to them with injuries, risk factors, or symptoms (e.g., depression) that suggest the possibility of IPV (Feder et al., 2013; WHO, 2013c). Clinical social workers are among these clinicians and, as they may spend more time with IPV survivors than physicians or other clinicians, they may be the first to detect IPV. It is imperative that clinical social workers extend screening services to heterosexual men and LGBTQ individuals as well. Focusing efforts solely on heterosexual women and girls would be violating the rights of others to equal protection. One of the challenges with screening for IPV is that there may be few appropriate or accessible services in the community to serve the survivors identified if the state has not adequately funded services. This can be an ethical and a human rights problem.

### *Practice Guided by the Evidence Base*

Clinical social workers who work with men and women who have experienced IPV should be guided by the evidence base. They can also play a valuable role in contributing to research that informs practice. The level of current research evidence regarding the responses to care provided for women who have experienced IPV is deemed to be low to moderate (Feder et al., 2013). In comparison, there is nearly non-existent research worldwide on men's and boys' experience of and treatment for IPV. Cognitive behavioral therapy (CBT) and its variants (e.g., trauma-focused CBT), however, are among the most commonly endorsed evidence-based treatments for survivors of a wide variety of traumas. It is not surprising, therefore, that the WHO recommends CBT for the treatment of women with PTSD from past IPV. The WHO guidelines emphasize, however, that CBT is not recommended in situations where the IPV is ongoing (WHO, 2013b). Rights-based clinical social workers are cautioned that CBT may not always be appropriate or the most effective intervention for all those who have experienced IPV or other traumas. When selecting a trauma-specific or other intervention it is imperative that clinicians examine whom the intervention was normed on and whether it is appropriate for the given person (i.e., depending on the person's individual clinical picture, whether the person is a survivor of complex trauma, and whether the intervention was validated for use with individuals from the person's cultural background). One of the challenges that can complicate safety and treatment options for some survivors of IPV is that they may experience ongoing stalking or other forms of abuse (Warshaw, Sullivan, & Rivera, 2013). A systematic review of trauma-focused treatments developed or modified for use with survivors of IPV found that CBT, including versions modified for use with IPV survivors such as cognitive trauma therapy for battered women (CTT-BW) (e.g., Kubany, Hill, & Owens, 2003; Kubany et al., 2004), and an integrative intervention showed promise (Warshaw, Sullivan, & Rivera, 2013). The authors concluded that more research is needed to determine which treatments are more effective for which survivors, including for those from particular cultural populations and those who have experienced more than one kind of trauma.

Some of the other approaches that have been effectively used with diverse survivors of complex trauma including IPV include, in part: the self-trauma model (Briere, 2002), narrative exposure therapy (NET) (Schauer, Neuner, & Elbert, 2011), and various group modalities (Sax, 2012). Group may be the best modality of treatment for survivors from collectivistic cultures, aligned with a culturally appropriate way of seeking support (Akinsulure-Smith, 2012). The treatment of male and female IPV perpetrators is also often conducted in groups (Bowen, 2011; Dutton & Sonkin, 2013; Meichenbaum, n.d.). In the words of one woman participant in a rights-based support group for battered women that also engaged in activism to further the cause of similarly situated women:

> Just to have someone believe my story, literally saved my life. Because it was framed as a human rights issue, I felt less isolated. I was part of a larger group. If I couldn't get custody of my kids, at least I can be part of a process that can help other women (Ford Foundation, 2004, p. 63).
>
> —Dawn Faucher, support group member, Battered Mothers' Testimony Project

Treatment models to address the impact of complex trauma (defined in Chapter 1) typically are empowering and emphasize establishing emotional and physical safety before in-depth trauma work can begin (Briere, 2002).

## *Safety—No Guarantees (the Case of Castle Rock vs. Gonzales)*

A rights-based practitioner must be aware of and attentive to the risks to the survivor of disclosing the IPV (WHO, 2013a). There remains a problem of impunity for some perpetrators of IPV. In other instances, a perpetrator may be arrested and locked up temporarily. He or she may become enraged and retaliate against the survivor who discloses the IPV, particularly if the authorities take action against him or her.

It is essential that practitioners never make false promises or guarantees of safety, including if the survivor decides to take out a restraining order against their perpetrator. There are many reports of continued incidents of IPV and even murder occurring despite having a restraining order in place. The US Supreme Court case of *Castle Rock vs. Gonzales*, 545 U.S. 748 (2005) made this abundantly clear (Siegel, 2012). The Court ruled, 7–2, that the town and police department of Castle Rock, Colorado could not be sued for failure to enforce a restraining order under 42 U.S.C. § 1983. In the absence of enforcement of the restraining order, Jessica Lenahan's estranged husband murdered their three minor children, Rebecca, Katheryn, and Leslie Gonzales. This ruling led to an outcry from human, women's, and civil rights activists and organizations and legal scholars and practitioners in the United States. The National Organization for Women (NOW), for example, denounced the Supreme Court's decision, stressing that it made restraining orders less effective and, "gives law enforcement a green light to ignore restraining orders" (Kline, 2005). The denigration of the experiences and lives of survivors of IPV was underscored by these events, as manifested when the law enforcement officer did not believe Lenahan's report that her children were in danger and when the US Supreme Court failed to hold the authorities accountable (Park, 2013). By emphasizing the inherent dignity of all human beings, a human rights framework resists such treatment of survivors (Park, 2013).

An important human rights victory came in 2011 when the Inter-American Commission on Human Rights (IACHR) found that the United States (a member of the IACHR) violated its obligation to provide equal protection before the law and not discriminate by not acting with due diligence to protect Jessica Lenahan (Gonzales) and her three daughters. The IACHR also found that the United States' failure to, "adequately organize its state structure to protect [the Gonzales girls] from DV not only was discriminatory, but also constituted a violation of their right to life under Article 1" of the American Declaration (IACHR, 2011, p. 44). The IACHR held that the United States had failed to uphold international human rights standards, such as that regarding due diligence (Siegel, 2012). Lenahan, represented by the ACLU, made history as the Commission's ruling was the first against the United States in a case brought by a survivor of IPV (Park, 2013).

There have been some positive developments following this landmark ruling. The Department of Justice (DOJ) and police departments in Puerto Rico, Missoula, and New Orleans have worked together to improve police practices and policies and police officers in Colorado have been training on how to respond to IPV (Park, 2013). Miami-Dade County, Cincinnati, and Baltimore adopted ordinances stating that it was a human right not to be subjected to IPV (Park, 2013), lending support to anti-violence initiatives in their localities and elsewhere throughout the United States.

The 2013 reauthorization of the VAWA by Congress (and its signature into law by the president) was another victory, providing more inclusive protection, including for LGBTQ individuals, Native Americans, and undocumented immigrants subjected to IPV (Violence Against Women Reauthorization Act of 2013, 2013). For example, the power of tribal courts was expanded to allow for the prosecution of non-Native

Americans accused of sexual and violent gender-based crimes. Despite these positive developments, clinical social workers are urged to be cautious when exploring intervention and safety options with IPV survivors given that they cannot guarantee the survivor's safety and the potentially severe consequences.

## *Holding Perpetrators Accountable*

Much discussion and debate has been devoted in recent decades to what the response should be to IPV, including the legal response (Morgaine, 2011). Holding the perpetrator(s) accountable is generally deemed to be a key component, yet it is also recognized that a number of factors may contribute to the reluctance of some survivors to report IPV including: cultural influences, fear of retaliation from the perpetrator(s), fear that laws protecting them from the perpetrator(s) may not be consistently or adequately enforced making the situation even more dangerous, embarrassment, shame, and concern that they may not receive needed support from law enforcement or others (Black, et al. 2011).

Dominant legal responses in the United States to IPV have been criticized on numerous grounds, including the disproportionate negative impact on males and women of color (Bohmer, Brandt, Bronson, & Hartnett, 2002; Morgaine, 2011; Presser & Gaarder, 2000). Morgaine, (2011) makes a compelling argument that, when the criminal justice system becomes involved in cases of IPV, immigrant communities and communities of color have a more complex situation than some other communities. She discusses the responsibility some in the community may feel about contributing to further community disintegration if they report the IPV. In some of these situations, the person subjected to IPV may avoid reporting due to fear that they or the person they report may be deported as a result. In addition, rather than protecting victims, the arrest and prosecution of their perpetrators may disempower victims and put them in more danger while failing to decrease the incidence of IPV or address the fundamental causes of IPV. Clinical social workers can explore the complexity and intersectionality of these concerns with those subjected to IPV and support survivors in coming to terms with how they wish to proceed.

The WHO's (2013a) recommendation against mandatory reporting by clinicians to the police in cases of IPV when the victim is a competent adult as well as the issue of mandatory arrest and prosecution, and batterers' programs are controversial (UN Special Rapporteur on Violence Against Women, 2011). The laws in his or her jurisdiction bind each social work clinician. Some countries and US states mandate that health care providers (and sometimes social workers) report IPV to law enforcement. If the victim is a child, child abuse laws are relevant. The clinical social worker should make sure that the person targeted by IPV knows his or her rights and support them in making a report to the authorities (or offer to report on their behalf) if they so wish. The WHO guidelines support this approach, noting the importance of preserving or supporting the victim's self-determined decision making and autonomy (WHO, 2013b).

## Working with Perpetrators

As Gilligan (1996, 2001) and others who have devoted their considerable expertise to the treatment of violent offenders model for us (Glendon Association, 2011), clinicians can (and should from a human rights perspective) treat these individuals with dignity, recognize their humanity, and refrain from condemning a whole person for one or more acts of violence. Perpetrators of IPV and other violent offences also have rights as human beings even though they have violated the rights of others. They have potential for rehabilitation. Some can experience transformation and even contribute to the effort to reduce violence in their communities.

Clinical social workers, depending on their area of practice, may encounter or choose to work with perpetrators of intimate partner violence or other forms of human-perpetrated violence. This topic is less commonly covered and social work graduate students and seasoned practitioners are not often prepared to work with those who perpetrate IPV. Sometimes, as in the case of Claire above, social workers discover in the course of working with a person over time that they have engaged in one or more acts of harming another. Considerable research indicates that some individuals who have engaged in violence have experienced significant prior trauma themselves, such as child abuse, although violence exposure as a child does not predetermine violent behavior later in life (Gil-Gonzalez, Vives-Cases, Ruiz, Carrasco-Portino, & Alvarez-Dardet, 2008; Gilligan, 1996, 2001; Watt & Scrandis, 2013). Male participants in the Adverse Childhood Experiences Study were increasingly at risk for engaging in IPV the greater the number of traumas they had been exposed to as children. Those who had been exposed to childhood physical abuse, childhood sexual abuse, and growing up with a mother who was battered were 3.8 times more likely to perpetrate IPV as adults compared to those who had not experienced all three of these types of violence in childhood (Whitfield, Anda, Dube, & Felitti, 2003).

As is true in work with any person, it is important to conduct a holistic assessment of perpetrators, rather than a narrower one focused solely on their act(s) of perpetration. The assessment should include, among other things, exploration of traumas they may have experienced earlier in life. Clinical social workers must attend to the ethical and other complexities presented from a rights-based framework including with those perpetrators who may have been mandated to receive services (Barksy, 2010; Rooney, 2009). It is essential at the outset of clinical work to explicitly and clearly identify all possible exceptions to confidentiality. This includes situations where mandated reporting exists such as with child abuse, and if the social worker determines that there may be an imminent risk to the person or others (Cronholm, 2006). In addition, if the social worker is required to provide information or reports to a probation officer, judge, or another authority as a condition of the mandated treatment, or may be called to testify in a legal proceeding, he or she must disclose this at the outset (Rooney, 2009).

Social workers working with this population are at risk for experiencing difficult dilemmas and situations that challenge their ability to maintain a professional and ethical stance toward those they work with. A human rights-based approach facilitates effective and ethical practice in this domain by reminding the social worker that all persons have fundamental rights by virtue of being human. Ortega and Faller (2011) present a case of a social worker who, in using cultural humility in her work with a father ("Jung") accused of perpetrating IPV and physical and sexual child abuse, employs reflective listening to search for the meaning of the experience from the father's perspective. By reserving judgment, not making assumptions and coming to a premature conclusion, and opening herself to listening and hearing the father's perspective, the father shared important contextual and cultural information that facilitated the social worker's ability to engage with and work with the family.

Good supervision is essential for practitioners who work with IPV survivors and/or perpetrators given the host of challenging issues that may come up for beginning (and even experienced) clinical social workers. For example, those who engage in women-defined advocacy (Davies & Lyon, 1998) work to build on the woman survivor's perspective and strengths and support her self-determination even if they do not think that her decision will lead to a positive or healthy outcome. A clinician or advocate in that situation will discuss his or her concerns with the survivor, offering alternatives to consider, but will ultimately respect the survivor to make her own decision and continue to provide support. Social workers in this difficult position are at risk for the blurring of boundaries with those they serve and letting their personal opinions or biases influence their interactions with a survivor (see Chapter 5 regarding self-awareness and a rights-based use of self). Social workers, keenly aware that they can never ensure the safety of a survivor or his or her children, may experience anticipatory fear for the survivor if he or she chooses to remain with or return to their batterer. It is vital for social workers to remember that leaving one's spouse may not be considered a culturally or personally viable option for some (Blagg, 2002). Effective supervision and training can facilitate the social worker in being able to put aside their own biases and opinions and engage with cultural humility to support the rights of the survivor. The social worker's focus then becomes enhancing safety in the context of each person's situation and choices. Supporting the survivor's right to make his or her own choices and decisions also works to counteract part of the dynamics of the IPV, namely that of being controlled or disempowered by the perpetrator, even to the extent sometimes of not being allowed or feeling able to express his or her own desires or opinions.

Working with those who batter may leave social workers with intense feelings including of anger, fear, and/or helplessness. Supervision can help a social worker be able to anticipate and develop strategies to maintain his or her professional role, demeanor, and skills. It is important, although at times difficult, to not judge those they work with, even if the person has perpetrated violence on another. Not judging does not mean that the social worker should condone the person's behavior. Regardless of what the person has done, a professional social worker (rights-based or not) must cultivate within themselves and demonstrate respect for the person as a human being, recognizing their dignity and humanity and working to safeguard their rights, consonant with Article 10 of the ICCPR (UN General Assembly, 1966).

## *Restorative Justice*

Some clinical social workers and other practitioners work with perpetrators and survivors of IPV in the same group. This is typically true, for example, for those who apply a restorative justice approach (Frederick & Lizdas, 2003; Mills, 2008). Restorative justice advocates recognize the necessity to hold perpetrators accountable yet hold that this, on its own, may not be enough to promote healing and justice for survivors. Restorative justice approaches include a diverse array of programs.

> In general, restorative justice proponents seek a holistic, integrated sense of justice and healing for victims, as well as personal accountability from offenders. For some, the concept of restorative justice extends to the broader communities affected, the idea being that healing and justice are interconnected for everyone. (Witness Justice, 2014)

There is a rich tradition of the use of restorative justice practices around the world (PFI Centre for Justice and Reconciliation, 2014). Examples from Africa include the South African Truth and Reconciliation Commission and the use of the *gacaca* community justice mechanism (a modified version of a traditional form of communal justice) following the Genocide in Rwanda[7] (Powers, 2011). National reconciliation initiatives that sought to create cultures of peace in parts of Latin America following civil war are another example. Traditional processes to resolve conflict and promote restorative justice are being used in North America, the Caribbean, and the Middle East. Peacemaking and Healing Circles is an example of a restorative justice approach to IPV that involves everyone who is part of the violence, engaging the whole family system in treatment (Mills, 2008). These approaches are designed for those who want to find a way to stop the IPV and stay in the relationship.

Restorative justice approaches to IPV are controversial, with prominent supporters and detractors (Edwards & Sharpe, 2004). As mentioned earlier, it is important to recognize that not all who are subjected to IPV want to leave the relationship or even conceptualize that as a possibility. Culture and personal values can shape one's perception of viable choices. As Blagg (2002) elaborates:

> For many Indigenous women, choosing to leave 'family'—with all its complexly embedded ties of responsibility and obligation, connection with country and culture—is not an option. The capacity to exit family relationships (indeed, the very concept of 'choice' in such matters)—to repackage and reconstitute one's identity as an autonomous individual in some new location—is a profoundly eurocentric construction. (p. 198)

For some survivors, IPV may well be occurring within a larger system of extended family violence made more complex by a legacy of systemic injustice rather than being contained within a single relationship (Blagg, 2002; Edwards & Sharpe, 2004).

---

[7] The use of the *gacaca* system to try those accused of genocide in Rwanda received mixed reviews. From a human rights and safety perspective, critics of the *gacacas* decried the intimidation and/or murder of some who testified (or were scheduled to testify) against alleged perpetrators (Brounéus 2008, 2010; Powers, 2011; Waldorf, 2006).

Further, the IPV may be an ongoing phenomenon rather than an isolated event, resulting in further marginalization of those targeted (Coker, 1999; Edwards & Sharpe, 2004). Power imbalances between survivor and perpetrator have sometimes been perpetuated in restorative justice arenas that are designed to be egalitarian, leaving some victims such as Aboriginal women experiencing dual discrimination (Goel, 2000). Aboriginal women and others who see members of their community disproportionately imprisoned and otherwise affected by the criminal justice system may not trust that system or welfare agencies to be part of the solution and may be perceived as betraying their family and community if they report IPV (Blagg, 2002). Safety concerns have also been raised by some in relation to restorative justice efforts in cases of IPV, particularly related to the risk for further violence from angry or defensive perpetrators after a dialogue (Edwards & Sharpe, 2004). As this discussion demonstrates, the experience of IPV is multifaceted and complex, and rights-based clinical social workers must carefully assess the situation and engage survivors in the process of determining the best course forward to promote healing while safeguarding the rights of those involved.

## Conclusion

This chapter has explored the definition of IPV and contextual factors associated with this problem from a human rights-based perspective. Relevant human rights mechanisms and tools were described and selected core principles and clinical considerations for rights-based clinical social workers working with IPV survivors and perpetrators were examined. A variety of models of intervention were described and discussed, including restorative justice approaches. Rights-based practitioners who work with survivors of IPV should be vigilant in monitoring that the people they work with are afforded equal access to protection and services and in advocating for non-gendered and non-heterosexist implementation of VAWA and other legislation.

There are many possible benefits of employing a human rights-based approach to IPV. Morgaine's (2011) research with diverse experts from IPV advocacy groups found that a human rights approach could strengthen the mainstream IPV movement in the United States—a movement that she argues has long grappled with issues of oppression, power, and privilege, especially in relation to racism. Specifically, Morgaine (2011) recommends making the IPV movement more holistic (addressing the complexity and intersectionality of concerns such as the survivor's economic, social, and cultural rights rather than focusing narrowly only on the immediate impact of the violence), more engaging of the community, and with expanded coalition building (including organizing across issues and engaging men as allies). Engaging with the community includes, in part, addressing human rights concerns *from the bottom up* (Morgaine, 2009) in a grassroots fashion.

Given the widespread prevalence of the problem of IPV, perhaps it is necessary for rights-based clinical social workers to think outside of the box in their approach to preventing and combating the problem of IPV. Rather than focusing all of their energies on individual, group and family therapy, there is much to be learned from creative community-based prevention strategies, and a role to play for clinical social workers in these efforts. One promising example is the projects in central Asia and eastern Europe supported by the United Nations Population Fund (UNFPA) that have engaged men in preventing GBV (UNFPA, 2009). These projects have achieved success in regions of the world with high rates of IPV and other forms of GBV affecting one in three women at some point in her life. Norms and attitudes of acceptance toward GBV and impunity for the perpetrators have contributed to its prevalence in these regions. Examples of such projects include work among Turkish police to change officers' perception of IPV and a coordinated institutional level response in Romania that aims at curbing IPV and serving survivors. In some jurisdictions, law enforcement has teamed up with battered women's advocates to leverage their expertise to inform police response to IPV (Sadusky, 2004). Clinical social workers can play active roles in training and supportive roles in advocacy and policy campaigns based on their clinical knowledge and experience working with survivors (and in some cases perpetrators).

Clinical social workers that work with survivors or perpetrators of IPV may be at risk for vicarious traumatization. These reactions may be further complicated when the social worker learns that the person he or she is providing therapy to who was victimized by IPV or other violence has also perpetrated violence on others, such as in the case of Claire. Some social workers may find it difficult or choose not to work with perpetrators, or not to work conjointly with perpetrators and victims of IPV or from a restorative justice perspective. A rights base is invaluable in sorting through these potential challenges. Effective and healthy clinical social workers are needed who are able to work as part of interdisciplinary teams to address the widespread problem of IPV, intervening in both micro and macro domains. There is an important role for clinical social workers in providing clinical support to those who may experience vicarious trauma by engaging in IPV work. The impact of engagement in rights-based clinical social work on the self and strategies to address that is a topic covered in the next chapter.

## Suggested Activities/Resources

*Case Discussion* Have students read the following case vignette and engage in discussion in small groups, reflecting on the discussion questions provided.

> Maria, 27, has sought therapy with you at the urging of her best friend Ann. Ever since Maria and James married last year, their long-term relationship has deteriorated. Maria reports that recently James has been calling her derogatory names, including in public, and has started to force her to have sex with him in ways and at times that she does not want. He has slapped her in the face when she refused to have sex and threatened to humiliate her at work if she did not do what he ordered. In the past 6 months, James has stayed out very late several times a week without telling Maria what he is doing and yells at her if she asks. Maria recounts that before they got married, James was always quite charming and kind to her.

Upon questioning, Maria admits that at times before the marriage James could be a little jealous and possessive of her but that she was flattered by this, viewing it as evidence of his deep love for her. When Maria became pregnant 6 months ago, James refused to believe that it was his child, despite Maria's insisting that she had not been with any other man. James sent repeated text messages to Maria while she was at work calling her a "whore" and a "traitor" and Maria discovered that he was following her on multiple occasions when she went out to do errands. Maria reported that James forced her to have an abortion despite her pleading with him to let her keep the baby because abortion was against her religious beliefs. Maria grieved the loss of her unborn baby and tried to separate from James after he beat her badly and broke her arm one night when she told him of her grief. On that occasion, Maria went to her friend Ann's house. James banged on the front door of Ann's house in the middle of the night, drunk and demanding that Maria come home or she would regret it. Maria did return home with James, fearful of what he might do. James has since threatened to kill himself if Maria ever tries to leave him again. Maria has started to have panic attacks and cannot sleep well at night. She begins to sob in session with you and asks, "What should I do?"

Discussion Questions: The Case of Maria

1. What are some of the key risk and human rights issues in Maria's case?
2. What additional information would you want about Maria and her situation to guide you in your work with her?
3. Where would you begin with Maria and why?
4. How do the core principles of a rights-based approach to clinical social work presented in this chapter help us to understand Maria's case from a rights-based perspective?
5. How would you work with Maria from a rights-based perspective? In what way(s) might this differ from a more traditional needs-based social work approach?
6. What human rights instrument(s) may be particularly relevant to your work with Maria? Discuss which principles apply and how.
7. In what way, if at all, might the use of CEDAW shape your perspective and guide your work with Maria?

## *Additional Classroom Discussion Activities or Assignments*

- Imagine that you have been hired as a consultant to an agency that provides clinical social work services to those convicted of IPV. Many of those served by the agency are there on an involuntary basis. Drawing on the principles of a rights-based approach to clinical practice and on relevant human rights documents and tools, what guidance would you give to the clinical team members at this agency?
- How would you design an intervention or prevention campaign for your community related to IPV, keeping in mind the rights-based practice principles and models presented in this chapter?
- Break into groups of two students and role-play the case of Claire presented at the beginning of this chapter. One student plays the role of Claire and the other, the clinical social worker. As the role-play begins, Claire has just pronounced to her social worker (as per the end of the opening vignette), "*I never wanted to grow up*

*to be like my dad*." After you role-play the social worker's efforts to explore and understand the situation more deeply, debrief in your group (and later with the class as a whole). Explore any ethical issues or dilemmas that arose and the skills that a clinical social worker could use to navigate these challenges in keeping with a rights-based approach.

## *Video Suggestions for Class Instruction (Selected)*

- ***Domestic Violence & Human Rights: Lenahan v. USA*** (7:57 min. YouTube video): A video of Jessica Lenahan speaking about the DV she experienced at the hands of her husband who ended up murdering their three children. She was the first survivor of IPV to sue the US government before an international human rights tribunal. Her case is discussed in this chapter. The IACHR found that the United States violated the human rights of Jessica and her children and failed its legal obligation to protect girls and women from DV. To view the video: https://www.aclu.org/womens-rights/domestic-violence-human-rights-lenahan-v-usa
- ***Strong at the Broken Places: Turning Trauma into Recovery*** (38 min. video from Cambridge Documentary Films). This short documentary tells the stories of four survivors of diverse types of trauma and loss who share their journeys to recovery and the factors that contributed to their resilience. Class discussion can focus on the case of Marcia Gordon, a woman who experienced multiple types of family violence since she was a child, who turned her life around and is resilient. The video can be ordered and the discussion guide downloaded at: http://www.cambridgedocumentaryfilms.org/filmsPages/strong.html
- **Two videos depicting Dr. James Gilligan's work with perpetrators of violence: Hidden Victims of Domestic Violence** (*Voices of Violence* video of a DV perpetrator group (http://www.psychotherapy.net/video/therapeutic-treatment-violence) and *Resolve to Stop the Violence Program* (http://www.resolvetostoptheviolencesf.org/news/)

## *Resources (Selected)*

- Anti-Violence Project (includes reports and resources for LGBTQ and HIV-infected individuals): http://avp.org/resources/avp-resources/273
- Stop Violence Against Women: A project of the Advocates for Human Rights: http://www.stopvaw.org/Stop_Violence_Against_Women
- Stop Abusive and Violent Environments (SAVE): Following the reauthorization of VAWA in 2013, SAVE has established the *Inclusive-VAWA Resource Center at* http://www.saveservices.org/inclusive-vawa/resources/

- National Online Resource Center on Violence Against Women: http://www.gov/vawnet.org/research/MeetingSurvivorsNeeds/
- Special Collection (3 parts): Trauma-Informed Domestic Violence Services: Understanding the Framework and Approach: http://www.vawnet.org/special-collections/DVTraumaInformed-Overview.php
- MINCAVA Electronic Clearinghouse: http://www.mincava.umn.edu/categories/889
- CDC's Injury Prevention and Control, Intimate Partner Violence: http://www.cdc.violenceprevention/intimatepartnerviolence/index.html

## References


Akinsulure-Smith, A. M. (2012). Using group work to rebuild family and community ties among displaced African men. *Journal for Specialists in Group Work, 37*(2), 95–112.

Akinsulure-Smith, A. M., Chu, T., Keatley, E., & Rasmussen, A. (2013). Intimate Partner Violence among West African Immigrants. *Journal of Aggression, Maltreatment & Trauma, 22*(1), 109–129.

American Civil Liberties Union. (2013, August 7). Jessica Gonzales v. U.S.A. Retrieved from http://www.aclu.org/womensrights/violence/gonzalesvusa.html. Accessed 18 Feb 2014.

Amnesty International. (2004, June 2). Turkey: Women confronting family violence. AI Index: EUR 44/023/2004 (Public). Media Briefing. News Service No: 131. Retrieved from http://webcache.googleusercontent.com/search?q=cache:bqbfTb6y8zoJ:www.amnesty.org/en/library/asset/EUR44/022/2004/en/d4ad9023-fab2-11dd-b6c4-73b1aa157d32/eur440222004en.pdf+&cd=3&hl=en&ct=clnk&gl=us&client=firefox-a.

Amnesty International. (2005). Women' human rights. Domestic violence as torture. Retrieved from http://www.amnestyusa.org/women/pdf/domestic_violence_as_torture.pdf.

Appel, A. E., & Holde, G. W. (1998). The co-occurrence of spouse and physical child abuse: A review and appraisal. *Journal of Family Psychology, 12*(4), 578–599.

Anderson, L. (2011, November 23). UN women's Bachelet outlines policies to end violence against women. *Thomson Reuters Foundation*. Retrieved from http://webcache.googleusercontent.com/search?q=cache:ZtJa6_YNqj0J:www.trust.org/item/20111123174500-mt7sv?view%3Dprint-+&cd=3&hl=en&ct=clnk&gl=us&client=firefox-a.

Barksy, A. (2010). *Ethics and values in social work: An integrated approach for a comprehensive curriculum*. New York, NY: Oxford University Press.

Beasely, M. E., & Thomas, D. Q. (1994). Domestic violence as a human rights issue. In M. A. Fineman & R. Mykitiuk (Eds.), *The public nature of private violence: The discovery of domestic abuse* (pp. 323–346). New York, NY: Routledge.

Black, M. C., Basile, K. C., Breiding, M. J., Smith, S. G., Walters, M. L., Merrick, M. T., & Stevens, M. R. (2011). *The National Intimate Partner and Sexual Violence Survey (NISVS): 2010 summary report*. Atlanta, GA: National Center for Injury Prevention and Control, Centers for Disease Control and Prevention.

Blagg, H. (2002). Restorative justice and aboriginal family violence: Opening a space for healing. In H. Strang & J. Braithwaite (Eds.), *Restorative justice and family violence* (pp. 191–205). Cambridge, MA: Cambridge University Press.

Bohmer, C., Brandt, J., Bronson, D., & Hartnett, H. (2002). Domestic violence law reforms: Reactions from the trenches. *Journal of Sociology and Social Welfare, 29*(3), 71–87.

Bookey, B. (2013). Domestic violence as a basis for asylum: An analysis of 206 case outcomes in the United States from 1994 to 2012. *Hastings Women's Law Journal, 24,* 107–148.

Bowen, E. L. (2011). Domestic violence treatment for abusive women: A treatment manual. Retrieved from http://www.eblib.com.

Bragg, H. L. (2003). *Child protection in families experiencing domestic violence*. Washington, DC: Office on Child Abuse and Neglect, Children's Bureau.

Briere, J. (2002). Treating adult survivors of severe childhood abuse and neglect: Further development of an integrative model. In J. E. B. Myers, L. Berliner, J. Briere, C. T. Hendrix, T. Reid, & C. Jenny (Eds.), *The APSAC handbook on child maltreatment* (2nd ed., pp. 175–202). Newbury Park, CA: Sage.

Brounéus, K. (2008). Truth telling as talking cure? Insecurity and retraumatization in the Rwandan gacaca courts. *Security Dialogue, 39*(1), 55–76.

Brounéus, K. (2010). The trauma of truth telling: Effects of witnessing in the Rwandan gacaca courts on psychological health. *Journal of Conflict Resolution, 54*(3), 408–437. doi:10.1177/0022002709360322.

Bunch, C. (1990). Women's rights as human rights: Toward a re-vision of human rights. *Human Rights Quarterly, 12*(4), 486–498.

Coker, A. L. (1999). Enhancing autonomy for battered women: Lessons from Navajo Peacemaking. *UCLA Law Review, 47*, 1–111.

Cronholm, P. F. (2006). Intimate partner violence and men's health. *Primary Care Clinics in Office Practice, 33*, 199–209.

Davidson, M. M., & Duke, A. (2009). Same-sex intimate partner violence: Lesbian, gay, and bisexual affirmative outreach and advocacy. *Journal of Aggression, Maltreatment & Trauma, 18*, 795–816.

Davies, J., & Lyon, E. (1998). *Safety planning with battered women*. Thousand Oaks, CA: Sage.

Dutton, D., & Sonkin, D. J. (2013). Intimate violence: Contemporary treatment innovations. Retrieved from http://www.eblib.com.

Edwards, A., & Sharpe, S. (2004). *Restorative justice in the context of domestic violence: A literature review*. Edmonton, Alberta, Canada: Mediation and Restorative Justice Centre. Retrieved from http://mrjc.ca/documents-publications/restorative-justice-domestic-violence/.

Feder, G. S., Hutson, M., Ramsay, J., & Taket, A. R. (2006). Women exposed to intimate partner violence: Expectations and experiences when they encounter health care professionals: A meta-analysis of qualitative studies. *Archives of Internal Medicine, 166*(1), 22–37.

Feder, G., Wathen, C. N., & MacMillan, H. L. (2013). An evidence-based response to intimate partner violence: WHO guidelines. *Journal of the American Medical Association, 310*(5), 479–480.

Ford Foundation. (2004). *Close to home: Case studies of human rights work in the United States*. New York, NY: Author.

Frederick, L. M., & Lizdas, K. C. (2003). *The role of restorative justice in the battered women's movement*. Minneapolis, MN: The Battered Women's Justice Project.

Freedom House. (2014). Turkey: Freedom in the world 2014. Retrieved from http://www.freedomhouse.org/report/freedom-world/2014/turkey-0.

Freedom Network. (2012). Human trafficking and domestic violence. Retrieved from http://freedomnetworkusa.org/wp-content/uploads/2012/05/FN-Factsheet-Human-Trafficking-and-Domestic-Violence-Updated-Sept-2012.pdf.

Gil-Gonzalez, D., Vives-Cases, C., Ruiz, M. T., Carrasco-Portino, M., & Alvarez-Dardet, C. (2008). Childhood experiences of violence in perpetrators as a risk factor of intimate partner violence: A systematic review. *Journal of Public Health, 30*(1), 14–22.

Gilligan, J. (2001). *Preventing violence*. New York, NY: Thames & Hudson.

Gilligan, J. (1996). *Violence: Our deadly epidemic and its causes*. New York, NY: G. P. Putnam.

Glendon Association (Producer). (2011). *Effective treatment of violent individuals. Part two of the voices of violence series* [DVD]. Santa Barbara: The Glendon Association.

Goel, R. (2000). No women at the center: The use of the Canadian sentencing circle in domestic violence cases. *Wisconsin Women's Law Journal, 15*, 293–334.

Hawkins, D., & Humes, M. (2002). Human rights and domestic violence. *Political Science Quarterly, 117*, 231–257.

Inter-American Commission on Human Rights [IACHR]. (2011, July 21). Report No. 80/11 case 12.626. Merits Jessica Lenahan (Gonzales) et al. United States.

Kelley, M. (2013, October 29). Addressing the intersections between domestic violence & human trafficking: FVPSA supports ACF efforts to assist survivors. Retrieved from http://www.acf.hhs.gov/programs/fysb/news/trafficking-fvpsa-supports-acf.

Ki-Moon, B. (2008). Secretary-General says violence against women never acceptable, never excusable, never tolerable, as he launches global campaign on issue. New York, United Nations Department of Public Information, News and Media Division, 2008 (SG/SM/11437WOM/1665). Retrieved from http://www.un.org/News/Press/docs/2008/sgsm11437.doc.htm.

Klevens, J., Kee, R., Trick, W., Garcia, D., Angulo, F. R., Jones, R., & Sadowsk, L. S. (2012). Effect of screening for partner violence on women's quality of life: A randomized controlled trial. *Journal of the American Medical Association, 308*(7), 681–689.

Kline, M. (Summer/Fall 2005). Gonzales ruling endangers women and children. National NOW Times. Retrieved from http://www.now.org/nnt/summerfall- 2005/gonzalesvcastlerock.html.

Krug, E. G., Mercy, J. A., Dahlberg, L. L., & Zwi, A. B. (2002). The world report on violence and health. *Lancet, 360*(9339), 1083–1088.

Kubany, E. S., Hill, E. E., & Owens, J. A. (2003). Cognitive trauma therapy for battered women with PTSD: Preliminary findings. *Journal of Traumatic Stress, 16*(1), 81–91.

Kubany, E. S., Hill, E. E., Owens, J. A., Iannce-Spencer, C., McCaig, M. A., Tremayne, K. J., & Williams, P. L. (2004). Cognitive Trauma Therapy for Battered Women With PTSD (CTT-BW). *Journal of Consulting and Clinical Psychology, 72*(1), 3–18.

Libal, K., & Parekh, S. (2009). Reframing violence against women as a human rights violation: Evan Stark's Coercive Control. *Violence Against Women, 15*(12), 1477–1489.

MacMillan, H. L., Wathen, C. N., Jamieson, E., Boyle, M. H., Shannon, H. S., Ford-Gilboe, M., & McNutt, L. A. (2009). Screening for intimate partner violence in health care settings: A randomized trial. *Journal of the American Medical Association, 302*(5), 493–501.

McDowell, T., Libal, K., & Brown, A. L. (2012). Human rights in the practice of family therapy: Domestic violence, a case in point. *Journal of Feminist Family Therapy, 24*(1), 1–23. doi:10.1080/08952833.2012.629129.

Meichenbaum, D. (n.d.). Family violence: Treatment of perpetrators and victims. Retrieved from http://www.melissainstitute.org/documents/treating_perpetrators.pdf.

Migliaccio, T. A. (2002). Abused husbands: A narrative analysis. *Journal of Family Issues, 23*(1), 26–52.

Migliaccio, T. A. (2001). Marginalizing the battered male. *The Journal of Men's Studies, 9*(2), 1–18.

Mills, L. G. (2008). *Violent partners: A breakthrough plan for ending the cycle of abuse*. New York, NY: Basic Books.

Morgaine, K. (2009). "You can't bite the hand..." Domestic violence and human rights. *Affilia, 24*(1), 31–43.

Morgaine, K. (2011). 'How would that help our work?' The intersection of domestic violence and human rights in the United States. *Violence Against Women, 17*(1), 6–27.

Moyer, V. A. (2013). Screening for intimate partner violence and abuse of elderly and vulnerable adults: U.S. preventive services task force recommendation statement. *Annals of Internal Medicine, 158*(6), 478–486.

Musalo, K. (2010). A short history of gender asylum in the United States: Resistance and ambivalence may very slowly be inching towards recognition of women's claims. *Refugee Survey Quarterly, 29*(2), 46–63.

National Association of Social Workers [NASW]. (1996, revised 1999). Code of Ethics of the National Association of Social Workers. Retrieved from http://www.naswdc.org/pubs/code/code.asp.

National Coalition of Anti-Violence Programs (NCAVP). (2013). *Lesbian, gay, bisexual, transgender, queer, and HIV-affected intimate partner violence in 2012* (2013 release ed.). New York, NY: New York City Gay and Lesbian Anti-Violence Project.

National Task Force to End Sexual and Domestic Violence Against Women. (2006). Frequently asked questions about VAWA and gender. Retrieved from http://www.ncdsv.org/images/FAQ_VAWA%20and%20Gender.pdf.

New Tactics in Human Rights. (n.d.). *Victim services: Promising practices in Indian country*. Washington: Author. (Website. www.newtactics.org http://www.newtactics.org Office for Victims of Crime (2004))

Office for Victims of Crime. (2004). *Victim services: Promising practices in Indian country*. Washington, DC: Author.

Ortega, R. M., & Faller, K. C. (2011). Training child welfare workers from an intersectional cultural humility perspective: A paradigm shift. *Child Welfare, 90*(5), 27–49.

Park, S. (2013, August 13). Advancing the human rights of survivors of domestic and sexual violence in the U.S.: Progress report. [Blog post]. Retrieved from https://www.aclu.org/blog/womens-rights/advancing-human-rights-survivors-domestic-and-sexual-violence-us-progress-report.

PFI Centre for Justice and Reconciliation. (2014). Restorative justice around the world. Retrieved from http://www.restorativejustice.org/university-classroom/02world.

Powers, S. E. (2011, June 23). Rwanda's gacaca courts: Implications for international criminal law and transitional justice. *Insights, 15,* 17.

Prasad, N. (2014). Teaching the use of complaint mechanisms of UN treaty bodies as a tool in international social work practice. In K. R. Libal, S. M. Berthold, R. L. Thomas, & L. M. Healy (Eds.), *Advancing human rights in social work education*. Alexandria, VA: Council on Social Work Education.

Presser, L., & Gaarder, E. (2000). Can restorative justice reduce battering? Some preliminary considerations. *Social Justice, 27,* 175–194.

Public Health Agency of Canada. (2009). Intimate partner abuse against men. Retrieved from http://www.phac-aspc.gc.ca/ncfv-cnivf/publications/mlintima-eng.php.

Rooney, R. (2009). (Ed.). *Strategies for work with involuntary clients* (2nd ed.). New York, NY: Columbia University. Press.

Roth, K. (1994). Domestic violence as an international human rights issue. In R. Cook (Ed.), Human rights of women: National and international perspectives (pp. 326–339). Philadelphia, PA: University of Pennsylvania Press.

Sadusky, J. (2004). Bridging domestic violence intervention and community policing: Partnership and problem-solving tools. Minneapolis, MN: The Battered Women's Justice Project. Retrieved from http://www.bwjp.org/articles/article-list.aspx?id = 24.

Sax, K. (2012). Intimate partner violence: A group cognitive-behavioral therapy model. *The Group Psychologist*. Retrieved from http://www.apadivisions.org/division-49/publications/newsletter/group-psychologist/2012/11/partner-violence.aspx.

Schauer, M., Neuner, F., & Elbert, T. (2011). *Narrative exposure therapy: A short-term treatment for traumatic stress disorders*. Cambridge, MA: Hogrefe Publishing.

Siegel, M. D. (2012). Surviving Castle Rock: The human rights of domestic violence. *Cardozo Journal of Law and Gender, 18,* 727–751.

Stop Abusive and Violent Environments. (2010). Domestic violence programs discriminate against male victims. Rockville: Author. Retrieved from http://www.google.com/url?sa=t&rct=j&q=&esrc=s&source=web&cd=1&ved=0CC0QFjAA&url=http%3A%2F%2Fwww.saveservices.org%2Fpdf%2FSAVE-VAWA-Discriminates-Against-Males.pdf&ei=pHo3U_TLIoLQsQSF_YDgCw&usg=AFQjCNGbpycLEeyOaGD7ZOpILkp3lETTPQ&bvm=bv.63808443,d.cWc.

Stotzer, R. (2009). Violence against transgender people: A review of United States data. *Aggression and Violent Behavior, 14,* 170–179.

Taft, A., O'Doherty, L., Hegarty, K., Ramsay, J., Davidson, L., & Feder, G. (2013). Screening women for intimate partner violence in healthcare settings. *Cochrane Database System Review, 4*(4), CD007007. doi:10.1002/14651858.CD007007.pub2.

UN Committee on the Elimination of Discrimination Against Women. (1992). Committee on the Elimination of Discrimination Against Women General Recommendation No. 19: Violence against women. Retrieved from http://www.refworld.org/docid/52d920c54.html.

UN General Assembly. (1966). International Covenant on Civil and Political Rights, 16 December 1966, United Nations, Treaty Series, vol. 999, p. 171. Retrieved from http://www.refworld.org/docid/3ae6b3aa0.html.

UN General Assembly. (1989). Convention on the Rights of the Child, 20 November 1989, United Nations, Treaty Series, vol. 1577, p. 3. Retrieved from http://www.refworld.org/docid/3ae6b38f0.html.

UN General Assembly. (1979). Convention on the Elimination of All Forms of Discrimination Against Women, 18 December 1979, United Nations, Treaty Series, vol. 1249, p. 13. Retrieved from http://www.refworld.org/docid/3ae6b3970.html.

UN General Assembly. (1993). Declaration on the Elimination of Violence against Women, 20 December 1993, A/RES/48/104. United Nations 85th Plenary Meeting. Retrieved from http://www.un.org/documents/ga/res/48/a48r104.htm.

UN General Assembly. (1999). Optional Protocol to the Convention on the Elimination of All Forms of Discrimination Against Women, 6 October 1999, United Nations, Treaty Series, vol. 2131, p. 83. Retrieved from http://www.refworld.org/docid/3ae6b3a7c.html.

UN Special Rapporteur on Violence Against Women. (2002). Report of the special rapporteur on violence against women, Ms. Radhika Coomaraswamy: Cultural practices in the family that are violent towards women. Retrieved from http://www.unhchr.ch/huridocda/huridoca.nsf/%28Symbol%29/E.CN.4.2002.83.En?Opendocument.

UN Special Rapporteur on Violence Against Women. (2011). Report of the special rapporteur on violence against women, its causes and consequences, Ms. Rashida Manjoo. Addendum: Mission to the United States of America. Retrieved from http://daccess-ods.un.org/TMP/7492507.69615173.html.

UN Special Rapporteur on Violence Against Women. (2013). Report of the special rapporteur on violence against women, its causes and consequences, Ms. Rashida Manjoo. Retrieved from http://www.ohchr.org/Documents/HRBodies/HRCouncil/RegularSession/Session23/A_HRC_23_49_English.pdf.

United Nations Population Fund [UNFPA]. (2009). *Partnering with men to end gender-based violence: Practices that work from Eastern Europe and Central Asia*. New York: United Nations Population Fund.

UN Women. (n.d.). COMMIT initiative. Retrieved from http://www.unwomen.org/en/what-we-do/ending-violence-against-women/take-action/commit.

Violence against Women Reauthorization Act of 2013. (2013). 127 STAT. 54 PUBLIC LAW 113–4.

Waldorf, L. (2006). Rwanda's failing experiment in restorative justice. In D. Sullivan & L. Tifft (Eds.), *Handbook of restorative justice: A global perspective* (pp. 422–432). London, UK: Routledge.

Warshaw, C., & Brashler, P. (2009). Mental health treatment for survivors of domestic violence. In C. Mitchell & D. Anglin (Eds.), *Intimate partner violence: A health-based perspective* (pp. 335–387). New York, NY: Oxford University Press.

Warshaw, C., Sullivan, C. M., & Rivera, E. A. (2013). *A systematic review of trauma-focused interventions for domestic violence survivors*. Chicago, IL: National Center on Domestic Violence, Trauma, and Mental Health.

Watt, M. E., & Scrandis, D. A. (2013). Traumatic childhood exposures in the lives of male perpetrators of female intimate partner violence. *Journal of Interpersonal Violence, 28*(14), 2813–2830.

Whitfield, C. L., Anda, R. F., Dube, S. R., & Felitti, V. J. (2003). Violent childhood experiences and the risk of intimate partner violence in adults: Assessment in a large health maintenance organization. *Journal of Interpersonal Violence, 18,* 166–185.

Witness Justice (2014). Definitions of restorative justice by victims and their advocates. Retrieved from http://www.restorativejustice.org/victim-support/definitions-of- restorative-justice-by-victims-and-their-advocates.

World Health Organization. (2013a). *Global and regional estimates of violence against women: Prevalence and health effects of intimate partner violence and non-partner sexual violence.* Geneva, Switzerland: Author.

World Health Organization. (2013b). *Global and regional estimates of violence against women: Prevalence and health effects of intimate partner violence and non-partner sexual violence. Executive Summary*. Geneva, Switzerland: Author.

World Health Organization. (2013c). Responding to intimate partner violence and sexual violence against women: WHO clinical and policy guidelines. Retrieved from http://apps.who.int/iris/bitstream/10665/85240/1/9789241548595_eng.pdf.

# Chapter 5
# The Use and Care of Self when Engaging in Rights-Based Clinical Practice

> Ellen[1] is a 35-year-old clinical social worker and trauma specialist at a nonprofit that offers a wide range of services for women. Many of the women with whom Ellen works have experienced intimate partner violence (IPV), rape, and/or other traumas. Ellen has been providing psychotherapy to these women for the last 10 years. She has difficulty in sleeping and has become increasingly isolated from her old friends, feeling no interest in activities that she used to enjoy doing with them, such as going to movies and dancing. Ellen feels that her old friends cannot understand the pain she feels each day at work when she hears about the traumas of the women she serves. The women's stories trigger memories from her childhood, when she witnessed her parents fighting and had to go stay at a shelter more than once with her mother and brother. Ellen has started to pick up extra assignments at work, and finds that she cannot stop thinking about the women's traumas at night. She feels helpless at times, unable to distance herself from the women's pain or see any solutions to their problems. Ellen does not feel a lot of support within her agency, although she senses that she must not be alone in feeling affected by her work. Already licensed, she receives only occasional supervision and that only to address immediate crisis situations with little follow-up. When she tries to talk to her coworkers about the stressful work, they typically make a joke and avoid having in-depth conversations about the impact of the work on them. Ellen recently was diagnosed with high blood pressure, a surprise to her, since her family members have no history of hypertension.

Have you ever experienced some of the reactions that Ellen has? Do you sometimes have trouble sleeping or find yourself thinking about the traumatic experiences of those you work with after work hours? Are not social workers supposed to be able to remain strong in the face of anything we encounter at work? Is it a sign of weakness to acknowledge our vulnerabilities? If we find ourselves affected by the experiences of the survivors we work with, does it mean that we should not be social workers? Are you already doing things to take care of yourself? If so, what works for you? Is self-care consonant with a rights-based approach to clinical social work? If no, why not? Is self-care a luxury? Do any human rights instruments support our right to self-care? Do we have a right to have support for our well-being from our employer? If so, what form(s) should that take?

[1] This is a fictitious case of a therapist drawn from the many years of training experience the author has had with clinicians related to vicarious trauma and self-care.



S. M. Berthold, *Human Rights-Based Approaches to Clinical Social Work*,
SpringerBriefs in Rights-Based Approaches to Social Work, DOI 10.1007/978-3-319-08560-9_5

Social work practitioners use themselves as a tool and medium in their practice with diverse individuals, including with those who have experienced or are at risk of experiencing human rights violations. Like Ellen, many clinical social workers have experienced some traumas in their lives, sometimes similar in nature to aspects of the life experiences of those who they provide therapy to. Social workers also tend to have (or hopefully have) strong capacities for and inclination toward empathy. Both of these phenomena can put social workers at risk for having difficulty maintaining professional distance, having unhelpful countertransference reactions (CTRs), and for being negatively affected by their work with people in distress (Wilson & Thomas, 2004). These challenges can also arise even if the clinician has not experienced significant trauma himself or herself. In the absence of effective tools to prevent and manage these effects, clinical social workers may find their abilities to provide appropriate services and safeguard the rights of those they serve to be compromised. In addition, social workers may find that they leave work exhausted, with little time or energy to devote to their own interests or taking care of themselves. Rights-based clinicians may feel overwhelmed with not enough time or sufficient resources for addressing the enormity of the problems they face in their work. In comparison to the human rights violations they are dedicated to combat, taking care of themselves may seem less important, selfish, or impossible.

This chapter identifies human rights instruments that support all persons' (including social workers') right to leisure, health, and well-being. It examines the use of self by social workers engaged in rights-based practice. The practitioner's ethical duty to remain deeply self-reflective and aware of the impact of his or her work and approach on self and those they work with is also highlighted. Application of cultural humility and other core principles of a rights-based approach to practice are infused throughout this chapter. The vital need for social workers to deepen their skills of self-awareness and continually reflect on their own values, biases, assumptions, and prejudices is promoted in order to safeguard and realize the rights of those they serve. Individuals, families, and groups served by clinical practitioners frequently are in distress when they seek or are mandated to receive services from social workers and may have a significant trauma history, including sometimes trauma as a result of seeking or obtaining services from social workers or other service providers not operating from a rights framework. The impact of rights-based practice on the social work practitioner is explored. It is essential that every clinician working with trauma survivors develops and nurtures ongoing self-awareness and the ability to manage his or her own reactions to the person's trauma material in order to minimize the risk of retraumatizing the survivors they work with (Piwowarczyk, Moreno, & Grodin, 2000; Wilson & Lindy, 1994). If not aware of their secondary traumatic stress, clinical social workers may do harm to the survivors they serve, even unintentionally. Attention to assessing, preventing, and attending to the practitioner's vicarious or secondary trauma and the impact of CTRs on the therapeutic relationship is included, and readers are introduced to the concept of vicarious resilience. Recommendations are presented to advance self-care and the clinical practitioner's ability to engage with the pain, distress, and trauma of those they serve in a therapeutic fashion in keeping with a rights-based approach to practice. Finally, a call for the importance of creating an organizational culture of self-care is made.

Social work and allied professions increasingly are preparing their practitioners to engage in what is referred to as "self-care." While it is vital for clinical social workers to develop the awareness, skills, and commitment to take care of themselves, this does not take away from the obligation of organizations and governmental authorities to ensure their rights to health and leisure are protected and realized. New Tactics in Human Rights (2010), a global community of human rights defenders, defines self-care as the "ability to engage in human rights work without sacrificing other important parts of one life .... Self-care can also be understood as a practitioner's right to be well, safe, and fulfilled" (para. 4). Rather than framing self-care as an individual endeavor, a goal that does not fit culturally for many, identifying self-care as a collective concern of the individual, the organization he or she works for, and his or her community is recommended (New Tactics in Human Rights, 2010). Ensuring the well-being of the practitioner is consistent with the human right to leisure and health.

## Relevant Human Rights Instruments

Various international human rights instruments affirm the rights of all humans to leisure, health, and well-being. The Universal Declaration of Human Rights (UDHR) states that "Everyone has the right to rest and leisure, including reasonable limitation of working hours and periodic holidays with pay" (UN General Assembly, 1948, Article 24). The right to health is also set forth in the UDHR: "Everyone has the right to a standard of living adequate for the health of himself and of his family, including food, clothing, housing, and medical care and necessary social services" (UN General Assembly, 1948, Article 25.1). The right to health is also supported by the International Covenant on Economic, Social and Cultural Rights (UN General Assembly, 1966) that holds, "Everyone has the right to the enjoyment of the highest attainable standard of physical and mental health" (Article 12.1). The United Nations' Committee on Economic, Social and Cultural Rights, in its General Comment 14 (2000) stresses that the highest standard of health is something that every human is entitled to and that this indispensable right supports the ability of human beings to live in dignity and to exercise their other human rights. States are obligated to fulfill and implement the right to health and the United Nations has appointed a special rapporteur to examine and report on the implementation of this right and violations by State parties. The codes of ethics adopted by the International Federation of Social Workers and the National Association of Social Workers in the United States also affirm these rights. This body of instruments and ethical codes supports the right of social workers to leisure, health, and well-being. In practice, many factors contribute to making the realization of these rights challenging.

## Use of Self and Self-Awareness

Clinical social workers enter into professional relationships with the people and communities they serve. In the process, they seek to become change agents, using themselves (in part) to effect positive change and growth in those they work with. For decades, social workers have spoken about the key role of the use of self in their work, and that the social worker himself or herself becomes the instrument of change through the development of an effective therapeutic relationship (Chapman, Oppenheim, Shibusawa, & Jackson, 2003; Heydt & Sherman, 2005). By this, social workers mean that they deliberately and determinedly interact with those they serve to facilitate change using his or her abilities, energy, and enthusiasm (Sheafor & Horejsi, 2003; Heydt & Sherman, 2005). Sometimes, this means containing distress through the social worker's demeanor and interventions. This can be particularly challenging when the social worker finds that he or she becomes distressed in the session himself or herself (a topic addressed later in this chapter).

Social workers must remain aware of and in control of their feelings and motivations in their work, and be attentive to how they are perceived (Neuman & Friedman, 1997). Postgraduate training and ongoing clinical supervision by a seasoned licensed clinician with relevant experience is strongly recommended to develop one's ability to do this and monitor and address challenges as they emerge in practice. Chapman et al. (2003) teach MSW students a model of peer supervision given the reality that many public organizations do not have the resources to provide as in-depth and frequent clinical supervision as is needed. Self-knowledge and awareness are essential in order for social workers to discern the countertransference, transference, and other key dynamics in their relationships such that they can engage in effective helping relationships at both the micro and macro levels (Jacobson, 2001).

At times, the way the person seeking services perceives and reacts toward his or her social worker (the person's transference) may be hard for the social worker to tolerate or know how to respond to. Sometimes the situation may become volatile.

> Nguyen[2], a 46-year-old South Vietnamese former officer, who had been detained and tortured for more than 5 years in North Vietnam by the military after the fall of Saigon, was seen by a therapist in the United States for his depression and post-traumatic stress disorder (PTSD). As Nguyen walked with the therapist toward her office when they first met, he swore loudly at the therapist over and over, so all in the clinic could hear. Once in the office, he refused to sit down for most of the session, clenching his fist as he expressed anger toward the therapist. He was livid that he had come to a clinic specialized in treating Southeast Asians, but had been assigned to the only non-Southeast Asian clinician. Nguyen identified (correctly) the therapist as American and a feminist (although she did not confirm this later assumption on his part). He did sit down eventually that first day. Over time, Nguyen revealed to his therapist that his torture had begun when he was "abandoned" by the American military forces he was fighting alongside. His wife was now divorcing him. She had arrived in the United States long before he did, while he was still detained. She had adopted "feminist ideas" in

[2] The names and other identifying information in all case material have been changed to protect confidentiality, and aspects of each case are a composite from more than one person.

> the United States and he feared that his female American therapist would take the side of his wife. Nonetheless, Nguyen engaged in therapy with this therapist for several years. The therapist had to have strong skills and self-awareness in order to contain the situation and build a positive therapeutic relationship over time with Nguyen. Ultimately, the very things about the therapist that triggered a negative reaction in Nguyen appeared to become, over time, key ingredients in his healing process.

The interactional social work practice theory of Shulman (1999) relates to the clinical social worker's skilled use of self to create a therapeutic relationship and positively influence the outcomes of his or her interventions. Chapman et al. (2003) explicate the key features of a course designed to teach MSW students in their final semester how to effectively, ethically, and professionally use themselves in their practice. Social work students are taught to deeply understand the difference between conscious and unconscious use of self (Chapman et al., 2003; Heydt & Sherman, 2005). Through experiential activities, they are guided to examine how their personal characteristics and history serve as the basis of their emotional reactions to those they provide therapy to (countertransference) and affect their work together (Chapman et al., 2003). Some may have had little exposure in their coursework to process-oriented training and, in contrast, may have encountered media images of therapists such as in the films *Good Will Hunting* and *The Prince of Tides* that depict unethical and sometimes dangerous clinicians who violate ethical boundaries, yet the people they work with get better (Chapman et al., 2003). Social workers who rely on their gut to guide their clinical interventions, no matter how well intentioned and desirous of being helpful, are not acting professionally (Heydt & Sherman, 2005). They may well violate the rights of those they serve in doing so. Lacking self-awareness, a social worker may engage in behaviors or display emotions that are harmful to the very people they are trying to assist (Cournoyer, 2000). A Jamaican social work educator describes how student prejudices toward and perceptions of marginalized populations (e.g., individuals who are LGBTQ, disabled, living in severe poverty, and/or living with HIV/AIDS) shaped by what she calls *anti-rights socialization* in society, can be confronted and transformed in the curriculum (Chadwick-Parkes, 2014). If left unexamined, the social worker may be at risk for having his or her personal beliefs, attitudes, interactional patterns, values, and prejudices affect his or her ability to be helpful or sustain a therapeutic relationship. Enhanced and conscious awareness of these factors enable social workers to make effective use of self as an instrument of positive change (Heydt & Sherman, 2005).

Ellen, the social worker in the opening vignette in the chapter, might be at risk of engaging in a nontherapeutic fashion with the women she serves if she does not make conscious use of herself. For example, suppose that she still feels fragile about the severing of her relationship with her father, as a result of the long-term violence she witnessed him inflicting on her mother, when she was a child. Imagine that Ellen continues to have nightmares about the times she and her mom and brother spent in the shelter. If Ellen is not fully aware of these continued impacts of her own traumatic childhood, she may be in danger of imposing her own choices on the women she works with. She may, for example, try to persuade them not to go to a shelter rather than ensuring that the women are fully aware of their rights and full range of choices and supporting their self-determination.

Since clinical social workers cannot avoid using themselves in their work (as described above), it is vital that they work to make it a priority to continually enhance their self-awareness throughout their career. The potential risks for the people they serve of not doing this, or not doing it effectively, are great. Among the various factors that may impede the development of a therapeutic relationship, particularly if the social worker is not aware of them, are behaviors and attitudes that are degrading or devaluing of others and personal issues (Sheafor & Horejsi, 2003). Personal issues may include such matters as dealing with one's own or a family member's mental or physical health problem or addiction; going through a divorce and child custody issues; healing from a rape or other assault; experiencing financial stress; undergoing a spiritual or religious transformation in one's own life and trying to impose one's own beliefs and values on others; and a tendency to become defensive about one's own views with an inability to hear or consider the perspectives of others.

The imperative of self-awareness as a clinical social worker, including in relation to one's own stereotypes and biases "about self and self in relationship to other cultures" (Ortega & Faller, 2011, p. 34), is also a part of what is required in approaching one's work with cultural humility (one of the core principles of a rights-based approach to practice). Self-awareness not only promotes connectedness with oneself but also with others, including the people one works with (Ortega & Faller, 2011). Social workers "must assess the barriers their own attitudes and behaviors present to learning from others about others since personal knowledge alone will not sustain new insights, awareness, and behavioral change" (Ortega & Faller, 2011, p. 34).

Rights-based practitioners are encouraged to engage in therapy of their own, even if they do not have pressing or significant issues to address, in order to enhance their self-awareness. Becoming aware of one's vulnerabilities or unhealthy behaviors without becoming defensive, and remembering and revisiting painful events from the past can be stressful and emotional experiences. These issues are more appropriately addressed in depth in therapy than in supervision. Engaging in one's personal therapy may also be helpful in addressing the impact of intense clinical work with those who have had their rights violated. Crenshaw (2008) stresses that a therapist's self-awareness and healing of his or her own vulnerabilities is:

> . . . not an isolated task undertaken for a relatively brief period of personal therapy but rather a life long journey in which self-monitoring, personal therapy, supervision, consultation with colleagues, and continuing training and education are vital . . . . We can't afford to undertake this work with blind spots, unhealed damage, or unresolved trauma. (pp. 123 & 124)

Social workers must attend to their own healing to be able to serve others effectively.

Therapist's self-awareness can also extend to the somatic and emotional sensations the therapist experiences as he or she hears a story of trauma or sits with someone in great distress in his or her office. Consciously being aware of and transforming these sensations can be helpful to the therapist in containing his or her own distress while also enabling him or her to remain present and available to attend to the distress of the person they are conducting therapy with. The example of Rose, below, illustrates a piece of this work.

> Rose, an adolescent torture survivor from a country in West Africa, experienced a dissociative flashback in her therapist's office as she recounted searching through a pit of dead bodies looking for her father. Rose began to hyperventilate. The therapist split her awareness, remaining attentive to Rose while bringing a portion of her awareness to her own body. The therapist became aware that her stomach was tightening up and that her breathing was more rapid and shallow than usual. This gave the therapist the opportunity to consciously deepen and slow down her breath, while at the same time, grounding and orienting Rose back to the safe environment of the therapy room with her, half way around the world from the pit and those who tortured her and killed her father. The therapist also gently but firmly encouraged Rose to slow her breathing and match the therapist's breath—in and out . . . in and out. Then the therapist added a visualization of a safe place that she and Rose had developed together in an earlier session prior to doing any trauma work. Rose was gradually able to regain her equilibrium and return to being present with the therapist, no longer hyperventilating or flooded with images and sensations of her trauma.

Rose's therapist found that her training in meditation was a powerful and valuable tool that enabled her to navigate this challenging moment in therapy.

Given the important influence the social worker can exert on the person he or she is engaged in psychotherapy with, positive or negative or mixed, it is essential that the social worker strive to be continuously and consciously self-aware. For example, a trauma survivor may shut down or stop sharing important details or feelings if the clinician starts to grimace or gasp (or otherwise become visibly distressed) when the survivor reveals a particularly sensitive or gruesome part of his or her experience. That is not to say that the clinician should sit with a blank expression on his or her face or smile throughout the session, as that would also not be therapeutic. Acknowledging and validating the pain and rights violation (verbally and nonverbally) is essential, yet maintaining one's empathic engagement and professional demeanor will facilitate the exploration of difficult aspects of the survivor's experience.

Trauma survivors often utilize avoidance strategies (e.g., substance abuse and dissociation) in order to cope with trauma memories and associated emotional distress (Briere, Hodges, & Godbout, 2010). A therapist may also consciously or unconsciously seek to avoid hearing about or processing the traumatic experiences of survivors they provide psychotherapy to. Awareness of this response and the development of skills and abilities by the therapist so that they are not avoidant are essential. While such avoidance may be a protective response, it can hinder the positive aspects of treatment survivors may derive from exposure to and working through the traumatic memories, and consequently, interfere with recovery (Briere & Lanktree, 2013; Briere, Scott, & Weathers, 2005; Polusny, Rosenthal, Aban, & Follette, 2004).

## Vicarious or Secondary Trauma

Clinical social workers, exposed at high rates to the trauma material of others, are at risk for developing vicarious traumatic stress (also known as secondary traumatic stress) (Bride, 2007). Rights-based clinical social workers must be able to engage empathically with the trauma material of those they serve. In doing so, their inner experience is transformed and in the absence of appropriate boundaries, they may be at risk for developing vicarious trauma (Saakvitne, Pearlman, & Staff of TSI/CAAP, 1996). Their assumptions about benevolence in the world, trust, safety, and control can be shattered and radically changed in the process of working with trauma survivors (McCann & Pearlman, 1990; Stamm, 1999). Sometimes also called compassion fatigue (Bride & Figley, 2007), vicarious trauma usually takes time to develop and is often the cumulative result of working with many traumatized individuals. It may develop quickly, however, in cases that are particularly challenging or traumatic for the clinician. The clinician may develop some of the same symptoms of post-traumatic stress or depression that those he or she works with experience (Stamm, 1999). Saakvitne et al. (1996) identified a wide range of common signs and symptoms of vicarious trauma including: disruption and a sense of powerlessness; damaged sense of personal control and safety; disconnection from loved ones; social withdrawal; reduced ability to trust; lack of energy or time for oneself; increased sensitivity to violence; widespread feelings of hopelessness and despair; and cynicism.

There are numerous indicators of vicarious trauma. Having one or two of these may not mean the social worker has developed this condition. A clinical social worker may find himself or herself spacing out and having difficulty concentrating while meeting with a traumatized person. He or she may hope that a particular individual will not show up to the next session. The social worker may have nightmares of the traumas they learn about when conducting therapy or find that thoughts or images from a trauma story told by someone he or she is providing psychotherapy to interferes with his or her functioning. He or she may stop reading or watching the news, exercising, and/or going out with friends. Low likelihood events like plane crashes may preoccupy his or her thoughts. The social worker may become extra cautious when leaving his or her office or home, and/or feel uncharacteristically depressed, irritable, or out of sorts. He or she may feel emotionally numb or begin to use (or increase his or her usage of) drugs or alcohol to cope with the intense reactions he or she feels. Some social workers may begin to feel guilty about carrying on with their own daily lives while knowing how badly the lives of others have been disrupted by trauma. Some may even come to feel that they should change professions to gain distance from or avoid being surrounded by trauma.

Vicarious trauma can be very distressing and rights-based clinical social workers should be supported in developing strategies to prevent its development. At the same time, these social workers need to know that if they do develop vicarious trauma, it does not have to last forever and that they can achieve vicarious transformation or resilience (described later in this chapter) as well.

## Countertransference Reactions

Empathy, a key therapeutic factor, is the ability to be aware of, understand, and vicariously experience the perspective, experiences, and distress of another (McCann & Colletti, 1994; Wilson & Thomas, 2004). Therapists often develop empathic strain, struggling to sustain their empathic attunement and therapeutic equilibrium when working with traumatized people (Wilson & Thomas, 2004). In the absence of effective intervention, empathic strain may lead to burnout, vicarious traumatization, and strong countertransference processes. Certainly, it can be painful and horrifying to hear accounts of children abused for years, adolescent teens sold into sexual slavery, women who have seen their husbands beheaded by rebels, and men and women who have been beaten and had their lives threatened by their intimate partners. Sometimes it can be hard to imagine how human beings can treat others as those we work with have been treated. Little in life may have prepared social workers to face such atrocities. Therapist avoidance, while understandable given the intensity of working with trauma material, does not facilitate the recovery of the survivor (Briere, 2010). Rather, a therapist with strong avoidance to the survivor's trauma material consciously or unconsciously discourages him or her from talking about his or her traumas, further reinforcing the person's own avoidance. This may be because the therapist wishes to protect the person from further distress in the therapy sessions, and/or protect himself or herself from feeling distressed.

Some survivors stimulate strong reactions in therapists. The person may remind the therapist of someone or the person's experiences may trigger a traumatic memory in the therapist. The therapist may form judgments about the person based on his or her own experiences. All of these reactions may be forms of countertransference (Walsh, 2011). Countertransference, in its contemporary sense, involves the therapists' reactions to the person they are conducting therapy with based on the characteristics, experiences, and behavior of the person, and/or the therapists' own present or past experiences and inner unresolved conflicts (Hepworth, Rooney, Rooney, Strom-Gottfried, & Larsen, 2010). The therapist may not be aware of his or her CTRs in the absence of overt problems. Left unexamined and unaddressed, countertransference may result in perceptions, emotions, and behaviors by the therapist that are counterproductive to the therapy or are otherwise harmful to the person they are working with (Hepworth et al., 2010). CTRs are inevitable and may be especially intense when working with survivors of severe human rights violations. These reactions, when examined, can yield valuable information that may be useful for assessment and treatment.

Wilson and Lindy (1994) developed a model of the impact of two broad types of CTRs on PTSD treatment, viewing CTRs as the primary cause of failed PTSD treatment. This model is highly relevant for clinical social workers that treat survivors of human rights violations. Type I CTRs include avoidance/counter phobic and detachment reactions. This type of CTR may be manifested in such reactions by the therapist as intellectualization, misconception of dynamics, minimizing the trauma, shifting focus away from the trauma, and/or denial of the existence of some of the survivor's symptoms. Therapists most at risk of developing empathic withdrawal are those who have not personally experienced significant trauma, according to Wilson and Lindy (1994). Therapists with significant and unresolved trauma histories, particularly when their own trauma is similar to the trauma of the person(s) they are conducting therapy with, are most at risk for empathic repression.

Therapists who have Type II overidentification CTRs may: engage in too much advocacy for the people they are providing therapy to; have rescue tendencies; be enmeshed and have blurred role boundaries with the people they are serving; move the therapy along at too rapid a pace; develop an unhealthy bond with the persons they are working with; or may overly focus on the survivors' trauma experiences. Therapists who are relatively unaware of and unprepared for the powerful psychological and physiological arousal reactions they may experience as a result of working with trauma survivors are most at risk for empathic disequilibrium. These reactions are related to being exposed to such challenging aspects of the survivor's traumas as multiple and otherwise complex traumas, existential issues such as shame, the horror and inhumanity of the types of human-perpetrated violence experienced, and the impossible choices faced by the survivor during and after the traumatic experiences. These therapists may experience distressing somatic symptoms, graphic distressing images of the trauma, and/or overwhelming emotional distress (e.g., feeling vulnerable or insecure about their abilities, highly anxious, and/or uncertain about their treatment approach). Therapists who have not yet sufficiently healed from their own significant trauma histories are most at risk for developing empathic enmeshment as exhibited by loss of boundaries, overinvolvement with the survivor, and/or reciprocal dependency (Wilson & Lindy, 1994).

The various types of CTRs described above can have negative effects on the people served, including compromising their efforts to heal from the distressing experiences or situations that brought them into therapy, reinforcing negative feelings about themselves, and making it more challenging for them to develop healthy relationships. Social workers have an ethical duty to do no harm. Therefore, clinical social workers are encouraged to develop a prevention strategy and obtain appropriate training and ongoing supervision in order to address their CTRs and safeguard the rights of those they serve.

## Vicarious Resilience

Much of the literature in the field has emphasized the potential negative impact of engaging in clinical work with those who have encountered trauma or other stressful life experiences. Social workers may, alternatively or simultaneously, experience positive consequences from their work such as enhanced skills to reframe and cope with traumatic or otherwise adverse events (Hernández, Engstrom, & Gangsei, 2010; Hernandez-Wolfe, Killian, Engstrom, & Gangsei, in press). The concept of vicarious resilience grew out of qualitative research with psychotherapists treating survivors of political violence and their families and was further developed in research with torture treatment therapists (Engstrom, Hernández, & Gangsei, 2008; Hernández, Gangsei, & Engstrom, 2007). Vicarious resilience refers to the empowerment and positive transformation of therapists through their empathic engagement with the stories and displays of resilience of the survivors they work with in the face of adversity.

A number of factors have been found to be associated with the development of vicarious resilience in trauma therapists (Engstrom et al., 2008; Hernández et al., 2007). These therapists reported positive change in their perspectives about the world and their own lives, as reflected by: taking things less for granted and experiencing more appreciation for their freedoms; experiencing their own problems as less severe and more manageable; being better able to see the positive aspects of experiences that they previously only saw as negative; and feeling more motivated for life, more hopeful, and stronger. They also became better able to tolerate frustration and reported an enhanced appreciation for the role that spirituality and religion can play in trauma survivors' healing processes. Another valuable aspect of their vicarious resilience was gaining increased hope and understanding that it is possible for survivors of trauma to recover. The trauma therapists' vicarious resilience appeared toc promote their overall well-being and ability to continue to work with survivors of torture and other human rights atrocities. Finding an avenue to speak publically against human rights atrocities was also a positive outgrowth of their experiences with survivors.

While more study is needed of vicarious resilience, preliminary research findings (Engstrom et al., 2008) and anecdotal reports from trauma therapists suggest that it may contribute to preventing or counterbalancing the effects of vicarious trauma. What the survivors they work with teach them about resilience may help to sustain clinical social workers in their work and also in dealing with personal traumas and challenges. The well-being of rights-based clinical social workers is essential, not only for their own health but also so that they can continue to do their important work. Social workers in some fields of practice (e.g., child welfare) have relatively high rates of turnover, associated in part with worker burnout and vicarious trauma (Pryce, Shakelford, & Pryce, 2007). Preventing and combating the negative effects of vicarious trauma while nurturing vicarious resilience is part of what clinical social workers must do in order to take care of themselves.

## Self-Care

Clinical social workers that engage in human rights work are encouraged to make self-care a priority. This includes balancing their work with other facets of life and safeguarding their right to be safe and well (New Tactics in Human Rights, 2010). Individual self-care strategies include maintaining a long-term view, cultivating effective coping strategies, and engaging in a sustainable way of life that includes attention to overall health (New Tactics in Human Rights, 2010). Human rights practitioners may struggle to make it a priority to take care of themselves. Some think that, to be truly committed to their cause, they should be devoting all of their energies to caring for others. The very notion of taking care of oneself is viewed as selfish and contrary to some cultures' communal values. Without effective self-care, however, human rights activists cannot fulfill their roles effectively or, for some, sustain the ability to continue to engage in the work at all.

Cox and Steiner (2013) have conceptualized self-care as a state of mind, one that extends beyond isolated activities of care. These authors argue that it should be a fundamental aspect of training for all social workers, with an emphasis on the development of a comprehensive strategy that is implemented in a consistent and ongoing fashion rather than only in short bursts of activity or when the social worker happens to have free time. The plan may include such things as getting more sleep, exercising regularly, learning to meditate, joining a singing group, going on hikes in the mountains, or getting a massage. However, these activities should be integrated into an overall strategy of self-care. One social worker recommits each new year to a theme of self-care (Berthold, 2014), checking in with herself frequently to ask if what she is planning to do or is doing is in keeping with her own self-care or not. This is a commitment to self-care as a lifestyle change, one that includes setting boundaries and limits and being gentle with herself when she slips in her mission of self-care, using that as an opportunity to reflect and rededicate herself to her theme of self-care. Cox and Steiner (2013) have found that self-care is enhanced as social workers develop self-awareness, self-efficacy, and self-regulation. Strategies must be proactive, practical, feasible, and within their control to implement, otherwise social workers may set themselves up for failure and additional distress.

A questionnaire developed by Baker (2003) guides psychotherapists to reflect on the stresses and emotional demands in their lives, their experience with therapy, professional challenges they have faced, whether they have ever contemplated changing professions, and identifying what would most support their well-being. Practitioners examine their: own individualized definition of self-care; attitudes toward self-care and whether it is a priority in their life or not; understanding of their own self-care needs; and assessment of the most effective strategies of self-care in their life.

Additional resources for assessing one's current level of self-care and for developing self-care plans are included at the end of this chapter. As Saakvitne, Pearlman, and Staff of TSI/CAAP (1996) remind us, the following are essential to cultivate in all realms of self-care: self-nurturance; self-awareness and mindfulness; meaning and connection; and balance between work, play, and rest. In addition, a deep and personal motivation and commitment to engage in self-care are vital. Taking care of oneself is a right as well as a need; it is imperative in order to be able to continue to work effectively with others.

Developing the capacity to engage with the pain, distress, and trauma of others in a therapeutic fashion in keeping with a rights-based approach to practice is part of what is required for a comprehensive self-care plan. Adopting a long-term trauma stewardship approach, as developed by van Dernoot Lipsky (2009), can support social workers to remain healthy and to be able to continue to work with trauma survivors. Trauma stewardship encourages practitioners to deeply reflect on what led them to become involved in trauma work, the impact the work has on them, the lessons they have learned, and the meaning of the work. Individual efforts at self-care can only go so far to mitigate the effects of clinical social work with survivors of human rights violations when the organizational culture or structure is not supportive or is exacerbating the problem. The care of social workers or other human rights workers should be framed as a community or agency responsibility.

## Creating an Organizational Culture of Self-Care

Rights-based social workers attend to the structural and other macro forces affecting the people they are serving, and so to the organizational factors affecting themselves must be addressed. This should be a responsibility of administrators. That would also be in keeping with the human right to leisure, which includes, in part, the right to reasonable work hours and paid vacation days (UN General Assembly, 1948). Clinical social workers often are employed by organizations with limited resources, however, including insufficient resources to support their self-care. The social work staff members in these organizations are called upon to provide more services with fewer resources, a prescription for stress. Administrators may not believe that it is important to spend money on the care of staff members or even see that as part of the organization's responsibility. New Tactics in Human Rights (2010) advocates for creating an organizational culture of self-care. This would involve, in part, creating a positive vision of an organizational culture where the well-being of both staff and the persons receiving services is prioritized. Staff members would be supported in taking care of themselves, rather than the organizational leaders focusing instead only on the problems or what cannot be done. These organizations would proactively and intentionally invest in the development and well-being of their staff rather than reacting after the fact to staff crises.

There are a variety of ways that organizations can accomplish this. New Tactics in Human Rights (2010), for example, has identified measures that leaders of organizations can take to promote an organizational culture of self-care including: adopting a preventive approach; fostering confidence and trust within members of the organization; and ultimately holding the organization and its leaders accountable for the well-being of each staff member through investing in their self-care. In addition, the development of a staff support network can provide valuable support. This may be a network within the organization but also extending to human rights workers at other similar organizations that the staff may collaborate with. In this technological era, this network need not be confined to participants who reside nearby but can be national, regional, or international in scope. The networks developed by New Tactics in Human Rights and the consortium of torture treatment providers in the United States and internationally are good examples of this. A training of trainer's model may be valuable in spreading knowledge and skills regarding the impact of human rights work on workers and the importance of and tools for self-care to the broader network of providers in a community. Specialized rights-based social workers are well equipped to be trainers in this area as well as provide ongoing support to members of these networks.

A review of the literature regarding healthy workplace practices that promote employee well-being and organizational improvements across a broad range of organizations identified the following categories: health and safety, employee development and growth, work-life balance, and employee recognition and involvement in decision making (Grawitch, Gottschalk, & Munz, 2006). In addition, the literature suggested that these practices must be well aligned with the organization's context (i.e., the organization's structure, strategy, and values) and there must be effective communication in order for these workplace practices to have a beneficial effect on employee's well-being. Social workers may or may not be well matched with the culture and structure of their organization (Cox & Steiner, 2013). In a national sample of child advocacy center forensic interviewers, lack of job support was significantly related to their secondary traumatic stress (Bonach & Heckert, 2012). The forensic interviewers identified the following organizational factors that they perceived affected their work-related stress: insufficient teamwork and time for debriefing, having dual roles within the agency, inadequate education on secondary traumatic stress and self-care, and less than satisfactory leadership or supervision. Child welfare professionals who receive supportive supervision have been found to experience less burnout (Barth, Lloyd, Christ, Chapman, & Dickinson, 2008).

The availability of weekly supervision is one of the organizational interventions necessary to promote the well-being and self-care of trauma therapists (Saakvitne, Pearlman, & Staff of TSI/CAAP, 1996; Wilcox, 2012). It is also recommended that organizational leaders normalize their staff members' burnout, countertransference and vicarious trauma reactions, hold forums to address staff concerns, and promote open communication and attention to the staff safety and empowerment. The mentoring of new staff and regular multidisciplinary case conferences are valuable in order to facilitate the exchange of ideas and information, the provision of professional support, and a reduction of professional isolation. Organizational leaders are encouraged to provide support for continuing education for the staff, varied work duties, work-free periods, and mental health benefits. All of this must be done within a context of respect for staff and those served by the agency (Saakvitne, Pearlman, & Staff of TSI/CAAP, 1996).

## Conclusion

This volume has presented a model for rights-based clinical social work practice, provided examples of how this model can be applied to several populations, and addressed the social worker's use and care of self in human rights work. The focus throughout was not on providing a comprehensive guide to clinical interventions, but rather illustrating the principles and key aspects of a rights-based approach to clinical practice. For example, clinical social workers are encouraged to reflect on whether it is more important to get the people they serve to quickly sign all of the required legal documents at the beginning of the first session so they can move on to the "real work," or to ensure that the persons' rights are fully realized in the sense that they are afforded the time to fully know, understand, and ask questions about what they are signing. By operating from a rights' frame and slowing down and attending to the rights of those they serve, the clinical social worker is more likely to build a stronger therapeutic relationship in the process that ultimately enables deeper work and better outcomes. Rights-based clinical practice can also be helpful in navigating ethical dilemmas by providing a standard for therapists to consider the big picture regarding which path in the given situation is most in keeping with peoples' rights. Clinical social work from a rights-frame sets a high standard of care.

Rights-based clinical social work practice is not without its challenges such as the risk for vicarious trauma in working with survivors of human rights violations. The practitioners' empathy and use of self as they engage with the distress and trauma of the survivors they work with in a therapeutic fashion is part of what puts them at risk for developing vicarious trauma. These factors, however, also open the practitioner to experiencing vicarious resilience. This chapter has made the case for the vital need for clinical social workers to build self-awareness, have good ongoing supervision, and take care of themselves. Leaders of organizations that employ social workers also need to invest in the well-being of their staff, create a culture of self-care, and work to be trauma informed. The rights of individuals and communities served by an organization must always be in the forefront of the organization's priorities. In the absence of a strong rights-base, clinical social workers and the organizations they work for might inadvertently further violate the rights of already vulnerable individuals, families, and communities.

## Suggested Activities/Resources

*Case Discussion* Have students read the following case vignette and engage in discussion in small groups, reflecting on the discussion questions provided. Alternatively, this can be given as a journaling assignment. It is recommended that the professor/instructor addresses the topics covered by the discussion questions outlined below during class time so as to build the knowledge base and skills of students in these areas.

> Max, a 35-year-old man, has entered therapy with you after his 10-year marriage ended in divorce. In your second session, as you begin to explore his childhood history, Max starts to rock back and forth in his chair, slumping forward and moaning. His back shakes as he sobs for some minutes. After you are able to calm Max down, he shares that his father abused him for years, starting when Max was five. Max notes that he was hospitalized several times after particularly heavy beatings, including when he was ten and suffered a concussion. Max alludes to his father touching him inappropriately but you change the topic, telling yourself that Max is not strong enough to talk about possible sexual aspects of his abuse history. In the ensuing weeks of therapy, you avoid exploring Max's possible sexual abuse. It makes you anxious and nauseated to talk about and you feel overwhelmed when Max expresses his distress.

Discussion Questions: The Case of Max

1. What might it be like for you to work with Max? Might you experience some of the same reactions as the therapist in the vignette or would your reactions be different?
2. What are the human rights issues present in Max's case?
3. How would a rights-based approach guide your work with Max?

4. What has been your experience in providing psychotherapy with very distraught persons (e.g., types of issues and how distress was expressed)?
5. What was it like for you to sit with (and work with) these individuals?
6. Have you ever found yourself avoiding a difficult topic with someone you are providing therapy to or changing the subject if it comes up? If yes, under what circumstances? What is your understanding of the factors that may have contributed to your avoidance?
7. Some therapists express concern about not wanting to push those they serve too far. How have you approached addressing difficult topics? What strategies have you employed? How do you introduce the topic? Are there things you want to have in place before you launch into these areas? Do you monitor the person's state during the session? If so, how (and why)?
8. When is the "right" time to assess for a person's possible trauma history?
9. Is it always necessary to "work through" a survivor's trauma in order for some healing to take place?
10. Does "working through" a trauma always involve telling the story (in detail)? In one session?
11. What has helped you to be able to address difficult topics with those you provide therapy to (e.g., demeanor, preparation, skills to tolerate distress, and self-awareness)?
12. What types of situations or other factors trigger you when you are providing therapy?
13. What helps you to manage your own reactions/countertransference in those moments and tolerate and contain any distress you might feel so that you can continue to fulfill your professional role?

*Experiential Activities* The following suggested class activities draw from real-life and/or fictitious practice examples from film or literature. These activities are designed to promote the development of knowledge and skills to: enhance self-awareness, assess and attend to one's own vicarious trauma, and therapeutically address the distress and trauma of the survivors one serves grounded in an ethical and rights-based approach.

- **Reflection on therapists depicted in film:** Assign students to watch and keep a journal about two movies during the semester from a list of films provided (e.g., *Good Will Hunting; The Prince of Tides; Couples Retreat; Analyze This; Girl, Interrupted; Ordinary People*). Films should be selected that include in-depth depictions of therapy relationships and the course of therapy. Students can be asked to process the fictional therapists' ethical and/or unethical use of self in therapeutic relationships and the relevance of these issues for their own practice. They can be instructed to identify the rights-based issues depicted in each film and discuss how they would avoid ethical breaches and engage in a rights-based approach if they were the therapist in the film. The journals should be shared with the instructor who will provide detailed feedback to each student and incorporate some of the themes (anonymously) into class discussions. *Note: This assignment was adapted from* Chapman et al. (2003).

- **Love's Executioner—Honest reflection on own reactions to someone you have provided therapy to:** Assign reading of *Love's Executioner: And Other Tales of Psychotherapy* by Irving Yalom, first published in 1989 by Basic Books. This is a set of ten essays in which Yalom reflects on his strong positive and negative reactions to those he provides therapy to. Have students write an essay about their reactions to someone they have worked with in therapy (with no identifying information about the person) and how this influenced their work with the person. Some of the issues that may be explored would connect with issues discussed in this chapter such as: CTRs; vicarious trauma; self-awareness of biases, prejudices or values in conflict with the values of the person in therapy. Students should also be asked to reflect on human rights issues that are relevant to the therapy or the person's life and make a connection to a rights-based approach to practice. *Note: This assignment was adapted from* Chapman et al. (2003).
- **Reflection on vicarious trauma and resilience in own practice:** Provide each student with a blank piece of paper. Have them break into groups of two or three and do the following exercise:

1. On one side of a blank piece of paper, write down a few ways that working with trauma survivors is (or may be) difficult for you.
2. Turn the paper over. On the other side of the paper, write down a few of the positive effects you have experienced from working with trauma survivors.
3. Discuss in your small group, including regarding how rights-based clinical social workers may experience vicarious trauma and resilience simultaneously.

*Resources (Selected) Self-Assessment Measures:*

- **Professional Quality of Life Scale:** Compassion Satisfaction and Compassion Fatigue Version 5 (ProQOL). ©*B. Hudnall Stamm, 2009. (*www.isu.edu/ bhstamm/ *or* www.proqol.org)
- **Self-Care Self-Assessment Worksheet:** Developed by Saakvitne, Pearlman, & Staff of TSI/CAAP (1996), this assessment worksheet covers the following five domains of self-care: physical, psychological, emotional, spiritual, and workplace or professional self-care. An online version can be found at: https://files.counseling.org/wellness_taskforce/PDF/ACA_taskforce_assessment.pdf
- **Self-Care in Social Work website:** http://www.selfcareinsocialwork.com/. The website includes assessment tools, worksheets, examples of stories, and a link to Cox and Steiner's (2013) book on self-care in social work.
- **The Secondary Traumatic Stress Scale** (STSS): measures 17 intrusion, avoidance & numbing, and arousal symptoms in professionals associated with their indirect exposure to the traumatic experiences of the survivors they are working with (Bride, Robinson, Yegidis, & Figley, 2004).
- **Post Traumatic Growth Inventory:** growth as a result of therapy work. Five subscales: new possibilities, relating to others, personal strength, spiritual change, and appreciation of life (Tedeschi & Calhoun, 1996).

- **Resilience Checklist by Meichenbaum:** Roadmap to resilience—resilience checklist. Meichenbaum, D. (n.d.). *Self-Care for Trauma Psychotherapists and Caregivers: Individual, Social, and Organizational Interventions,* training materials. Retrieved from http://www.melissainstitute.org/documents/Meichenbaum_SelfCare_11thconf.pd.
- **Vicarious Resilience Scale:** At the time of this writing, Hernandez-Wolfe and colleagues are in the process of development and validation of the Vicarious Resilience Scale (Killian & Hernandez-Wolfe, 2013; Hernandez-Wolfe, Pilar, email to the author, April 28, 2014).

***Vicarious Trauma and Vicarious Resilience:***

- **Beth Hudnall Stamm's website** (http://www.isu.edu/ bhstamm/) includes a wealth of information, measurement tools (e.g., ProQOL 5), and resources related to professional quality of life, compassion satisfaction and fatigue, burnout, secondary trauma, and vicarious transformation for clinicians.
- **Comprehensive bibliography compiled by Beth Hudnall Stamm:** Stamm (2010, November). Comprehensive Bibliography of the Effect of Caring for Those Who Have Experienced Extremely Stressful Events and Suffering. www.proqol.org
- **Continuing education course on vicarious trauma and resilience:** Berthold (2014). *Vicarious trauma and resilience* (2nd ed.). Peer-reviewed CME course published by NetCE Continuing Education Online. Retrieved from http://www.netce.com/courseoverview.php?courseid=1060.

## References

Baker, E. K. (2003). *Caring for ourselves: A therapist's guide to personal and professional well-being*. Washington, DC: American Psychological Association.

Barth, R. P., Lloyd, E. C., Christ, S. L., Chapman, M. V., & Dickinson, N. S. (2008). Child welfare worker characteristics and job satisfaction: A national study. *Social Work, 53*(3), 199–209.

Berthold, S. M. (2014). *Vicarious trauma and resilience* (2nd ed.). Peer-reviewed CME course published by NetCE Continuing Education Online. Retrieved from http://www.netce.com/courseoverview.php?courseid=1060.

Bonach, K., & Heckert, A. (2012). Predictors of secondary traumatic stress among children's advocacy center forensic interviewers. *Journal of Child Sexual Abuse, 21,* 295–314. doi:10.1080/10538712.2012.647263.

Bride, B. E. (2007). Prevalence of secondary traumatic stress among social workers. *Social Work, 52*(1), 63–70.

Bride, B. E., & Figley, C. R. (2007). The fatigue of compassionate social workers: An introduction to the special issue on compassion fatigue. *Clinical Social Work Journal, 35*(3), 151–153.

Bride, B. E., Robinson, M. M., Yegidis, B., & Figley, C. R. (2004). Development and validation of the secondary traumatic stress scale. *Research on Social Work Practice, 14,* 27–35.

Briere, J. (2010, July 1). Self-Trauma model: Applications for torture survivors [webinar]. Advance Clinicians Peer Consultation Group. Retrieved from www.healtorture.org.

Briere, J., & Lanktree, C. B. (2013). *Integrative treatment of complex trauma for adolescents (ITCT-A): A guide for the treatment of multiply-traumatized youth* (2nd ed.). Los Angeles, CA: USC

Adolescent Trauma Treatment Training Center, National Child Traumatic Stress Network, U.S. Department of Substance Abuse and Mental Health Services Administration.

Briere, J., Scott, C., & Weathers, F. W. (2005). Peritraumatic and persistent dissociation in the presumed etiology of PTSD. *American Journal of Psychiatry, 162,* 2295–2301.

Briere, J., Hodges, M., & Godbout, N. (2010). Traumatic stress, affect dysregulation, and dysfunctional avoidance: A structural equation model. *Journal of Traumatic Stress, 23,* 767–774.

Chadwick-Parkes, S. (2014). Integrating human rights into the Jamaican social work curriculum. In K. R. Libal, S. M. Berthold, R. L. Thomas, & L. M. Healy (Eds.), *Advancing human rights in social work education.* Alexandria, VA: Council on Social Work Education.

Chapman, M. V., Oppenheim, S., Shibusawa, T., & Jackson, H. M. (2003). What we bring to practice. *Journal of Teaching in Social Work, 23*(3–4), 3–14. doi:10.1300/J067v23n03_02.

Cournoyer, B. (2000). *The social work skills workbook* (3rd ed.). Belmont, CA: Wadsworth.

Cox, K., & Steiner, S. (2013). *Self-care in social work: A guide for practitioners, supervisors, and administrators.* Washington, DC: NASW Press.

Crenshaw, D. A. (Ed.). (2008). *Child and adolescent psychotherapy: Wounded spirits and healing paths.* New York, NY: Jason Aronson.

Engstrom, D., Hernandez, P., & Gangsei, D. (2008). Vicarious resilience: A qualitative investigation into its description. *Traumatology, 14*(3), 13–21.

Grawitch, M. J., Gottschalk, M., & Munz, D. C. (2006). The path to a healthy workplace: A critical review linking healthy workplace practices, employee well-being, and organizational improvements. *Consulting Psychology Journal: Practice and Research, 58,* 129–147.

Hepworth, D., Rooney, R., Rooney, G. D., Strom-Gottfried, K., & Larsen, J. A. (2010). *Direct social work practice: Theory and skills.* Belmont, CA: Brooks/Cole.

Hernández, P., Gangsei, D., & Engstrom, D. (2007). Vicarious resilience: A new concept in work with those who survive trauma. *Family Process, 46,* 229–241.

Hernández, P., Engstrom, D., & Gangsei, D. (2010). Exploring the impact of trauma on therapists: Vicarious resilience and related concepts in training. *Journal of Systemic Therapies, 29*(10), 67–83.

Hernandez-Wolfe, P., Killian, K., Engstrom, D., & Gangsei, D. (in press). Vicarious resilience, vicarious trauma and awareness of equity in trauma work. *Journal of Humanistic Psychology.* Advance online publication. doi: 10.1177/0022167814534322

Heydt, M. J., & Sherman, N. E. (2005). Conscious use of self: Tuning the instrument of social work practice with cultural competence. *Journal of Baccalaureate Social Work, 10*(2), 25–40.

Jacobson, W. B. (2001). Beyond therapy: Bringing social work back to human services reform. *Social Work, 46*(1), 51–62.

Killian, K., & Hernandez-Wolfe, P. (2013, June 7). Development and validation of the vicarious resilience scale. Presentation at the Annual American Family Therapy Academy (AFTA) Conference, Chicago, IL.

McCann, I. L., & Colletti, J. (1994). The dance of empathy: A hermeneutic formulation of countertransference, empathy, and understanding in the treatment of individuals who have experienced early childhood trauma. In J. P. Wilson & J. D. Lindy (Eds.), *Countertransference in the treatment of PTSD* (pp. 87–121). New York, NY: Guilford Press.

McCann, I., & Pearlman, L. (1990). Vicarious traumatization: A framework for understanding the psychological effects of working with victims. *Journal of Traumatic Stress, 3*(1), 131–149.

Neuman, K. M., & Friedman, B. D. (1997). Process recordings: Fine-tuning an old instrument. *Journal of Social Work Education, 33*(2), 237–243.

New Tactics in Human Rights. (2010, September 22 to 28). Self-care for activists: Sustaining your most valuable resource. Retrieved from https://www.newtactics.org/conversation/self-care-activists-sustaining-your-most-valuable-resource.

Ortega, R. M., & Faller, K. C. (2011). Training child welfare workers from an intersectional cultural humility perspective: A paradigm shift. *Child Welfare, 90*(5), 27–49.

Piwowarczyk, L., Moreno, A., & Grodin, M. (2000). Health care of torture survivors. *Journal of the American Medical Association, 284*(5), 539–541. doi:10.1001/jama.284.5.539.
Polusny, M. A., Rosenthal, M. Z., Aban, I., & Follette, V. M. (2004). Experiential avoidance as a mediator of the effects of adolescent sexual victimization on negative adult outcomes. *Violence and Victims, 19,* 109–120.
Pryce, J., Shackelford, K., & Pryce, D. (2007). *Secondary traumatic stress and the child welfare professional.* Chicago, IL: Lyceum Books.
Saakvitne, K. W., Pearlman, L. A., & Staff of TSI/CAAP (1996). *Transforming the pain: A workbook on vicarious traumatization.* New York, NY: Norton.
Sheafor, B. W., & Horejsi, C. R. (2003). *Techniques and guidelines for social work practice* (6th ed.). Boston, MA: Allyn & Bacon.
Shulman, L. (1999). *The skills of helping individuals, families, groups, and communities* (4th ed.). Itasca, IL: F. E. Peacock Publishers, Inc.
Stamm, B. H. (Ed.). (1999). *Secondary traumatic stress: Self-care issues for clinicians, researchers, & educators* (2nd ed.). Lutherville, MD: Sidran Press.
Tedeschi, R. G., & Calhoun, L. G. (1996). The Posttraumatic Growth Inventory: Measuring the positive legacy of trauma. *Journal of Traumatic Stress, 9*(3), 455–471.
UN Committee on Economic, Social and Cultural Rights (CESCR). (2000, August 11). General Comment No. 14: The right to the highest attainable standard of health (Art. 12 of the Covenant). Geneva, Switzerland: Author. Retrieved from http://www.refworld.org/docid/4538838d0.html.
UN General Assembly. (1948). Universal Declaration of Human Rights, 10 December 1948, 217 A (III). Retrieved from http://www.refworld.org/docid/3ae6b3712c.html.
UN General Assembly. (1966). International Covenant on Economic, Social and Cultural Rights, 16 December 1966, United Nations, Treaty Series, vol. 993, p. 3. Retrieved from http://www.refworld.org/docid/3ae6b36c0.html.
van Dernoot Lipsky, L., & Burk, C. (2009). *Trauma stewardship: An everyday guide to caring for self while caring for others.* San Francisco: Berrett-Koehler Publishers.
Walsh, J. (2011). Countertransference with clients who have schizophrenia: A social work perspective. *Families In Society, 92*(4), 377–382. doi:10.1606/1044-3894.4156.
Wilcox, P. (2012). *Trauma-informed treatment: The restorative approach.* Fitchburg: NEARI Press.
Wilson, J. P., & Lindy, J. D. (Eds.). (1994). *Countertransference in the treatment of posttraumatic stress disorder.* New York, NY: Guilford Press.
Wilson, J. P., & Thomas, R. B. (2004). *Empathy in the treatment of trauma and PTSD.* New York, NY: Brunner-Routledge.

CPSIA information can be obtained
at www.ICGtesting.com
Printed in the USA
BVHW041820280120
570747BV00007B/115